Willingness-to-pay surveys

– A streamlined approach –

Willingness-to-pay surveys
– A streamlined approach –

Guidance notes for small town water services

Alison Wedgwood & Kevin Sansom

Water, Engineering and Development Centre
Loughborough University
2003

Water, Engineering and Development Centre,
Loughborough University,
Leicestershire, LE11 3TU, UK

ISBN 13 Paperback: 978 1 84380 014 9
ISBN Ebook: 9781788533751
Book DOI: http://dx.doi.org/10.3362/9781788533751

A catalogue record for this book is available from the British Library.

A reference copy of this publication is also available online at:
http://www.lboro.ac.uk/wedc/publications/

Wedgwood, A. and Sansom, K. (2003)
Willingness-to-pay surveys – A streamlined approach:
Guidance notes for small town water services
WEDC, Loughborough University, UK.

WEDC (The Water, Engineering and Development Centre) at Loughborough University in the UK is one of the world's leading institutions concerned with education, training, research and consultancy for the planning, provision and management of physical infrastructure for development in low- and middleincome countries.

This edition is reprinted and distributed by Practical Action Publishing.
Since 1974, Practical Action Publishing has published and disseminated books and information in support of international development work throughout the world. Practical Action Publishing trades only in support of its parent charity objectives and any profits are covenanted back to Practical Action (Charity Reg. No. 247257, Group VAT Registration No. 880 9924 76).

Designed at WEDC

About the authors

Alison Wedgwood is a natural resources economist specialising in water, sanitation and rural livelihoods. She previously worked for DFID in both the Water and Sanitation and Rural Development offices in India and has private sector experience working as an economist for ERM and Metroeconomica. Alison has worked for herself since 1999 under the company name Environmental Economics UK. Key interests include the use of demand assessment techniques in planning sustainable water and sanitation services, integrating streamlined economics techniques within poverty focused participatory programmes and planning and designing water programmes to ensure sustainable and equitable cost recovery. Alison has played a key role in a number of research programmes including "Designing Water and Sanitation Projects for Demand", "Building Sustainable Livelihoods for the Poor into Demand-Responsive Approaches" and "Optimised Management of Small Towns Watsan Services" and has recently lead a consortium of four consultancies in the economic, social and environmental evaluation of three major hydro-power projects in Malaysia for the Japanese Bank of International Co-operation.

Kevin Sansom specialises in management and institutional development and is a programme manager at WEDC. He has particular interests in: urban and rural water and sanitation services, utilities management, policy and reform, public private partnerships, services for the poor, facilitating change, and participatory training and research. Other research programmes he has co-ordinated include: 'Contracting out water and sanitation services', 'Marketing approaches for all urban water consumers' and 'Optimised management of small town watsan services'. He has taken a key role on capacity development programmes in India, including the 'Change Management Forum for the urban water sector' and the associated management development programme. Water sector capacity development work has also been undertaken in Tanzania and Nigeria. He lectures on post graduate programmes on 'water utilities management' and 'community and management'. Previously he was a project co-ordination manager for a large DFID funded integrated rural water supply project in Maharashtra, India.

Acknowledgements

The authors would like to thank Joseph Oriono Eyatu and other members of the Uganda field research team including Silver Sewanyana and Edward Kazibwe. They provided valuable assistance in field testing the streamlined willingness-to-pay methodology.

Valuable comments and corrections were received from Clarissa Brocklehurst, Sam Kayaga and Peter Barker. We appreciate the assistance of Sue Coates when drafting the sections on community negotiations. We would also like to express our appreciation to DFID for funding the research and Ian Curtis in particular, for providing detailed comments on an earlier draft of the document.

Contents

List of boxes

List of figures

List of tables

Glossary

AIC	Average Incremental Cost
CV	Contingent Valuation
CVM	Contingent Valuation Method
CVS	Contingent Valuation Survey
DAWASA	Dar es Salaam Water and Sewerage Agency
DFID	Department for International Development, UK
IBT	Increasing Block Tariffs
IRR	Internal Rate of Return
KVIPs	Kumasi Ventilated Improved Pit Latrines
LC5s	A small area which has been sub-divided from a larger council area in Uganda
LMICs	Low- and Middle-income countries
NOAA	National Oceanic and Atmospheric Administration
NPV	Net Present Value
O&M	Operation and Maintenance
PV	Present Value
RUM	Random Utility Models
Tsh	Tanzanian shillings
UCPC	Unit Cost Per Capita
Ush	Ugandan shillings
VIP	Ventilated Improved Pit
WC	Flush toilet
WSP	Water and Sanitation Program, World Bank
WTP	Willingness-to-pay

Chapter 1

Introduction and overview

1.1 Purpose of this document

The aim of the streamlined approach to contingent valuation method (CVM) Surveys, is to encourage wider use of CVM Surveys to inform key decisions in the water sector in developing countries. The specific objective of these guidelines is to promote the facilitation of high-quality contingent valuation surveys in small towns, which will then be used to inform important planning decisions concerning the type, scale and cost of improved water supply schemes and the methods for ensuring cost recovery and hence sustainability.

In its purest form, the contingent valuation methodology is a tool used to elicit the potential service users' maximum willingness-to-pay (WTP) for carefully selected water supply service options such as house connections, standposts, protected springs, public kiosks, etc. Carefully constructed contingent valuation scenarios describe a hypothetical market where the user 'buys' a particular level of service, using a specified payment method. The water system can be managed by a choice of institutions. Therefore, the CVM Survey can collect useful data on individuals' preferences for the exact type of improved water supply, their ability and willingness to pay for this system and the types of organisation that users would like to see managing the system. This information can then be used to determine an appropriate tariff policy and financing package for the improved water supply system, often involving the allocation of appropriate subsidies to poorer households.

These guidelines describe a framework and good practice for conducting a reasonably robust CVM Survey for use in small towns.[1] It covers how the data obtained could be used by policymakers, engineers, financial specialists and administrators.

[1] Many CVM surveys have been carried out in large urban areas. These tend to be more complex, statistically robust and costly exercises, which are used to determine WTP for improved water supply for large populations, often more than 100,000 people. A recent good example of a detailed study was done in August 2001, 'Willingness to Pay For Improved Water Supply In Kathmandu Valley, Nepal' for WSP–South Asia.

It is envisaged that this guidance document will be used to support the training of future survey managers and enumerators in focus countries, possibly through implementing a number of contingent valuation (CV) studies simultaneously and combining the facilitation of CV training with actual willingness-to-pay studies.

The urban water sector in low- and middle-income countries (LMICs) requires good quality data in order to:

- justify future investment proposals;
- develop a better understanding of user perceptions and preferences;
- support the selection of preferred service options; and
- set out the scope for future tariff increases and subsidy reduction plans.

Well-designed CVM Surveys are a reliable means of generating such valuable information. When key decision-makers and planners have valuable information that is also reliable, they can confidently proceed with the implementation of projects. In order to ensure sufficiently reliable data is obtained, the use of a robust survey methodology is proposed, together with accurately priced and technically viable options. This will help to ensure that the results can be easily interpreted to produce useful design, implementation and policy recommendations.

1.2 Target audience and uses for this guide

These guidelines are intended for use in the field by researchers, government staff, water sector managers and other practitioners based in developing countries and working in the water and sanitation sector. They may also be of use to donor staff involved in evaluating consultancy bids for demand assessments and CV Surveys and for consultants based in developed countries.

Experience of carrying out high-quality contingent valuation surveys is currently limited to a small number of development professionals. A 1999 study led by the Water and Sanitation Programme (WSP) – South Asia[2] found that only seven India-based research organisations had the required experience to carry out CV Surveys to an international standard. Experience can be developed, however, and the comparatively small base of expertise available in most developing countries may have more to do with the reluctance of economists and other CV 'experts' to

[2] 'Willing to Pay but Unwilling to Charge', WSP – South Asia. Field Note

share the necessary skills and approaches. This is partly to do with a wide-spread perception that CV Surveys must be carried out to meticulously high standards and involve statistical techniques beyond the reach of most local consultancy firms. Section 4.1.2 suggests that complex econometric analysis might not be required for CV Surveys in small towns, and that reasonably skilled development professionals, consultants and government staff familiar with the water sector should be able to conduct them. Often it is not the methodology that is wrong but the interpretation of the results and weak policy guidance. Consequently, many CV Surveys simply become unused academic papers or consultancy reports.

These guidelines focus on how to carry out Contingent Valuation Surveys (CVS) to assess demand and willingness to pay for water supply services in small towns. The guidelines encourage a rigorous approach, but also explain clearly how to develop the hypothetical CV scenario to ensure that the results are used as the link between future policy developments and investment decisions for small towns, water supply systems. Section 4.1 outlines appropriate techniques for using straight-forward methods to analyse the data collected during the survey.

It is assumed that readers have some previous knowledge of the water sector and the concept of demand-led approaches. Furthermore, they should understand the basic ideas behind the contingent valuation methodology (CVM) but require more systematic guidance to explain, in more detail, how to carry out a successful CV study. It is important that those people who carry out the CV study know how to interpret the results to ensure that the full policy and design implications are understood by planners and designers involved with future stages of the project.

Although there are many papers available which describe the results of CVM Surveys carried out by researchers and project planners, there are very few guidelines that help practitioners in the field to undertake their own CV Survey without external assistance from skilled experts (Altaf 1992, Whittington 1990, Vaidya 1995). There is an inherent risk that poor-quality CV Surveys will provide misleading data, which can do more harm than good – donor advice stresses the need for specialist skills to ensure a robust study.

However, many small consultancies, local government staff and agencies based in developing countries *are already conducting CV Surveys and using CVM* as a tool to assess demand for water supply and sanitation. The fact that there is very little guidance does not prevent many studies being commissioned, sometimes without clear terms of reference or exact understanding of the types of information required, or how it could be used. The overall weight of evidence suggests that there is demand for relatively simple practical guidance on CV Surveys.

Clearly, there is an inherent danger that inexperienced staff may attempt their own CV Surveys and produce spurious, unreliable results. It is also clear that many poor-quality CV Surveys have already been undertaken in the water supply sector because policymakers and programme designers see the obvious advantages of the techniques – and hence commission work – without understanding the levels of skills required to undertake reasonable surveys. Therefore, if there are sections of this guidance that the new, less experienced, CV practitioner finds difficult, confusing, or off-putting then this should not be a deterrent to using the approach. Any difficult sections *should not be ignored*, but instead the CV practitioner should focus on them and request specialist help from colleagues, government departments, local consultants, social scientists and statisticians from local universities. These specialists may be able to provide assistance with managing surveys, logistical support for writing, printing and sorting questionnaires, software support in using Excel or SPSS, or even policy advice to ensure that when the data is analysed it is converted into useful facts for the project design.

If specialist help is sought, it is also important to remember that those involved in the project who are familiar with water sector policies and practice in that country can provide most of the useful skills and data necessary to set up the survey questionnaire and manage the survey. If the CV practitioner is a key part of the project team, and experienced in the water sector, these skills should be considered very valuable, and he/she should ensure that any external specialist help is focused and managed very carefully to ensure that it remains useful.

1.3 Key concepts

1.3.1 Demand

The term 'demand' has different meanings to different people (Webster 1999). Three interpretations of demand are commonly used by different stakeholders:

- *felt needs:* The 'felt needs' or aspirations of communities. Projects might be driven by political or equity considerations to meet this demand.
- *consumption*: Engineers in particular tend to see demand as directly proportional to consumption. Consequently, water supply schemes are often designed according to volumes of water supplied per household. The long term cost of these schemes, including maintenance and financial sustainability are often not fully considered.

- *effective demand*: Effective demand is a term used by White (1997) and Pearce (1981) and can be defined as 'demand for goods and services which is backed up with the resources to pay for it'.

If people merely *'want'* something it may not be backed up by a willingness to pay for that service. Hence the need to ascertain people's maximum willingness to pay for proposed service options. Effective demand is sometimes referred to as economic demand, and it is the most meaningful definition of demand for these guidelines. It essentially means that a water supply user must be able to support their expressed desire for improved water supply services by an ability to pay the required contribution towards this service.

In rural schemes this might not always involve paying cash towards construction costs, instead a contribution of time and labour during construction and on-going operation might be required to ensure the physical and financial sustainability of the supply. For more discussion on demand and demand-responsive approaches refer to *Designing Water Supply and Sanitation Projects To Meet Demand in rural and peri-urban communities* (Paul Deverill et al 2002).

1.3.2 Willingness to pay

The issue that is most important for project designers and planners is how to ensure the financial sustainability of a project. This can involve predicting what users will be able and willing to pay for water in the future.

Consumers are often willing to pay a higher price for water than the tariffs charged. How much higher depends on how much water is being used. People are willing to pay very high prices for basic minimum water requirements to ensure the survival of the household. Willingness to pay diminishes rapidly with non-essential levels of water use, therefore the relationship between WTP and water use can be shown by a downward sloping demand curve.

There are various definitions of willingness to pay (WTP), but the most common one states that:

'WTP is the maximum amount that an individual states they are willing to pay for a good or service' (DFID 1997).

The term willingness-to-pay can be confusing in a non-economic paradigm. Users may not be 'happy' paying a certain tariff, but they are *willing* to pay this amount rather than go without, just as householders in the UK might not be happy paying their gas bills but know that they must pay them, or go without. (Webster 1999).

There are three ways to estimate WTP:

1. Observe the prices that people pay for goods in various markets (i.e. water vending, buying from neighbours, paying local taxes).

2. Observe individual expenditures of money, time, labour, etc. to obtain goods – or to avoid their loss. This method might involve an assessment of coping strategies and involve observations, focus group discussions and even household surveys.

3. Ask people directly what they are willing to pay for goods or services in the future.

The first two approaches are based on observations of behaviour and are called REVEALED PREFERENCE techniques. The third technique is based upon STATED PREFERENCES and includes the contingent valuation methodology.

1.3.3 Contingent Valuation Methodology

Contingent Valuation Surveys simulate a market for a non-marketed good[3] and obtain a value for that good, contingent on the hypothetical market described during the survey. Put more simply; facilitators carry out house-to-house surveys and ask users a range of questions about their existing water supply system plus other socio-economic characteristics and then present a hypothetical scenario, involving one or many improved water supply options which are offered to the respondent at various prices. This is done to determine what kind of water and sanitation services users want and are able to pay for.

The economic concept that CV Surveys are trying to capture is the maximum amount that a respondent would be willing to pay for the proposed improvement in water services in the context of the existing institutional regime within which households are free to allocate their financial resources. (Whittington 2001).

The most important part of the Contingent Valuation Methodology is creating a realistic contingent valuation scenario, which has accurately priced water supply 'options' that reflect the levels of prices that the water service provider would

[3] Although sometimes there is an existing market for water supply services, whether through water vending, established piped connections or purchasing from neighbours.

have to charge in order to provide the service. The respondent is asked about their preferences and is effectively asked at what price they would be willing to 'buy' the water, based on the level, quantity and quality of service. Critics claim that respondents will not answer truthfully, and what they *say* they will pay does not reflect what they would actually pay. It is true that some respondents might bias their answers: selecting expensive options in the hope that the government would eventually pay for them if the consumer could not or would not pay. Bias may also occur because the respondents did not really understand the CV scenario discussed during the survey. Various techniques have been developed to try and eliminate biased responses. In particular, the way that the CV scenario is presented to the respondent and how the willingness-to-pay question is asked can be very specifically designed to reduce bias.

CVM has been increasingly advocated by economists and sector specialists as a useful tool for gathering reasonably accurate data about how much a household can afford and is willing to pay for particular water and sanitation options presented to them. Early research in the 1980s found that '*when the CV method is used to estimate the use of goods and services with which the individuals are familiar…CV surveys that are carefully designed and administered can yield accurate and useful information on households' preferences*' (Cummings et al., 1986).

In the summary statement of the 'Small towns water supply and sanitation conference held in Addis Ababa on 11–15 June 2002 it is stated that:

The Contingent Valuation Methodology allows planners to assess people's willingness to pay for service options and provides the necessary basis for projecting sales and revenues. This information is essential to support community participation and enable "informed choice" at the household level as well as for the community as a whole. WTP surveys provide the parameters to underpin financial models needed to evaluate expansion plans and to set tariffs. The relative high cost of WTP tools is likely to come down as they are systematically applied and as the local consulting profession builds up its capacity (WSP, 2002).

An alternative term for CVM that is commonly used in developing countries is willingness-to-pay surveys (or WTP surveys). This term is not entirely accurate because the contingent valuation method is one of many methods which can be used to determine an individual's maximum willingness to pay for an improved or new water supply service. A willingness-to-pay survey might simply be an assessment of household coping strategies, or a survey of the time it takes to collect water each day.

1.4 WTP and investment planning

WTP surveys that have been carefully conducted provide valuable information for investment planning for water services. Figure 1 sets out a typical investment planning process leading to implementation. Such a process enables the design team and stakeholders to adequately consider:

- the most suitable technical options;
- the right size of facilities;
- the consumer's willingness/ability to pay; and
- long-term sources of funding for construction, O&M, expansion and rehabilitation.

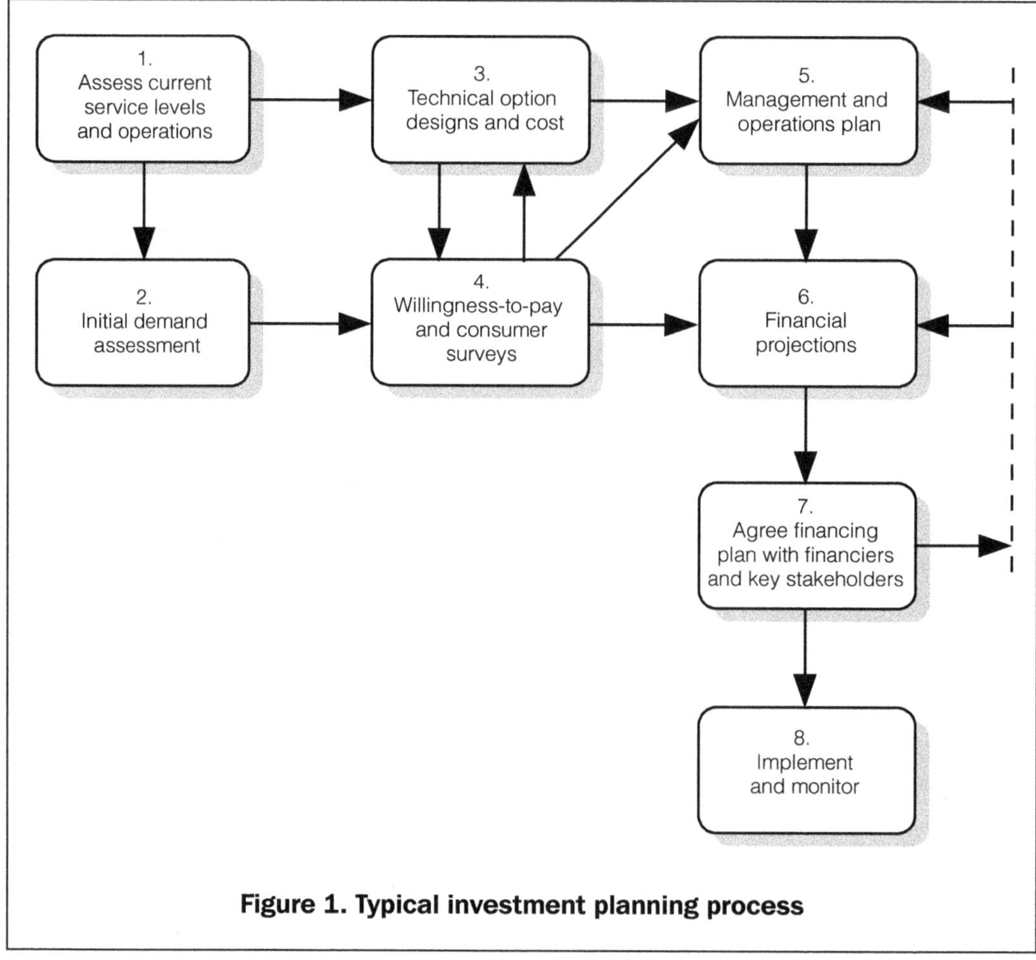

Figure 1. Typical investment planning process

Source: K. Sansom adapted from C. Revels (2002)

The process begins with an assessment of current service levels and operations, which should reveal if there are problems and any need for service improvements. It is useful to carry out informal demand assessments from time to time, such as participatory focused group discussions with different consumer groups. In a small town situation, if there is a demand for better services involving significant investment, such as a piped water supply system or a large extension, then it is recommended that a willingness-to-pay survey be conducted.

The development of 'outline' technical option designs and costs are necessary for the WTP survey. It is important to be flexible in terms of design standards and to also consider technical options other than piped water, in order to determine the most viable options for each area of the small town. The WTP survey results in turn provide the best information to inform the selection of the preferred technical options. It is for this reason that two arrows are shown between Boxes 3 and 4 in Figure 1, to represent this iterative process.

The preferred options and costs, as well as the management and operations plan (Box 5) and the willingness-to-pay results, all provide key information for developing the financial projections (Box 6) over 10 years or more from when the proposed project is completed. The WTP results indicate the likely take-up rates for each option at given water charge rates.

In doing the financial projections and finalising designs it is important to make some allowance for the likely future demands for expansion. If technical, management and financial plans are agreed by key stakeholders and the proposed financiers, then there are good prospects for proceeding to implementation. If not, then there should be feedback loops (showed by the broken lines in the diagram) to allow adjustment to the plans.

1.5 Outline CVM process

Good quality contingent valuation surveys require both a series of skills and knowledge, including: survey skills, knowledge of how to develop different CV scenarios for population groups with different water supply or housing/income conditions, how to train enumerators, analyse results, etc. A number of steps are advocated in these guidelines for an effective CVM Survey and dissemination of results, and these are set out in the flow diagram below (Figures 2 and 3):

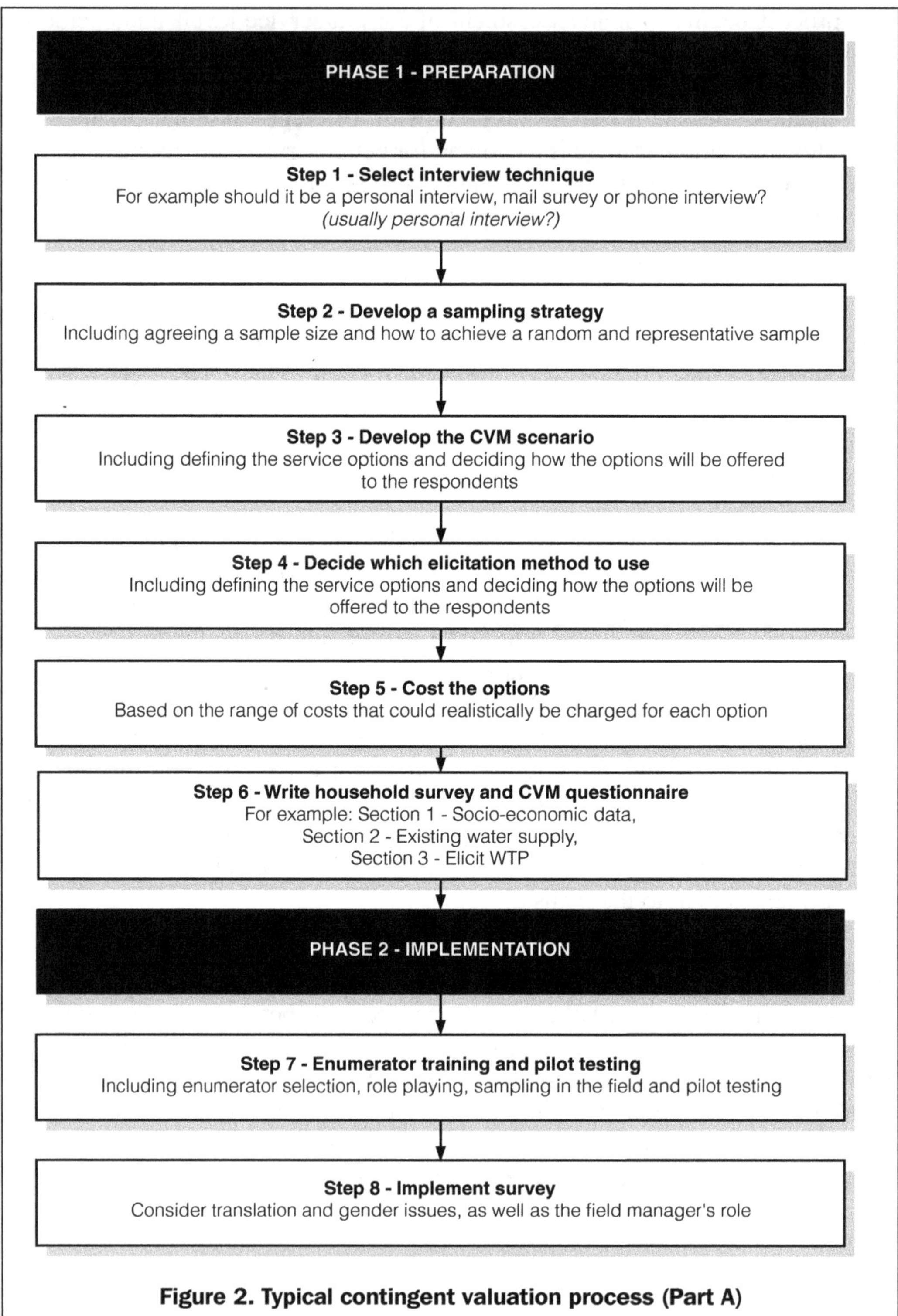

PHASE 1 - PREPARATION
Step 1 - Select interview technique
For example should it be a personal interview, mail survey or phone interview?
(usually personal interview?)
Step 2 - Develop a sampling strategy
Including agreeing a sample size and how to achieve a random and representative sample
Step 3 - Develop the CVM scenario
Including defining the service options and deciding how the options will be offered to the respondents
Step 4 - Decide which elicitation method to use
Including defining the service options and deciding how the options will be offered to the respondents
Step 5 - Cost the options
Based on the range of costs that could realistically be charged for each option
Step 6 - Write household survey and CVM questionnaire
For example: Section 1 - Socio-economic data,
Section 2 - Existing water supply,
Section 3 - Elicit WTP
PHASE 2 - IMPLEMENTATION
Step 7 - Enumerator training and pilot testing
Including enumerator selection, role playing, sampling in the field and pilot testing
Step 8 - Implement survey
Consider translation and gender issues, as well as the field manager's role

Figure 2. Typical contingent valuation process (Part A)

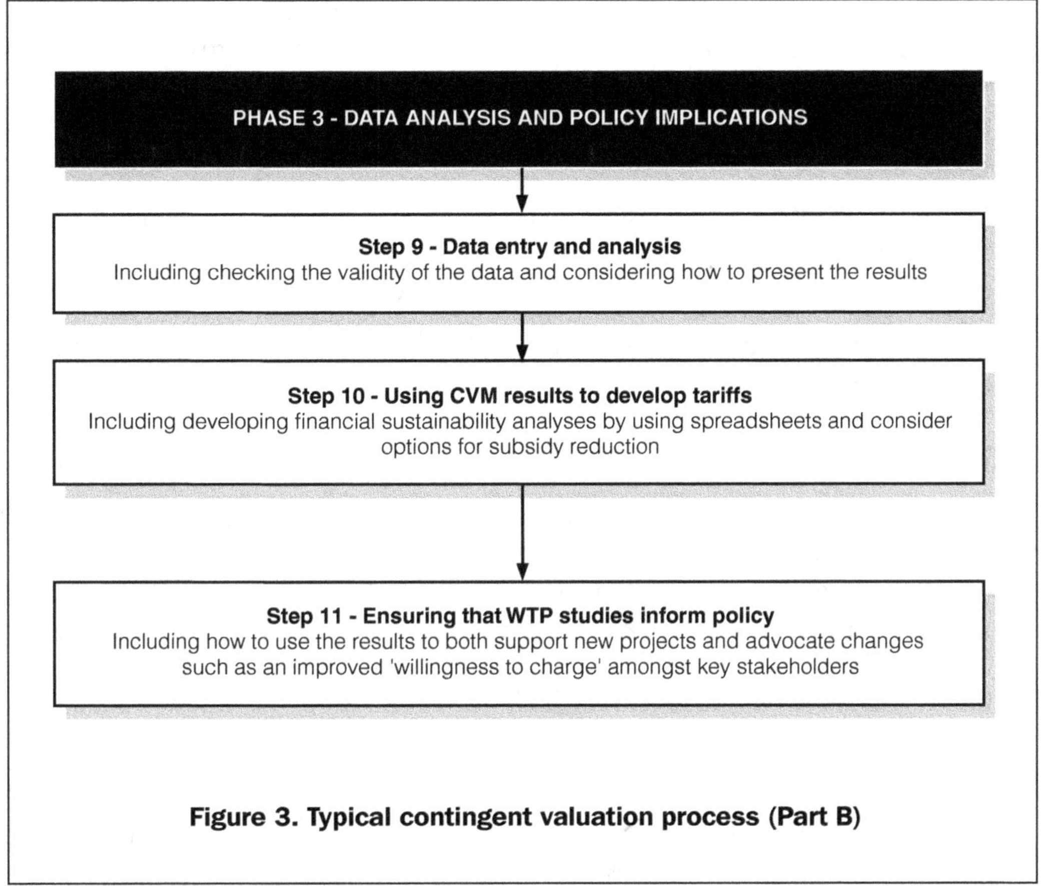

PHASE 3 - DATA ANALYSIS AND POLICY IMPLICATIONS
Step 9 - Data entry and analysis
Including checking the validity of the data and considering how to present the results
Step 10 - Using CVM results to develop tariffs
Including developing financial sustainability analyses by using spreadsheets and consider options for subsidy reduction
Step 11 - Ensuring that WTP studies inform policy
Including how to use the results to both support new projects and advocate changes such as an improved 'willingness to charge' amongst key stakeholders

Figure 3. Typical contingent valuation process (Part B)

1.6 Why use CVM?

CVM has many advantages over other techniques:

- It can be used to investigate peoples' maximum willingness to pay for different levels of service that *are not currently available*. Therefore, it should capture a fuller range of the benefits of the service improvements and can accurately estimate what proportion of households are likely to switch to improved service levels at given tariff levels.
- Consumers can bid on a range of different service options, thus users are defining projects designs and technology choices which are demand led.
- The technique generates information on household ability and willingness to pay for ongoing O&M and can guide tariff and cost-recovery policy, and hence improve the financial sustainability of the project.

- More specifically, the technique will enable simple financial models to be developed. This enables the government and local service providers to understand clearly the types of subsidies which may be needed, including cross-subsidies to the poorest households and realistic service levels that can be sustained.
- The respondents answers can be easily understood by non-economists and therefore used by social development, environmental health, and engineering experts for other aspects of demand responsive planning.
- Similarly, the results of a CVM Survey, if presented clearly, are conceptually easy for non-specialists, politicians and administrators to understand.

1.6.1 Disadvantages of CVM

- The DFID Guidance Manual on Water Supply and Sanitation Programmes (WELL, 1998) state that 'using CVM adds significantly to the cost and time needed for small survey demand assessment studies, but the incremental costs will be relatively modest if a large random sample is to be undertaken in any case' (1998:110). This argument is refuted in the section below, but it is true that to ensure robust results, relatively rigorous survey techniques need to be employed, requiring a skilled survey manager and six to eight trained enumerators.

  The technique does not test consumers' effective demand, i.e. Will they really pay the tariffs they said they would in the survey?
- The results are not often transferable, even between apparently very similar locations.
- There may be problems involved with the aggregation of responses, particularly if the sample size is too small.
- Individuals may answer inaccurately (biases), giving answers that are either too high or too low in order to deliberately mislead the design of the new system and tariff calculations.

1.7 When to use CVM?

The first issue to consider is whether using CVM is appropriate. What is it being used for? There are other techniques available to determine demand for water and sanitation services (these are not discussed in this guide). The choice of the right technique depends on the size and complexity of the programme being planned. As reported in the *DFID Guidance Manual on Water Supply and Sanitation Programmes* (WELL, 1998):

> *If resources are available, the Contingent Valuation Method is the most reliable...however, in different circumstances, less costly options can yield worthwhile results.*

The same document suggests that the case for using a CVM approach at some stage in the project design is stronger whenthe conditions described in Box 1 prevail:[4]

Box 1. Reasons for using the CVM approach

- There is likely to be some demand for feasible options even when charged at full cost.
- There is a range of different technical service options, which can feasibly be made available to consumers in the town. These should have significantly different implications for project design, e.g. whether to plan for public standposts, or private connections, or both and whether to use groundwater or a local reservoir etc.
- The charges that users will be required to pay for the higher service-level options are likely to be high. In this case the financial viability of potential projects and the whole justification for the project may be highly dependent on how users respond to the options at the prices to be charged.
- There are richer households and commercial and industrial users who may have higher WTP and thus can cross-subsidise poor households. Capturing this information can be crucial in setting equitable, sustainable tariffs.
- There is the possibility of providing metered private connections to households that are willing to pay for the full costs and are likely to sell on to neighbours.

Many of these points apply to water service improvements in small towns. CVM has been used as a tool to evaluate an existing project[5], but ideally CVM should take place very early on in the project cycle, and used as an integral part of the design process. CVM activities then become intertwined with other programme activities, including institutional processes, responding to new policy initiatives, engineering design and financial planning.

[4] Examples adapted from the DFID Guidance Manual on Water and Sanitation. 1998:110

[5] Dar es Salaam Community Managed Water and Sanitation Programme. Demand Assessment in 4 Street Communities: Alison Wedgwood and Water Aid. 2000

1.8 Who can do CVM?

How can CVM studies be carried out to a high standard and yet not always involve international consultants at prohibitively higher costs? A fine balance needs to be struck between statistical rigour and the need to use a technique that has many obvious advantages and which conceptually can provide project planners with useful information. It may not always require an external specialist to ensure that the options are designed and costed accurately, the questionnaire is well written and pre-tested, the random sample is sufficiently large, and the enumerators are well trained. The results will still be viable whether or not complex econometric tests are performed on them so long as the CVM process was carried out with enough careful planning. (See Section 4.1.2 for further discussion.)

To meet this goal, CV Surveys will need to be carried out using both central government/authority staff and consultancy contracts between 1993 and 1996, with the aid of skilled national, or occasionally international consultants, if and when necessary. It is envisaged that once enough precedents are set, use of CVM as a tool to assess demand in small towns may become commonplace. In Uganda the economist at the Directorate of Water Development commissioned five studies as part of the World Bank's Small Towns Water and Sanitation Project – although international consultants were used for the first study, local Ugandan and Kenyan consulting firms were the main contractors.

1.8.1 Skills required for a CVM Survey

The CV Survey manager should have some experience in carrying out traditional household surveys and some knowledge of social research methods, and should understand the water sector particularly in relation to small towns. The survey manager does not need to be an economist. It is more important that she or he, have a broad knowledge of project design and implementation, and is more likely to have a social science or even an engineering background. Collectively the team should:

- be familiar with technical issues, including the types of water supply service options that could be used in the hypothetical scenario;
- understand the socio-economic and cultural aspects of small town water supply services;
- appreciate managerial and institutional issues with relation to small town water supplies;

- be familiar with sampling techniques to ensure that the survey sample is random and unbiased;
- be able to write surveys to facilitate easy analysis, and have previous experience of pre-testing and managing household surveys;
- be able to train and manage a team of enumerators; and
- be able to use spreadsheets and analyse simple frequency graphs, etc.

1.9 How much will it cost?

Carrying out a Contingent Valuation Survey (CVS) can have significant time and cost implications compared to other techniques, however recent surveys carried out in Tanzania,[6] Uganda[7] and Kenya[8] indicate that robust CVS for small towns can be carried out for US$20,000. This may prove a controversial point, as other experts believe that a minimum price is $50,000 and that high-quality, large-scale urban studies can cost up to $150,000.[9] The price of a study is not the only factor that determines whether a CVS provides reliable data, which is *then used within the planning process.* A rapid assessment, carried out with the aid of one international consultant who has extensive CV experience in the water sector, can produce successful results for under $20,000 (assuming the consultant is not charged out at more than $500 per day).

Once in-country CVM study teams have demonstrated their ability to manage the entire survey and analysis process without external assistance, it should be possible to undertake surveys in small towns for considerably less than $20,000, depending on the charge rates of the local consultancy teams. The findings of this research suggest that it is the poor quality and lack of clarity of the final report that often undermines all the hard work of the field team who have undertaken an accurate, robust survey.

The incremental costs of a CVM study can be much less if a household survey is to be undertaken in any case. Large, random sample household surveys are often needed when the intention of the study is to inform politically contentious

---

[6] Dar es Salaam Community Managed Water and Sanitation Programme. Demand Assessment in 4 Street Communities: Alison Wedgwood and Water Aid. 2000

[7] Research carried out in Bushenyi Uganda by Joseph Oriono and Alison Wedgwood. Part of the optimisation of the management of small towns Knowledge and Research Programme conducted by WEDC for DFID 2001-2002

[8] DFID KaR still in progress. *Pricing and Service Differentiation of Utility Water Services in urban Areas. Mombasa Customer Survey and WTP DFID KaR Research Project.* 2001-2

[9] Guidance Notes for DFID Economists on Demand Assessment in the Water and Sanitation Sector. August 1998 Prof. Dale Whittington presented following a DFID seminar in December 1997.

decisions such as tariff structures, cost-recovery levels and how subsidies should be targeted. These often occur in larger cities in the developing world and may be linked to donor/ financial aid programmes. In such cases detailed CVM Survey may be used with international experts, such as the study conducted in Kathmandu, Nepal (WSP, 2001).

It is useful to remember that it is much cheaper and easier to administer contingent valuation surveys in developing countries than in industrialised countries (Whittington, 1997). Enumerators are relatively inexpensive; therefore the survey costs are normally considerably less than they would be in a developed country. This allows for larger sample sizes. The size of the survey and the cost will depend on the number of households included in the survey, although the marginal cost of each additional household can be quite small compared to the time taken to design the CV scenario, train enumerators and pay for international/ national experts.

There is an added advantage that most respondents are receptive to listening and talking about their needs. Response rates are often over 95 per cent. To date, there are no examples of respondents being paid to answer questions, which is often the case in industrialised countries. Researchers claim that paying respondents would make the random sampling very difficult because many people may offer to answer questions for a fee, and this would introduce bias into the results.

Time and human resources

The amount of time and human resources required will of course vary with the size and depth of the CVS required. Examples vary enormously. The World Bank research team spent at least four weeks assessing of 'Household Demand for Improved Sanitation In Kumasi, Ghana' (Whittington et al, 1993). Staff included 20 enumerators, field supervisors, plus six staff contracted by the World Bank. Similarly, in Kathmandu, a large detailed CVM Survey employed three international specialists, seven professionals from Tribhuvan University, Nepal, and 15 enumerators. But both Kumasi and Kathmandu are reasonably large cities. In South Africa, poor quality CVSs were carried out in a few days by a couple of engineers and involved a simple question: 'Are you willing to pay X? Yes or No?'

As a broad guideline, a reasonable CVS for a small town requires at least 30 days from the main staff member/consultant who is familiar with the technique, 20 days from a support person and 15 days for each of the enumerators. This includes time to:

- Work out the sampling strategy for the small town
- Write the questionnaire
- Select and cost options
- Select enumerators
- Train enumerators
- Carry out a pilot study
- Carry out the survey
- Input the data
- Analyse the data

It is not possible to set out a blueprint for the amount of time and resources that are needed. This will depend on the size of the project area, the size of the random sample deemed necessary to gauge demand accurately, and whether the results are to be used to set tariff and subsidy policy or just to provide useful information on preferred options and their affordability.

Chapter 2

Survey preparation

Chapter 1 provided a broad background to the Contingent Valuation Methodology and sought to explain why, when, and how much it should cost and who could carry out a CVM Survey. Chapters 2, 3 and 4 explain *how* a CVM Survey should be conducted in a small town, going through the steps shown in Figure 1. Chapter 5 of the guidelines then explains how the results can and should be used to influence the final design and planning of a small town's water supply, including how costs can be recovered to ensure the financial sustainability of the system.

For more general advice on how to conduct household surveys, the World Bank's Living Standards Measurement Study (LSMS) household surveys have become an important tool in measuring and understanding poverty in developing countries. The Development Economics Research Group (DECRG) of the World Bank, formerly the Policy Research Department, maintains a website to make available to researchers around the world the data sets and methodological lessons from a range of household surveys, including guidance on how to conduct surveys. The website is at http://www.worldbank.org/lsms/

2.1 Step 1 – Select interview technique

This step should be relatively easy for all practitioners wishing to implement a contingent valuation methodology survey to assess demand for improved water supply services in small towns in developing countries. The main question is 'what form should the survey take?'. Should it be a personal interview, a postal survey or a telephone interview?

Postal surveys have been used with some success in the US and UK, and there is an example of a CVM Survey to assess WTP for improved water quality in the River Ganges in India which used a postal vote to middle-class Indian families located in major cities throughout India (Markandya, 1997). This survey found that WTP to clean up the River Ganges was very high, and was possibly a result of the religious value that many Hindus placed on the sacred river.

Telephone surveys are not recommended because many households, particularly the poorest, will not have telephones.

For small towns in developing countries with possible mixed literacy levels and few telephones it is recommended that the surveys take the form of personal interviews. Postal surveys rely too much on the literacy of the adults in the household and would prevent less literate females and poor illiterate households from participating.

2.2 Step 2 – sampling strategy and background research

2.2.1 Collecting existing socio-economic reports

Once a CV Survey is to be conducted in a small town, the first task should be to visit the town to work out a sampling strategy and to gather information in order to develop the hypothetical CV scenario.

Preparation for a CVM Survey essentially entails developing a CVM scenario that includes viable options that are likely to meet the needs of different consumer groups. Opponents to the CV methodology believe that respondents do not answer questions accurately, and thus invalidate their answers. It is essential that from the outset CV researchers develop realistic and practical CV scenarios, with real options that have been carefully priced and that are likely to be familiar to the respondent. In order to do this, the researcher must understand the local water supply situation before designing the CV scenario. This will involve visiting the small town, meeting key staff involved in the management of the existing water supply system, and gathering relevant data to assist in developing an appropriate sampling technique.

Data of relevance to the development of the CV scenario and survey sampling will include local census data, government and local sources of population statistics, street maps, other utilities, billing records and any available data on incomes, employment, and education that might be compiled in other reports. It is often the case that other donor agencies or the government have already commissioned surveys, or used participatory approaches for gathering data. These reports provide extremely useful data on the socio-economic and cultural characteristics of the town's inhabitants.

2.2.2 Understand existing management systems

The CV researcher needs to understand the history and current situation of the water supply system in order to be able to develop an authentic 'story' describing the future, improved system for the respondent. The following information on the current and proposed future arrangements will be useful:

- What is the relationship between the key stakeholders, such as: the water service providers (formal and informal), government water departments, the local council water department, community and water user groups and others involved in the management of water services?

- What are the current prices of water from different sources, including vending, any piped system charges, water kiosks, etc.

- How will costs be recovered? Will the existing system be piped, or based on single point sources, and will O&M costs be fully or partially subsidised?

- Are there any problems with the supply, including power shortages, or a lack of chemicals or filters for cleaning?

- Are any plans being initiated to change the management of the services in a substantial manner, including distributing responsibilities for the management and co-ordination of services?

Any information on service levels and financial performance against key performance indicators will be very useful in comparing the current situation in the small town in question with other small towns. This can be used to determine the potential scope for improvements in service provision. Refer to the World Bank documents and website *Benchmarking water and sanitation utilities* for an explanation of the key indicators and how they can be used for benchmarking.

2.2.3 Use local information to improve credibility of the CV scenario

During this preliminary field visit, every effort should be made to meet with local water officers and engineers. Central government may have policies about appropriate types of water supply options for small towns, but local information on likely options may prove more useful. The engineers will be able to draw on their experiences of previous projects,[10] they will know whether, and how many,

[10] It is very rare now to find a small town that has not received some water supply intervention by either central government, local government, aid agencies, NGOs, religious organisations or the private sector. However, recent field visits to Tanzania by staff of WEDC suggest that some towns in Tanzania have had very little intervention and have no piped schemes at all.

boreholes have failed and the reasons why; whether there are problems with the main water source for the piped network; and whether hand-dug wells or protected springs are likely options. They will also hopefully understand the cultural and practical reasons and why certain options might be preferred by different socio-economic groups in the town. Using social scientists amongst the team of enumerators can also assist in the shared understanding of these issues amongst the survey team.

2.2.4 The importance of achieving a random sample

The Contingent Valuation Methodology involves the use of household surveys, which will always mean that a sample of the total *population*[11] of the town will need to be surveyed. Of course in an ideal world each household or individual adult would be questioned, but it is highly unlikely that there is the time or resources for this, unless very small villages are being surveyed. Therefore, a proportion of the population must be selected. Ideally, the CVM researcher will seek to question a *representative sample* of the town, i.e. a sample that reflects the population accurately so that it is a microcosm of the population; the researcher can then say that the findings apply to the population of the town as a whole.

It is very important when carrying out CVM that the researcher gathers information on a sample of the town's population that is representative of the whole population.

Whether you interview 1 per cent or 10 per cent of the total population, if the sample is poorly selected it may not be representative. Samples are only *estimates* of the corresponding *true* population. In this context, the purpose of sampling is to draw inferences about the population's demand for different water supply scenarios on the basis of sample information. The fundamental consideration is that any sample should be a *random* sample, i.e. *every member of the population should have an equal chance of being selected.*

A probability sample should be used, this is a sample that has been selected using random selection so that each unit in the population has a known chance of being selected. It is generally assumed that a representative sample is more likely to be the outcome when this method of selection is employed.

[11] In this case the population of the town also coincides with the population of the sample area. The subjects of any survey are collectively referred to as the population. Sometimes the population can be defined by fixed parameters, such as 'people in employment between the ages of 18 and 40' or 'females'.

2.2.5 Establish the sample size

An integral part of the sampling procedure is working out the sample size, which is clearly constrained by the budget and time. There is often a trade-off between budget and sample size. In order to decide how many interviews to do to complete the CV Survey, the field manager will need to take into account:

- the population of the town and estimates of average household size;
- the number of enumerators;
- the number of questionnaires that can be completed each day and the number of days budgeted for. Household surveys are hard work and require staff that are adept at dealing with strangers and able to concentrate for long periods of time. On average only six to eight questionnaires per enumerator should be completed each day; and
- the minimum proportion of the total population to be surveyed.

For example, if the original intention is to survey 10 per cent of all households in a large town with a population of 50,000 and an average household consists of five people, this will mean conducting 1000 surveys. If there are only five enumerators completing eight questionnaires a day this will require 25 days in the field. The original intention may have to be changed. The most likely technique to establish the sample size will be to use the budget to work out how many days the enumerators can work in the field, based on six to eight questionnaires per day.

Box 2. Working out the sample size

Assuming eight questionnaires per day are completed by 10 enumerators at a daily cost of $50 per day and that the total budget available for the survey is $3000, then six days of surveying can be afforded. Consequently, approximately 480 survey forms should be completed.

2.2.6 Simple random sample

The simple random sample is the most basic form of probability sample. If the researcher decides that they have enough money to sample 480 (n) households and the population of the town is 4000 households (N), this means that the probability of inclusion in the sample is:

4000/480 = 1 in 8.333 households

The key steps in devising a simple random sample are:

- Define the population. In most cases this will be the total population of the town, but sub-divided into households. The population may also need to be split into renters and owners. For large towns, the researcher may wish to focus only on one area of the town, such as the core area or slums.

- Devise a comprehensive sampling frame. This will normally involve using any local or national census that are available. Sampling can be more difficult in developing countries because of the lack of accurate census information, phone books, street names and addresses, etc. Simple random sampling requires that some form of census data, or listing of residents by ward or council area is available. It may be necessary to construct your own sampling frame by using simple mapping techniques (see Section 2.2.8).

- Decide on the sample size.

- Using the data on households provided, assign each household a number from 1 to 5000 (N) (assuming the total population of households is 5000).

- Using a table of random numbers, select 480 random numbers that lie between 1 and 5000.

- Assign the 480 random numbers to the corresponding households.

Two points are striking about this process. First, there is almost no opportunity for human bias to manifest itself. Households would not be selected on any subjective criteria such as whether they were friendly or approachable. Second, the process is not dependent on a member of the household being instantly available. The selection is done without their knowledge.

There are however, some serious drawbacks to this technique for conducting surveys in developing countries. The most obvious is the fact that in densely populated small towns, particularly the core areas, and with high labour mobility, not all households, families, or members of households are likely to be listed in any official government census or report. Addresses are often unclear if they exist at all and the enumerator may waste time trying to find a particular house that has been assigned a random number. In addition, the head of the household or head female may not be in and this will involve many repeat visits in order for the enumerator to complete their quota of questionnaires. Therefore, this method is only recommended in small towns where reasonable and recent data is available on the number and location of households in the town. If a recent census has taken place, or other surveys or research has taken place where this information was collected, then simple random sampling should be relatively easy. However, if this kind of information is not available, then systematic sampling with mapping is recommended.

2.2.7 Systematic sampling

A variation on the simple random sample is the systematic sample. With this kind of sample you select households directly from the sampling frame, without resorting to a table of random numbers.

Imagine you plan to survey 400 households from a total population of 8000 households. You know that you should select approximately 1 in 20 households. Therefore, make a random start between 1 and 20, simply by drawing one of the numbers out of a hat and then taken every 20th household. If the number drawn was 15, you would take the 15th , 35th, 55th house, etc.

This still assumes that there is an available list of households. If there is not, it will then be necessary to devise a list, or at least devise a means to identify each 20th household at random in the town. This might be done by using simple sketch maps devised by the team.

2.2.8 Using maps to assist sampling

Using a sketch map for sampling is an appropriate technique in small towns where there is incomplete census data. Refer to Figure 4, which shows the sampling sketch map of Ishaka town in Uganda. Note that the map has been used as a basis for deciding the sampling zones in which the enumerators will work.

The boundaries of different wards or informal (named) settlements can be included to give an overall impression of the socio-economic/geographical situation. A sketch artist should be employed to draw a rough map of the town. There may be existing maps with the local council, which can be used as the base. The map should include:

- a rough outline of the core and fringe areas of the town with main roads and streets;
- a rough outline of the density of housing in each area. Unless the town is very small it would be impossible to include every house accurately, but an idea of the density of housing can be demonstrated. For example, Figure 4 shows the area where there is high density low-income housing in Ishaka;
- indications of wealth. Many locals and staff of the local councils will be able to inform you of the poorer areas of the town compared to middle and higher income areas;
- all existing waterpoints. Water sources that are no longer operational (such as defunct handpumps) should also be marked, although a different symbol or code should be used; and
- other significant sites, such as the market place, taxi rank, local factories or mills, etc.

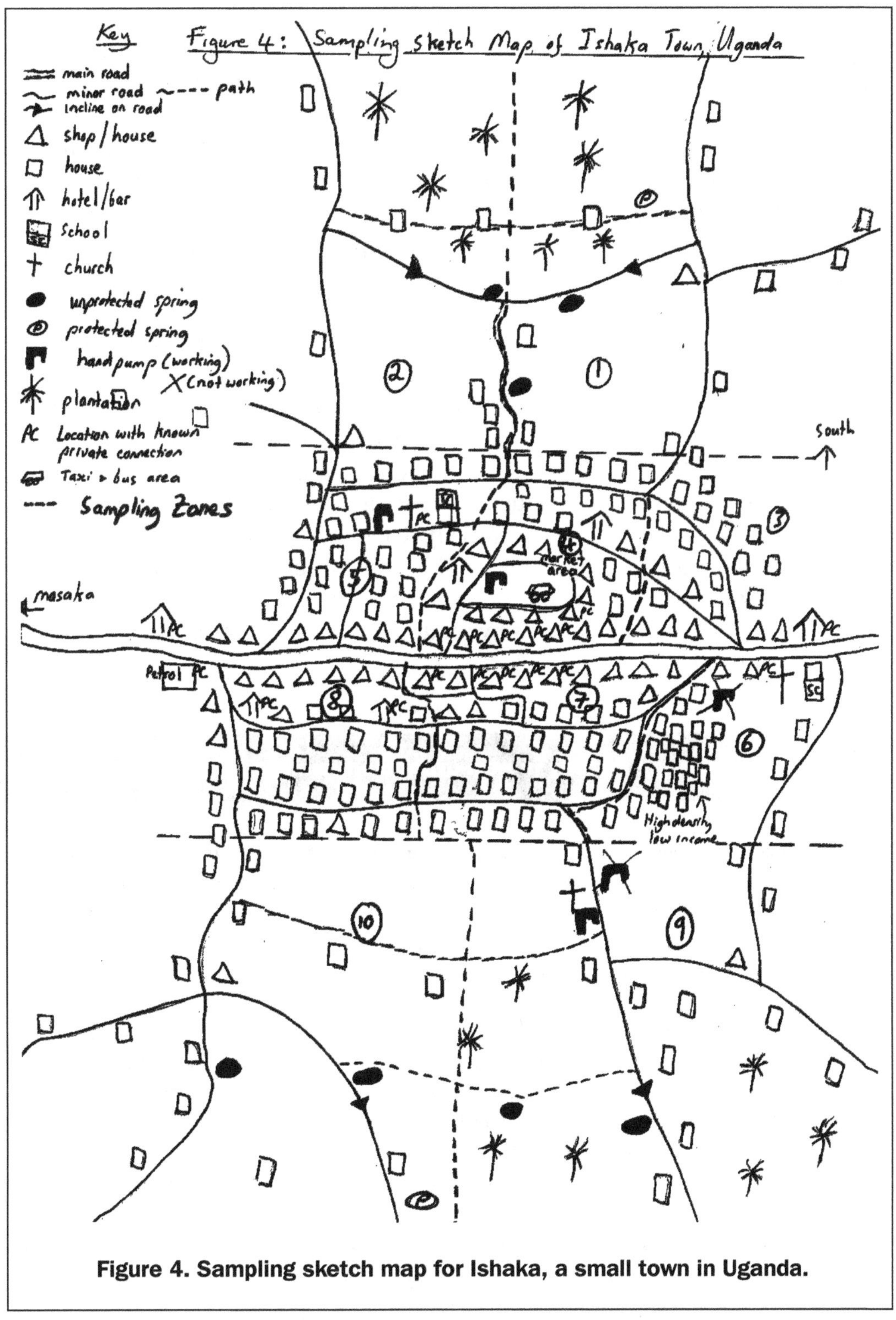

Figure 4. Sampling sketch map for Ishaka, a small town in Uganda.

Once the map has been drawn, it can be sub-divided into geographical areas containing similar numbers of households, for sampling purposes. To manage the survey more simply, it is recommended that the number of sub-divisions should match either the number of enumerators employed or the number of days over which the survey will take place. It is important that the household groupings are in proportion to the number of houses, not the size of the area. Densely packed housing should therefore appear as a much smaller sub-division in geographical area. The town has essentially been divided up into slices containing a similar number of people.

Each enumerator could survey one area, counting every 'nth' house according to the size of the survey and number of days available. This has the advantage that the enumerator becomes familiar with their area, and can cover back and side streets and small roads and becomes familiar with the location of houses that are not set out on the main streets. Each enumerator should be encouraged to draw a rough sketch map of their individual area showing roads, alley ways, waterpoints, shops, hotels, churches, etc. Alternatively, each sub-division could indicate one day of surveying for the whole team. This makes transport much easier. At the start of the morning the enumerators are designated a particular section of the sub-division and conduct their surveys by randomly counting houses according to the system developed.

Box 3. Sampling strategy in peri-urban communities, Dar es Salaam

The sampling procedure was not easy to design. Time was not available to reconstruct household lists and use these as a basis for sampling. In Keko Mwanga B, fortunately, a recent and high-quality aerial photograph had been taken of the area, which enabled the team to count exactly the number of households and devise a sampling strategy. This gave the team the idea for the other three streets.

Counting every nth house proved impossible initially because houses were not spread out in an ordered manner. In the end, following observation walks in the streets, an artist sketched a plan of each street which was used by the team to split up the area into eight blocks. The blocks were approximately equal in area. Within each geographical block the enumerator selected 12 houses spaced out at every 5th interval. The 12 interviews were conducted over two days. The sampling ensured an even geographical coverage within each street, which served very well as a proxy for more rigorous counting techniques.

Source: 'Dar es Salaam Water and Sanitation Programme, Assessment of Demand'. A. Wedgwood, 2000, p.9.

Alternatively, instead of drawing artificial lines on the sketch map the researcher could use pre-designated wards or council areas. In Uganda, for example, larger local council areas are also sub-divided into smaller areas called Local Council Level 1s, (LC1s). These are well known to the ward councillors, and the boundaries normally coincide with roads. A representative sample would take every LC1 and then carry out a number of surveys in each, depending on the size of the sample required. Alternatively, small towns can be sub-divided into wards, districts, or blocks. If there are 20 wards in a small town they may need to be grouped together on the map. If there were 10 enumerators, each enumerator could survey two wards counting every nth house depending on the number of surveys required. However, using wards or other political designations may not cover the population accurately because some wards might contain very few houses and others may be densely packed.

As a first point of information gathering, local ward leaders or councillors normally know how many households occupy their area and should be consulted during the first field visit. If this information is gathered and appears to be reasonably accurate, a systematic sampling strategy could be designed based on the populations in wards, especially if each ward contains similar numbers of people.

2.2.9 Stratified sampling

The problem with random sampling is that it might not be representative of the whole town simply because of the very nature of random sampling. It is entirely possible that a higher proportion of higher income households are interviewed, or households that own a private connection or house-owners. To reduce this risk the sample can be stratified according to a range of criteria. These criteria could be low-middle-and higher income groups or owner-occupied households compared to rented houses. However, stratified sampling is really only feasible when the relevant information is available; in other words, when data are available that allow the ready identification of members of the population in terms of the stratifying criteria it is sensible to employ this sampling method. However, in small towns it is unlikely to be economical because the identification of population sub-groups for stratification purposes will entail a great deal of work as there is likely to be no available listing in terms of strata.

2.2.10 Multi-stage cluster sampling

Cluster sampling is normally carried out in larger cities, (for example the Kathmandu Study by WSP, 2001) or across a number of cities where there is a wide geographical area, a range of urban and rural settings, etc. Clusters of household units are selected to reduce the amount of travel time by enumerators.

A step-by-step process is normally employed; the first stage of the sampling procedure involves groupings of units of houses or groups of wards. These are further sub-divided into several segments of a fixed number of households, and then one segment in each ward might be randomly selected using a lottery process. Every household in that segment might then be interviewed. For small towns, cluster sampling should not be necessary unless the town is very large or very spread out – to the extent that enumerators couldn't possibly walk between every nth house and so would require a vehicle, which would increase the price of the survey.

2.2.11 Summary of sampling procedures

In practice, a certain amount of flexibility and innovation is required by the researcher to ensure that the sampling strategy employed is as random and unbiased as possible. The sampling procedure may be difficult to design. Local governments often do not know the census data in the core or fringe areas and time is not available to reconstruct household lists and use these as a basis for sampling. Using simple maps is a suitable alternative.

Small towns often have a simple layout, as demonstrated in Figure 4 – the sketch map of Ishaka, which made a geographical/population split of the town relatively simple. Each enumerator was designated one area and counted every 5th house. The town's population was quite small and the 425 surveys completed represented 20 per cent of the total population. Therefore, sampling errors tended to be reduced because of the large relative sample size (as a proportion to the total population). In larger small towns, more care may need to be taken with the sampling because sampling error increases as sample size decreases.

2.3 Step 3 – Develop the Contingent Valuation scenario

2.3.1 Key steps in the Contingent Valuation scenario

The contingent valuation scenario should comprise the following four key steps:

Define the options being offered to the respondent.

Decide how the options offered to the respondent will be. Will all households be asked their willingness to pay for all options? Will the sample be split according to specified market segments such as the households' existing water supply, location (fringe or core area), or housing tenure?

Choose realistic payment method which sets out clearly how the respondent is being asked to pay for the improved/new services. This should include an institutional setting for the payment method and management of the new services.

Choose elicitation method. This depends on how the willingness-to-pay question is being asked and the number of options offered. The elicitation method can be quite detailed and so has been included as Step 4 this guide.

2.3.2 Select feasible water supply options

In terms of carrying out a robust CVM survey that is useful for making important planning decisions, it is imperative that appropriate, feasible and, accurately valued technical options form the central building block of the CV scenario.

Before completing this stage, the CV researcher should hold discussions with existing institutional partners and engineers, local committees and water user groups, local government, and any other stakeholders involved in the provision of water services. In addition, because the Contingent Valuation Survey should only form one part of the on-going demand responsive process, it is likely that other project stakeholders have suggested a range of options which they feel would be appropriate for each particular project. Using this knowledge, the first task is to draw up a checklist of water supply options. The most important physical characteristic is to ensure that these options are technically feasible. Suggesting private connections for households living in areas many kilometres from the nearest piped system for example, might prove prohibitively expensive.

How many options/scenarios?

An essential part of the survey is to devise a scenario that the respondent believes is credible and understandable. Ideally, there will only be a reasonably small number of feasible technical or service options that users may choose This makes analysis more simple and the questionnaire process easier for the enumerators and the respondents to understand.

In order to decide whether to try and offer only one water supply option or a range of different options, the first important criterion is to find out whether the options offered are really going to be part of a future project proposal by the key stakeholders and project funders. A CVM study carried out in Dar es Salaam for Water Aid, (Wedgwood, A., 2000) gave respondents the choice of private connections, (at a much greater price), or public kiosks. Over 50 per cent of respondents were willing to pay large proportions of their income (including US$100 capital cost contributions) to obtain a private connection. However, it then transpired that

Water Aid were not considering offering private connections to households. Water Aid had a policy of providing public kiosks through community committees and demand for private connections was never going to be met within the project. In hindsight, private connections should not have been included in the CV scenario and probably raised the expectations of community members unnecessarily.

Some poorly conceived CVM studies offer huge numbers of water supply options, which makes the interview and elicitation procedure difficult, the results difficult to analyse, and the consequent design of a water supply project that meets demand impossible. Offering eight to 10 different water supply options – all with different attributes and benefits and at a range of prices is – more likely to confuse the respondent, and lower the chance of obtaining a rationale response. Furthermore, if eight options are selected, the CVM manager will have to ensure that an engineer costs the options, that sketches are made, and very importantly, that they are all feasible. This will add time and money to the process and make the analysis much more complicated. If demand for all options is evenly spread within the survey, and geographically within the town, the project designer has an extremely difficult task, particularly if those selecting private connections are interspersed with those selecting point sources.

The second important criterion is to decide whether certain options should only be offered to specific population groups within the town according to the feasibility of providing that option and the household's existing supply.

Consumer groups

In many small towns, it is likely that the two main consumer groups or market segments will be based on the geographical location of the house, i.e. the core area and the fringe area, as identified in the sketch map of Ishaka Town. Other consumer groups or market segments in Ishaka (as can be seen from Figure 3) are the high-density low-income area and the shops. When developing a sampling strategy for a town it is important to capture the demands of all the various main consumer groups, so that more customers can be satisfied and hence there is a better chance of having financially viable schemes. This is because satisfied customers are generally more willing to sustain water charge payments. There may of course be other useful classifications of consumer groups such as different house types, tenure of housing, income groups, etc.

Research in Uganda (Wedgwood et al., 2001) has shown that both the water options available and the household's capacity to pay vary significantly between the core and fringe areas of a small town (see Figure 5). The core area often has urban characteristics with a limited piped system, whereas the fringe areas are often similar to rural areas using water sources such as springs, wells, and handpumps. When conducting willingness-to-pay surveys for improved services, the service options offered to the different consumer groups should include all the viable options that could be made available to those different consumer groups. Otherwise the survey will not represent the real choices the water users are likely to make.

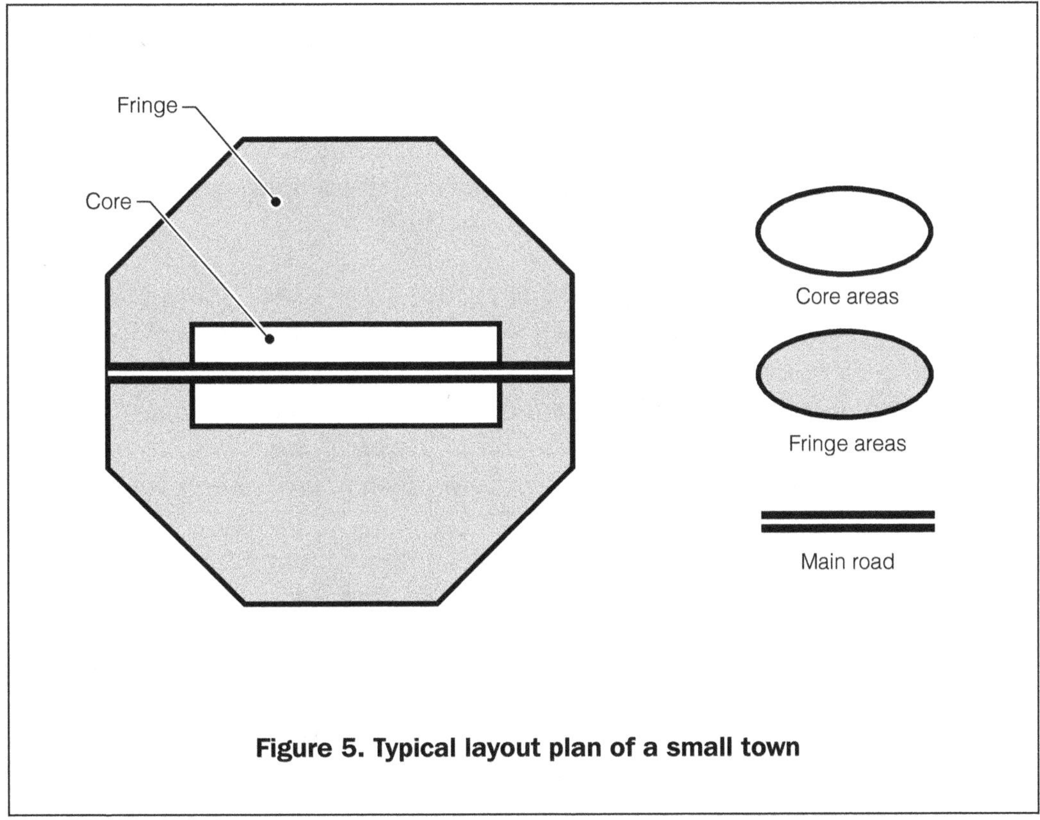

Figure 5. Typical layout plan of a small town

Source: J. Eyatu, 2000.

When conducting willingness-to-pay surveys for improved services, therefore, the *viable* service options to be offered are likely to be different for these two market segments.

There are examples where a large range of options are identified within the survey process, but not all respondents are asked their willingness to pay for all of the options, only those applicable to the household's circumstances. For example, during a sanitation CV Survey in Kumasi, Ghana (Whittington et al., 1993) if a household had a water connection but did not have a flush toilet WC it was asked about its willingness to pay for a WC with a connection to a sewer, as well as a ventilated improved pit (VIP). If the household did not have a private water connection, it was not sensible to ask them how much they would like to pay for a WC with a sewer connection, because they would have to obtain a water connection, which was outside the scope of that project.

Similarly, in Kenya (Nirju and Sansom, 2000) the WTP questionnaire was targeted at three types of respondents depending on the type and location of the house they lived in – the 'market segment'.

The recent survey in Kathmandu (WSP, 2001) varied the CV question depending on the existing water supply in the household. Households with a private or shared connection were first asked the following:

> *Now I want you to suppose that the improved water service for households in the Kathmandu Valley with a private Nepal Water Supply Corporation (NWSC) would result in a total monthly water bill for a typical household like yours of NPR (Nepalese rupees) 200/400/600/800/1000/1300/1600/2000. Let's assume that a water bill of this size would entitle a typical household to about 500 litres of water per day. Would you vote for the water supply improvement plan?*

Note that only one price was offered to each household uning a take it or leave it bidding method, which is discussed further in Section 2.4.

However, households that did not have a private connection but **could** possibly have one were first asked the following:

> *Now, I want you to suppose that the improved water service for households in the Kathmandu Valley with a private NWSC connection would provide the option of...*
>
> *A shared connection (with description and prices)*
> *or*
> *A private connection (with description and prices)*
>
> *Under these financial terms, would you vote for the water supply improvement plan if it gave households like yours the option of having either a shared connection or a private connection?*

However, for households that did not believe it was possible to install a private connection in their house, the private connection option was eliminated from the question and they were only offered the shared connection. In this case the enumerators had to make a decision about which questions to ask based on the previous socio-economic and water supply questions. This can make the process more confusing and prone to errors on the part of the enumerator, and also makes analysis more complicated.

In Uganda in the three small towns of Busia, Malaba and Luwero (van Nostrand and Associates, 1997 a,b) each house was assigned a particular market segment, and then high starting point bids were used to assess demand for *every* option. The elicitation of WTP must have taken some time, and the reliability and truthfulness of responses must have been reduced because each respondent was asked their WTP for every one of the five options. This method is very comprehensive and time consuming and would be difficult to manage and analyse in small towns.

Homeowner or renter?

It is always advisable to change the CV scenario slightly depending on whether the respondent is a homeowner or renter. This normally involves changing the wording of the question from a direct payment to the water authority to an increase in the monthly rent. However, it is not always appropriate to ask household renters questions about whether they would like to connect to a private connection if this is not their decision.

If a house has a private connection, it would make sense to offer improved reliability for this option. In technical terms this is probably the only feasible option. Similarly, it may not be economically or physically possible to offer households living in the distant fringe area a piped water connection, instead point sources might be the only realistic solution. Dale Whittington states in the (1998) Guidance Note For DFID Economists[12] that:

> *It would not be appropriate to ask a household with a private water connection how much it would pay to have a public tap installed in the neighbourhood.*

However, if half the town has a private connection, *but* the existing water supply is unreliable so that they are forced to use other sources as well, then it is probably worth offering those households with private connections other options as well. This may mean that you discuss using lower service options such as hand-pumps

[12] Guidance Notes For DFID Economists on Demand Assessment in the Water and Sanitation Sector. 1998

and kiosks with households that already have a private connection. This still makes sense because the private connections may be so unreliable that the household would prefer a different, reliable, clean source that does not depend on the poor piped network.

In conclusion, it is recommended that a flexible approach is taken when considering whether to design a number of CV scenarios and offer them to different market segments. At the very minimum the following factors should be considered:

- Is the house rented or owned?
- Where is the house located – in the core or fringe areas?
- What types of water supply system are feasible in the rural fringe areas.
- Are people living in the core areas likely to select a 'lower level of service' because their existing piped connections are so unreliable? (This may not be known and so the best advice would be to offer both levels of service if appropriate.)

Provide a detailed description of the water supply improvements

The main challenge in developing the CV scenario is to persuade the respondent to consider seriously the proposal. The description of the water supply improvement will play a large part in this. The CV researcher must consider what attributes of the water supply service matter to the respondent. These will normally include:

- the hours of service;
- the water pressure;
- the cleanliness/quality of the water; (is it safe to drink without boiling?)
- the location of the water source (private, shared, public kiosk, well, etc.);
- the regularity, fairness and predictability of the billing and cash collection systems;
- how the water will be provided from an upgraded piped system;
- whether a water operator will collect the fees? and if so at what times water will be available;

- whether bills will be monthly flat rate bills or whether the supply is metered?
- who will manages the system; and
- who conducts repairs on the system, including repairs if individual private connections fail.

The benefits of the option to the household should be emphasized, including where applicable:

- improved reliability, clean water, higher pressure;
- closer to the household, so less time spent collecting water;
- shorter queueing times; and
- paying by jerry can or bucket means that the household can control their own finances.

It would be unfair to offer a water supply system that will provide water 24 hours a day, seven days a week if engineers have advised that this is not feasible in the town (without unrealistic levels of expenditure). In Bushenyi, the private connection option offered was explained as described in Box 4.

Box 4. Description of private connection option used in the Bushenyi CVM

Option description

a) Option 5 is a private tap connection in your own home or yard. This will be a connection to the improved piped water system.

b) You – or others in your family – will not have to spend time each day collecting water and so will have time for other activities.

c) The water will be available between 7am and 10am in the morning and between 4pm and 6pm in the evenings – that is 5 hours per day.

d) You will not have to share the water with your neighbours or negotiate how to pay the bill because it will be your sole responsibility.

Payment method

e) There will be a contribution to building the system that will include improving the piped system in the town and the cost of additional pipes to your house. Your contribution will also cover the meter and tap.

f) Remember your family will be the only ones paying for the private connection so you will not be able to share the costs.

g) Also there will be operating and maintenance costs – the price of water will be about the same as the price of water sold at community kiosks. However, it is possible that you will use more water with a private connection and so will also have higher operating costs.

h) You will be issued with a monthly metered bill.

Source: Wedgwood et al, 2001.

In this case the private connection would provide water for only five hours per day, as this was the design preferred by the consulting engineers on the project. It represented a substantial improvement for those households that already had a private connection in the town because the existing water supply was so unreliable it often was not available for days at a time.

In the Kathmandu survey, households were told that if they voted for the improved water supply plan, they would receive the improved water service which operated 24 hours a day, water that was safe to drink and had accurate water billing.

Institutional and political factors

CV Surveys should be a practical tool to assist in planning sustainable water supply projects; therefore, the options presented in the CV scenario must reflect the political and institutional reality on the ground. This might mean that the range of technical options is reduced, as was the case for the Dar es Salaam Water Supply and Sanitation Project, discussed in Box 5.

Box 5. Dar es Salaam demand assessment – developing CV scenarios

The Dar es Salaam Water and Sewerage Agency (DAWASA) was content to let Water Aid discuss and design a water supply CV scenario for four poor communities based solely on groundwater sources. However, it would have been unrealistic if the CV scenario included options connected to the city's piped network. DAWASA are currently privatising the management of the system and could not guarantee that the water supply networks within the survey area could, or would be rehabilitated in the near future. Nor could they provide any estimates of the cost of rehabilitating the system because no investment appraisals or proposals had been developed. The subsequent CV scenario discussed kiosks and private connections linked to community-managed local boreholes. A separate question asked respondents whether, in the future, they would like to be connected to the city water system. The answers might prove useful for the company contracted to manage Dar es Salaam's water system, but did not bear much relevance to Water Aid's own project. Water Aid is now implementing improved water supply schemes in the four communities, based only on local groundwater sources.

In Ishaka Town (Wedgwood et al., 2001) respondents were so unsure of the local council's ability to deliver and maintain a reliable piped network that even comparatively richer households said that they are WTP for protected springs rather than an improved piped network. This raises an issue called *institutional bias,* because the respondents did not believe that the existing institution in charge of water supply could provide the level of service set out in the CV scenario. In this case, offering all households all options ensures that the full range of demand is captured. It should still be the case that households with higher incomes, and expectations, will state that they are WTP for the higher service levels.

If new institutional arrangements are being considered, this should be borne in mind when designing and conducting the survey. For example, the questionnaire could ask whether the respondent is in favour of private sector management of water services, if that is a realistic management option. Where possible the proposed future management arrangements should be stated to the respondents when conducting the survey.

Options should also be politically viable (i.e. do not suggest a technical option that has recently been lambasted by a politician, or received bad press because of problems in a neighbouring town).

Social and cultural factors

It is equally important to ensure that the options selected fit into the cultural context of that particular town. Box 6 below demonstrates what might happen if local concerns are ignored.

Box 6. Options which do not address cultural and social concerns

In Nourivier, Northern Cape Province of South Africa, engineering consultants Toen's built a surface dam in 1994. Water was pumped into two tanks using diesel pumps. An efficient reticulation system was designed and yard taps fitted for 90 per cent of the households. However, the community were not consulted about the scheme. They were extremely concerned because the reservoir was to be built on their ancestors' graves. They wrote to the Water Ministry, the Dept. of Local Government and Housing, and Toen Consulting, but were persuaded to 'give the dam a chance'.

The local people now believe that the water is dirty and polluted. The situation was further exacerbated because the activated-carbon filters are not replaced as frequently as they should be because they are too expensive. Consequently, households do not use the private connections installed in 1994 and have resorted to river water and springs (Wedgwood, 2000).

In order to be sensitive to cultural and social issues, it is worthwhile consulting the local authority, local community groups and any NGOs working in the area about the proposed survey and potential service options, prior to conducting the survey. By establishing these connections with local organisations, they can be useful links for when the results of the WTP survey are discussed with the community and key stakeholders.

It is also important that the survey captures the preferences of different consumer groups in the town, including low-income groups. A useful first step is to develop a comprehensive sampling sketch map of the town (as shown in Figure 3) and then consult local stakeholders, prior to conducting the survey, about whether all the significant groups in the town have been included on the sketch map.

The survey should also seek to obtain the demand, perceptions and preferences of both women and men in the community, as their interests and current experiences in collecting water may be very different.

2.3.3 Examples of water supply options

A wide variety of water supply options are usually feasible when considering a demand-responsive approach to improved water supply services in small towns. Figures 6 to 10 show a few widely used options. It must be stressed that these are not the only options, and that these options can also vary considerably; but they do present a few ideas for the engineers and CV researchers to consider. It is important to be open minded about the design of technical option, and not to stick rigidly to previous design standards, so that the most practical and affordable options emerge.

Note that the shared yard connection option (perhaps with onselling of water to neighbours) and the private connection option offer the prospect of selling more water in convenient locations to consumers, so higher levels of customer satisfaction and better revenues can be achieved with these options. However, private and shared connections may not always be affordable or practical in some situations, particularly for poorer people living on the fringe areas of towns. But until the option costings have been done and people have been consulted about their willingness to pay for various options, we cannot be sure what are the most suitable options.

Figure 6. Protected spring

Figure 7. Handpump

Figure 8. Water kiosk – standpost connected to a piped water system

Figure 9. Shared yard connection connected to a piped water system

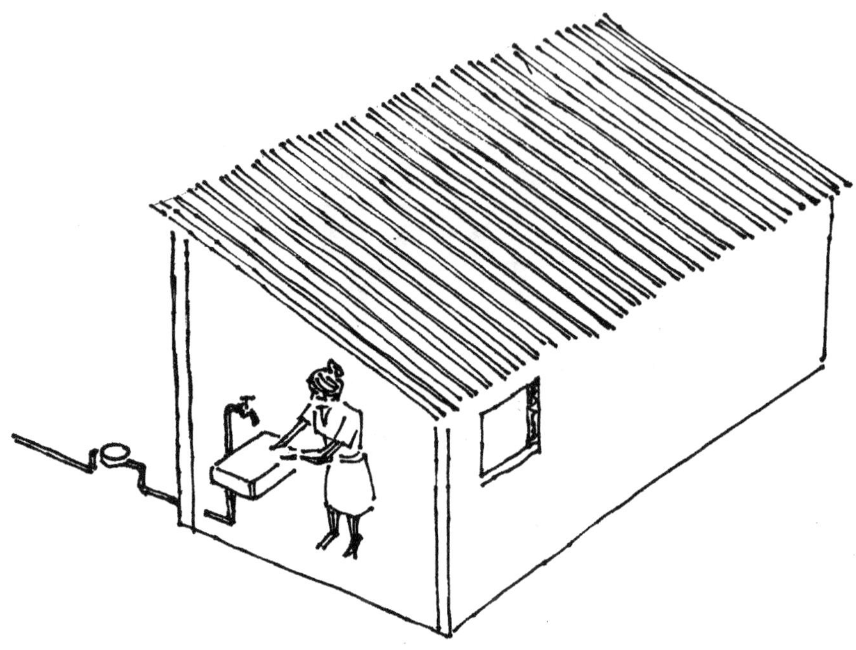

Figure 10. Private house connection connected to a piped water system

It is recommended that the number of service options offered are kept to a practical minimum, but also represent reasonable choice. Viable options in the range of three to five would generally be appropriate, depending on local circumstances. Note that even where technical options are limited, you can also offer different service-level options such as different hours of supply or within X or Y metres to the water kiosk or handpump.

The options should also comply with the objectives of the implementing organisation and if it turns out that demand is evenly spread amongst all options, it should be physically and financially possible to design a system that meets most householders' requirements.

2.3.4 Payment method and institutional setting

The second important aspect of the Contingent Valuation scenario is to include a realistic payment method which sets out clearly how the respondent is being asked to pay for the improved/new services. This should include an institutional setting for the payment method and management of the new services.

In Contingent Valuation Surveys, the description of the item offered for hypothetical purchase must include enough detail so as to ensure that respondents can realistically assess their willingness to pay for the service (Whittington et al., 1994). This description must convey the idea that the respondent would be required to pay something if the options were developed, and this payment method must appear to be realistic to the respondent.

The purpose of the CV questionnaire is to try and find out the maximum amount that respondents are willing and able to pay for their preferred choice of water supply option. WTP is therefore the amount of income, whether monthly, daily, etc. that the household could give up after obtaining the improved water supply and be just as well off as in the situation where the water supply had not been improved. It is unlikely, however, that the utility or water service agency would be able to extract the household's maximum willingness to pay. Most people who purchase a good or service receive a consumer surplus, which simply means the additional value they derive from the good or service over and above the actual real price paid. For example, when a person purchases a pair of trousers from a shop, normally they will feel that they have received an additional value over and above the price paid, particularly if the price of the trousers was reduced or of exceptional quality. For water supply services, for any given tariff structure most households will receive a consumer surplus.

Often the CVM question can explore more than one payment method to determine how households would prefer to pay for a particular water supply option. For example in Lugazi, Uganda (Whittington et al., 1994) the first set of questions asked respondents how much they would be willing to pay for water purchased by the jerry can from improved public taps. The respondents were next asked whether they would use the public taps if a different cost recovery mechanism were used: a fixed monthly fee for unlimited use of the public taps. Specifically, the following description of this option was read to respondents:

> *There is another way people may decide to pay for water from public taps. This would be for every household that wanted to collect water from the public tap to pay a monthly fee. In this case, the attendant would check to make sure that everyone that collected water had paid their monthly fee. Once a household had paid the monthly fee to the attendant, any member of the household could collect as much water as they wanted from the public tap.* (Whittington et al., 1994: 28)

Finally, respondents were asked about installing either a yard tap or in-house connection. Here the question and payment method was split according to whether the respondent owned or rented the house. Renters were told that it would be possible for their landlord to install a private connection and increase their rent by the amount of the water bill. They were then asked if they would want the landlord to install a private connection if the monthly water bill for a household like theirs would be one of two specified amounts. Homeowners were asked if they wanted a private connection if the monthly bill was one of two amounts.

Capital costs for private connections
It is also important to consider the capital costs of installing higher level options such as yard taps and private connections. It is unlikely that the funding institutions are able to pay for a 100 per cent subsidised private connection for each household in the small town, therefore respondents must be made aware that they will be expected to pay for some or all of the private connection. This might include the purchase of a tap and pipes from the main pipe, a meter, storage tanks, and often a connection fee is also charged. These costs can be significant and it is advised that an average cost is calculated to ensure that the respondent understands how much they will be expected to contribute over and above the monthly water fee.

It is generally better for water service providers to try and limit the connection charge amount and transfer some connection costs to the water bills, because connection charges can act as 'barriers to entering the market'. In other words, people may not be able to afford a big connection charge, but they may be able to pay regular water charges, particularly if they onsell some water to neighbours. A common problem in small towns is that there are not enough pipe connections to achieve financial viability. So more connections should be encouraged, provided there is sufficient water to distribute and the pipe system can cope with the additional flows.

The CV researcher should be aware of the availability of any micro-credit schemes available, or that might be made available within the project area, it may be possible for the respondent to pay off the capital costs over a 12-month period on top of their metered water bill.

2.4 Step 4 – Decide which elecitation method to use

The basic principle of a CV Survey is fairly simple: ask a random sample of residents how much they would like to pay for a variety of options. However, there can be complications: there are many examples in survey literature of how changes in wording or context will affect results based on questions about subjective phenomena. For example, in national surveys, close to a quarter of the population will choose the 'don't know' response to most attitude questions if it is explicitly offered; yet these same people will select a substantive alternative if 'don't know' is not specifically provided. More puzzlingly, a question about 'forbidding' a particular action tends to elicit less agreement than a question about 'not allowing' the same action, although the two questions are logically equivalent (NOAA, 1993).[13] CV studies seek descriptive information, thus they risk many of these same response effects that turn up regularly in attitude surveys.

A range of techniques have been developed to ensure that this process is more accurate, that the respondent's answer is rational and realistic and more likely to reflect what *they would pay* if given a *real* chance to contribute towards a particular service level.

There are essentially five elicitation methods:

- the direct open-ended question method;
- the bidding game;
- payment cards;
- take it or leave it (referendum voting); and
- contingent ranking.

Direct open-ended question

The direct open-ended question asks the respondent directly for his/her WTP for the improved water service option(s) offered. The advantage of this method is the lack of cues given to the respondent about the expected value of the service. However, for a similar reason this method does encounter difficulties in that people might not think much about valuing water supply services, particularly if they were previously free, and therefore find it difficult to estimate an economic value. The respondent might need some 'anchoring' as a framework for their decision.

Direct open-ended questions are therefore quite easy to set up and conceptually simple, but can be extremely difficult for the respondent to answer. The National Oceanic and Atmospheric Administration (NOAA, 1993) provided the first guidance on the validity of the results from CV Surveys to accurately value non-use

[13] NOAA (1993) Natural Resource Damage Assessments Under the Oil Pollution Act of 1990. The Use of CVM

values of natural resource areas in the US. The Contingent Valuation Panel concluded that the open-ended CV questions 'are unlikely to provide the most reliable valuations'. Two reasons were cited: in the first place the CV scenario lacks realism since respondents are rarely asked or required, in the course of their everyday lives, to place a monetary value on water supplies. Secondly, an open-ended request for WTP is more likely to invite strategic overstatements; i.e. the respondent increases their response value to make a point.

Bidding games

One of the most common techniques is termed the *bidding game*. Bidding games are slightly more sophisticated methods, requiring the respondent either to go through a series of bids until a negative response is generated and a threshold established, or to select from a range of values. The questioner suggests the first bid, called the starting point, and the respondent agrees or disagrees that they would be willing to pay that price. An iterative process follows: the starting point price is increased to see if the respondent would be willing to pay for it until the respondent declares that he/she is not willing to pay the extra increment bid. The last accepted bid is then the maximum willingness to pay.

This method provides the respondent with time to respond and the opportunity to develop an opinion about the payment for the improved water supply. However, by providing the initial starting price the technique is vulnerable to 'starting point bias' (discussed later).

An alternative to continuously raising the bid price until a negative response is reached is to start at a higher price and if a negative response is given, to lower the price by a specified increment until a positive response is given. At a UNICEF/ Water Aid workshop in Dar es Salaam (2000) to discuss the Socio-Economic Survey, 'CVM and Cost Recovery Planning for Dar es Salaam Water and Environmental Sanitation Programme' many participants thought that lowering the bids was a better procedure for Tanzania and other developing countries. This is because it more closely resembled familiar bargaining procedures that occur daily in the market place. This method is termed the 'High Starting Points' bidding game in this guide. An example questionnaire with a bidding game approach used is shown in Annex D.

Split sample bidding techniques involve using different starting points for randomly assigned sections of the survey. For example, one third of the sample might be given a low starting point, one third a mid-range point and one third a high starting point. This technique allows for a reasonably simple investigation to see if bias has been introduced into the sample. If the results show clusters of maximum WTP responses around the starting points then this suggests that the starting points massively influenced the respondents' answers. However, if the final WTP and the starting points appear to be random, with clusters of maximum WTP correlating with household incomes, or education levels, this suggests that the respondent has considered the real value of the improved service and their ability to pay for it.

The take it or leave it/referendum method

This method requires the respondent to indicate approval or disapproval for a single monetary sum, which is varied across the interview sample. It is very similar in nature to the *Referendum Style* method, sometimes called the *Dichotomous Choice* method because the respondent essentially has two choices, either 'yes I would be willing to pay that price' or 'no, I would not be willing to pay that price'. This technique only gives one answer, but it is possible to calculate the expected mean using statistical techniques, using the logit or probit models. This technique is only recommended for CV Surveys where an experienced statistician is a member of the team and able to analyse the results.

In Kathmandu this method was used and the results analysed using probit and logit models. Each household was offered a number of CV scenarios according to their existing water supply and house tenure, but only one of eight prices was given for the average monthly water bill. The bill might vary from NPR (Nepalese rupees) 200 to 2000 for a private connection to the improved supply for a 24-hour supply.

The NOAA panel preferred the referendum format because there is no strategic reason for the respondent to answer untruthfully.

Payment card

Respondents are shown a list of possible prices in the form of a payment card and asked to indicate their choice and willingness to pay. This runs a much greater risk of bias and the range of possible answers must be carefully determined. For example, a respondent might be shown a private connection and five different prices for the average monthly tariff. Experience in Bushenyi suggested that many households chose the lowest price on offer. More information is provided below.

The contingent ranking method

This method differs from other methods in that a list of multi-attribute alternative options are presented to the respondent. These will each have a WTP value or cost assigned to them. The respondent is then asked to rank the options according to their preferences. The calculations to analyse the results of contingent ranking can be more complicated. At a simple level the results can show the number of respondents that preferred Option A as a first choice, etc. and weights can be used to value second and third choice options.

Contingent ranking techniques are being explored for the water sector. For example, WEDC conference paper '*PREPP – improving utility water services to low income consumers*' (Coates et al., 2001) briefly describes a focus group discussion technique known as PREPP – Participation, Ranking, Experiences, Perceptions and Partnership – that has been field tested with positive results. It is a promising technique for encouraging dialogue between a water supply organisation and community groups, particularly in low-income areas.

Contingent ranking usually takes place in a focus group discussion, instead of personal interviews. Pocket chart voting can be used to derive participants' preferred choices. There is a greater risk of bias if the discussions are lead by stronger members of the group, who might hold more senior positions of responsibility in the community, but a good facilitator can reduce this effect.

Review and repeat procedures

For any of the elicitation techniques, if time permits, one useful idea is to review the answers given by the respondent. At the end of the survey the enumerators carefully repeat the questions, describe the CV scenario and payment methods again, and review the price that respondents said they were WTP towards their preferred option. The respondent might then wish to change their answer because they have had time to consider the implications for their household budget and may wish to lower or raise their bid. (This cannot take place for referendum style elicitation techniques, although the respondent can change their mind from a 'yes' to a 'no').

Table 1. Methods to elicit WTP values from respondents	
Type of bidding procedure	**Description of question**
Direct open-ended	What is the maximum amount that you are WTP?
Take it or leave it. Referendum model, dichotomous choice	Are you WTP $X ? Yes or No Prices can vary within the sample.
Referendum model with open-ended follow up	Are you WTP $X? If yes, what is the maximum amount you are WTP?
Double split sample bidding game	Sample 1: Are you WTP $X? If yes, are you WTP $X + Y? etc. Sample 2: Are you WTP $X+Y? If yes, are you WTP $X+ Y+ Z? If no, are you WTP Y-X?
Full split sample bidding game	Same as split sample with more sample sub-population groups. Keep raising the price over a number of intervals, although no more than five intervals should be necessary. Start one group at a low price and raise prices with yes responses, start another group at a middle price another at a higher price, etc.
High starting points	Referendum style bidding, but always start at the highest price. Are you WTP $Y? If yes, hold. If no, are you WTP $Y-X?
Payment cards	Show the respondent a card which has a selection of prices for a particular option. Cards can also show household expenditure to provide a perspective for the respondent.

2.4.1 Bias and how to avoid it

Opponents of the CV methodology believe that, for a variety of reasons, respondents will not answer truthfully. Misleading answers are said to introduce *bias* into the survey that undermines the validity of the results. Therefore, a basic intention of CV Surveys is to avoid the many biases that might occur.

Biases might arise at any stage in survey design and implementation: construction of the CV scenario; sample selection; development and application of the method and elicitation technique; or in drawing inferences from the results. The literature on CVM has focused on overcoming the many sources of bias in CVM studies. To do this involves careful survey design and pre-testing of questionnaires, competent management of the survey and enumerators, and the use of a range of tests and observations of the results during analysis.

Annex A sets out the option descriptions used in the Bushenyi CVM questionnaire which demonstrate a simple method to overcome some of the most common forms of bias.

Strategic bias

Strategic bias is intuitively the easiest for non-practitioners to understand, and is the bias most commonly cited by opponents of CVM. Strategic bias arises when respondents *deliberately* understate their true WTP for the water supply service, or deliberately exaggerate the amount they would be willing and could afford to pay for the hypothetical service.

Respondents might feel tempted to understate their true preferences in the hope of a 'free ride', i.e. in the hope that either the government, local council, donors, other agencies or other citizens in the town will provide the respondents' first choice without them having to contribute a meaningful amount. Conversely, respondents might overstate their own ability to pay and select higher level options such as private connections, knowing full well that they could not afford the capital cost contribution or the monthly water fees quoted by the enumerator. They may want to vote for the water plan or option to ensure that it is built and then they will worry about paying for it later, or hope that someone else pays for it.

To minimise the risk of strategic bias the CVM questions should be framed with incentives to prevent this type of behaviour from being induced. To help avoid these biases, the enumerators should *always* read out an introductory statement – which effectively sets up the CV scenario. This seeks to embed the bidding and discussion of options within a realistic framework to encourage accurate, reasoned responses and reminds respondents forcefully of their budget constraint. In particular the introductory statement should convey the realistic institutional setting for the provision of the improved water supply. If a private sector company is about to take over the management of the water supply system this should be made clear to the respondent.

Respondents should be made aware that the provision of services would depend on the demonstration of adequate WTP. They could be told that if they exaggerate the amount they would be WTP, they may not be able to afford it if that amount were charged and the new system would not be maintained and would fall into disrepair very quickly. This 'threat' would be very realistic and comprehensible to many respondents living in small towns in developing countries, familiar with the litany of new projects that fail, or never materialise. Conversely, if they willingly understate their ability to pay, then the service might not be provided and this would be the waste of an opportunity for the town.

In practice, in developing countries where water supply CVMs have been conducted, strategic bias problems have not been found to be significant so long as the enumerator explains clearly the CV scenario and payment method and emphasises why it is important to answer as truthfully as possible.

Hypothetical bias

Hypothetical bias in its simplest form refers to the fact that the respondent does not understand or believe in the hypothetical market that has been developed. In order to reduce the levels of misunderstanding the options should be presented with a hypothetical scenario that is familiar to the respondent. In particular the description of the options must be very clear particularly if the respondent has never seen or heard of them. Pictures and drawings help a great deal, although these need to apply to the particular town and often cannot be transferred from one country to another because the landscapes, people, house shapes, yards, courtyards, streets etc. can differ markedly. It is worthwhile engaging a capable local artist to prepare option drawings and to pre-test the level of understanding of the drawings produced.

Information bias

This is very similar to hypothetical bias and is dependent on the amount and quality of information provided to the respondent. Variations in the results of final bids were found to decrease as information increased (Pearce and Moran, 1994). Again offering respondents proper information about the proposed change and including photographs and sketches can reduce the likelihood of ignorant or flippant answers. It might be beneficial to offer more time to answer, either by reviewing the answers at the end of the interview or even returning the next day to complete the interview. At the very minimum, all respondents in the sample should be offered exactly the same information, which normally means that enumerators read from a 'script' and are then sparing with supplementary information they volunteer in response to questions.

Starting point bias

It is important to avoid hinting in the questions or in the manner of the interviewer about the level of expected WTP values. If respondents are asked their WTP for an ascending or descending range of values, the starting level might influence their answers. To isolate this problem, the starting points should be varied to examine whether they are influencing the final WTP. The same problem may arise from the use of payment cards with clearly visible different values printed on them. Respondents should be discouraged from guessing what level of WTP they are expected to produce or what answers their neighbours will be giving.

Interview and compliance bias

The way interviewers conduct themselves can influence responses. This can be identified by separately analysing the responses of each interviewer. If it is found that WTP is consistently higher or lower for all consumer groups when conducted by one particular interviewer, it is reasonable to infer that he/she has somehow influenced the respondent to increase their bid. These results should be discarded.

Another variant of the problem is compliance bias, which arises when the respondent tries to guess the correct answer or tries to answer in a way that they think will please the enumerator. To minimise the problem interviewers should be well trained, and they should following the exact wording of the questionnaire.

Payment method bias

The respondents' WTP may be biased by the choice of payment vehicle specified in the question, such as cash prices, indirect tax, property tax supplement, household rent supplement, one-off cash payments, monthly fees, etc. The bias between the various payment methods could also reflect people's genuine preferences, and so the responses should not always be disregarded or corrected for. To minimise misunderstanding and bias, controversial and unusual payment methods should be avoided and the payment method should be as realistic as possible.

Table 2. Main CVM biases and common errors

Bias	Characteristic	How to avoid
Low strategic bid	Respondent lowers their bid assuming that the state, or others, will pay more.	Emphasise policy on state/donor subsidies and mention that if the town is not prepared to pay sufficiently high water charges, then that scheme option may not get approval.
High strategic bid	Respondent raises their bid above real WTP to ensure that the project goes ahead.	Continually discuss household budget. Make it clear that there will be no subsidies, this is the *real* amount. Choose correct bidding model.
Hypothetical bias	Respondent does not understand or believe in the options.	Explain option clearly. Explain benefits and attributes. Use good sketches familiar to that particular town (not borrowed sketches).
Poor sampling	Non-random sample selected which might lead to poor-quality data collection.	Ensure study area is mapped out and a random sampling system designed to each town.
Starting point bias	Starting price for bidding game influences final WTP.	Vary starting prices within sampling frame.
Interview and compliance bias	Enumerator influences responses.	Analyse results by enumerator to identify influences and discard biased results. Ensure enumerators follow a script and do not deviate.
Payment method bias	Payment method somehow affects responses.	This might be realistic bias revealing preferences for a particular method so ignore. Do not use complicated or controversial payment methods.

The description of options used in Bushenyi are set out in Annex A. These explain the CV scenario, payment methods, etc and attempt to reduce the levels of most forms of bias.

2.4.2 Which elicitation method is best?

Recent research into types of CV bidding models carried out in Bushenyi, Uganda, suggested that different elicitation methods do affect the response values. In Bushenyi, four different elicitation techniques were tried with the same five options: protected spring, handpumps, public kiosks, shared yard taps and private connections. For all options, five price levels were assigned for both the capital cost contribution and the monthly maintenance/water charge. The four bidding models produced slightly different results, and varied in complexity. The enumerators themselves provided extensive feedback on the different methods, particularly in terms of how easy they were to conduct, and which of them appeared to provide an easy-to-understand, realistic CV scenario. Box 7 summarises the four elicitation techniques tested during the survey and discusses a variety of biases which may have occurred during the survey.

Box 7. Testing elicitation techniques

Elicitation Technique 1 – Payment card

This bidding model involved a payment card, and was the least successful of all methods. The danger with a payment card is that it introduces strategic bias and confusion because the respondent is given the opportunity to see all five prices set out on a card and often chooses the lowest price. This is similar to being offered a new car and the salesman sets out five prices that you can pay; naturally, for the same car you will always choose the lowest price. Only 1 per cent of respondents using this bidding model selected the highest price for each option, compared to over 50 per cent of respondents selecting the lowest price. Clearly, the payment card has introduced bias into the system and was not an appropriate elicitation method for Bushenyi.

Elicitation Technique 2 – Full split sample bidding game

Bidding model 2 is the split-sample bidding game, with a range of starting points and prices raised or lowered according to the response. Surprisingly, WTP for most of the options was slightly lower. There is no logical explanation for lower WTP using this model, the technique has been developed to reduce biases through the questioning procedure. During this survey, the team were required to systematically vary the starting points for each house visited. However, because of the risk of geographical bias, it was necessary to alternate different bidding models throughout the day. This led to some confusion, and the starting points were not sufficiently varied. Careful pre-testing and training must take place to ensure that the enumerators understand how to vary the starting point for each household and how to increase or lower the WTP value.

Box 7. continued

Elicitation Technique 3 – Full split sample with review

Bidding model 3 proved to be one of the most successful bidding methods because the enumerators carefully repeated the questions, discussed the CV scenario and payment methods, and then went back to review the price that respondents said they were WTP towards their preferred option. Generally, most households did not change their bid when given the opportunity to do so – 70 per cent of the bids from 109 households remained unchanged. The other 30 per cent of respondents either lowered or raised their bids with no overall pattern in the results. However, most of the enumerators thought that the additional time allowed to review the respondents choices, recap the option descriptions, and offer them the chance to raise or lower their bids, increased the credibility of the results.

Elicitation Technique 4 – High starting point

Starting point bias appears to have influenced a few results in bidding model 4. Average WTP values were very similar to the other bidding models except that there are generally one or two more households that were WTP the highest amount for each option using this model. However, this does not mean that the mean WTP was raised. For the monthly contribution for shared yard taps, 19 per cent of respondents were WTP sh2,500, and 30 per cent were WTP sh5,000 per month. These results were *exactly the same* for bidding model 3.

Summary

During the post-survey workshop, most of the enumerators said that they preferred bidding model 3, because it made the respondents take the survey more seriously and really consider how much they wanted – and could afford – to pay. Bidding model 4 was also popular because it suited the Ugandan market place bargaining system and because it took less time and was simpler for them to conduct because they did not have to constantly change the starting point for bidding.

It is recommended that either *full split sampling bidding games, possibly with a review section,* or *high starting point bidding games* are used for CVM Surveys in small towns. However, if skilled statisticians are available referendum-style techniques with split samples (as in Kathmandu) can help eliminate strategic bias (see below) but require more sophisticated analysis.

During the pilot testing, as part of the enumerator training and survey design, both elicitation techniques could be tested. If WTP values are significantly higher for the 'high starting point model' this suggests that the high starting point is introducing starting-point bias, and the results are not a true reflection of ability and WTP. Alternatively, the review provides respondents with the time to reflect on their answers, the opportunity to lower bids without 'losing face' and to ask more questions about particular options that they might not have understood clearly. It does take an extra 10 minutes per survey, but the marginal cost of employing the enumerators for an extra day is relatively small.

2.4.3 Sequencing options and elicitation procedures

By this stage the survey manager does not necessarily need to have estimates of the real prices of the options – that can be done later. Costing of options might take more time if engineers are involved and so the CV scenario can be designed and prices, or ranges of prices, put in afterwards. The elicitation technique should be decided, although again this might be revised during the field pre-testing.

CV practitioners will immediately realise why great care needs to be taken at this juncture, in order to present the options and prices to the respondent in a particular order, which encourages them to believe that the CV scenario is realistic and does not introduce any bias into the process. In Kumasi, Ghana (Whittington et al., 1993) a large-scale (1200 household) CV Survey was carried out to determine demand for two types of latrine – either a VIP or WC with sewer connection. The contingent valuation questions between the two options were always asked in the same sequence, first WTP for KVIPs and then for WCs. The World Bank Team running the research recommended that 'research is needed to develop cost-effective ways of determining how households would choose between two or more options presented simultaneously at alternative prices' (Whittington et al., 1993).

As many water supply Contingent Valuation Surveys actually offer four, five or even six water supply options, this problem is further exacerbated. Although many more Contingent Valuation Surveys have been completed in the last eight years in the water and sanitation sector, there has been very little constructive research to find the most effective solution to this dilemma. Consequently, as demonstrated in Table 3, methodologies to describe options and elicit bids vary considerably, with no particular method proven to produce the most reliable responses. Therefore, before completing the WTP section, the field manager should be aware that there are no 'right' or 'wrong' methods to elicit bids, but that careful consideration should be given to the way in which the options are presented to respondents and the method used to elicit a bid.

Table 3 implies that a very important decision needs to be made on how to present the options to the respondent; whatever bidding procedure is adopted these methodological issues need to be addressed:

- In which order are the water supply options described? Should they be presented in order of cost, or randomly?
- Should the respondent select only one option, or be asked their willingness to pay for each option in turn? (This can be very time consuming if there are more than two options). If there are four or more options this will involve a lot of descriptions. If the sample is divided and different options offered to each half, this effectively halves the sample size.
- Is the respondent asked to select their preferred option(s) just by the description of its characteristics alone, without revealing any of the prices for each option?
- Should *all* the options be described, and an initial price assigned to each option? If the respondent selects their preferred option on this basis they are implicitly stating that they are willing to pay at least the initial price. If so, which initial price is assigned to each option? If it is always the lowest price, when the enumerator initiates the bidding game they will always have to start at this price, and thus will not be able to conduct random split sample bidding. However, if the high price is assigned to each option, this will influence which options the respondent selects – forcing them to choose lower service levels than they actually could afford and would prefer.

Table 3. Examples of CVM studies with various options and prices

Example CVM study. Number of options and location of study	**Sequencing of options and bidding procedures**	**Reference paper**
Four water supply options in small towns in Uganda.	Describe each option, setting out the institutional environment and a fixed capital cost contribution for each option. Options are described simultaneously. Then ask referendum style questions for O&M contribution for all four options, starting with the most expensive option.	Van Nostrand, (1997a, b and c). 'Socio-economic and WTP Study – Busia, Malaba and Luwero Uganda.'
Small towns water supply in Uganda. Two options, two payment methods. Option 1a – Public taps by jerry can. 1b – Public taps fixed monthly charge. 2 – Private connection with various public tap prices.	1 – Each option was described and bids elicited for paying by jerry can. 2 – Bids elicited for monthly metered charge. 3 – Respondent asked to choose *between* monthly charge for private connection or pay by jerry can at taps (various prices). No lowering or raising of bids.	Whittington et al. (1998). 'Implementing a Demand Driven Approach to Community Water Supply Planning. A case study of Lugazi, Uganda'.
Jakarta, Indonesia. One water supply option to determine value of piped water option only.	1 – asked whether wanted a connection based on three types of charges. 2 – offered connection charge in instalments plus monthly charge for ordinary water quality. 3 – offered connection charge in instalments plus monthly charge for better quality water. 4 – offered real water authorities connection and monthly rates. All yes/no answers. 5 – repeated the above but with reverse ordering of all questions.	McGranahan et al.,(1997). 'Understanding Environmental Problems in Disadvantaged Neighbourhoods' Urban Environment Series Report No 3. SEI

Table 3. continued

Example CVM study. Number of options and location of study	**Sequencing of options and bidding procedures**	**Reference paper**
Anambra State, Nigeria. Public taps and private connections.	1 – described public taps, asked to bid. 2 – described private connections, asked to bid on unlimited quantity of water for fixed rate.	Whittington, et al.(1990). Strategy for Cost Recovery in the Rural Water Sector: A Case Study of Nsukka District, Anambra State, Nigeria.
Kerala, India. CVM to determine demand for piped connections	Two samples. Households with connections asked if they were WTP higher tariffs. Others asked WTP connection costs and monthly charges. Yes/no answers for quoted prices.	Griffin et al.,(1995). 'Contingent Valuation and actual behaviour: Predicting Connection to New Water Systems in the State of Kerala, India'. *World Bank Economic Review.* Vol 9. No 3
Dar es Salaam, Tanzania. Two Water Supply options – Piped connection or public kiosks.	1 – both options described in detail. Respondent asked to select preferred option. Split sample bidding on chosen option only.	Wedgwood (2000) 'Rapid Appraisal Using CVM and other Demand Assessment Techniques'.
Mombasa, Kenya. Six water supply options to three different market segments.	High starting point bids used to assess demand for each option.	Conducted as part of Strategic Marketing research for urban water services by Njiru & Sansom, 2000.
Bushenyi, Uganda. five water supply options.	1 – all five options described in detail, respondent chooses one without knowing exact price but knows relative prices. 2 – various bidding techniques on preferred option. 3 – respondent allowed to choose second option (not obligatory), bidding takes place.	Wedgwood et al., (2001).

Table 3. continued

Example CVM study. Number of options and location of study	Sequencing of options and bidding procedures	Reference paper
Kathmandu, Nepal. One main CV scenario with different market segments depending on existing supply.	Respondents ask 'Are you WTP X?' to join the water supply plan. Eight different prices offered by enumerators, only one price per house, no bidding.	WSP, 2001. 'WTP for Improved Water Supply in Kathmandu Valley'.

Two trends are apparent from Table 3: There are *comparative* CV scenarios based on one, or a maximum of two options. This gives the respondent the opportunity to select a preferred option relative to prices offered, for example, 'Are you WTP sh100 per jerry can or sh20,000 per month for a piped connection'. These surveys use referendum style questions, with 'yes' or 'no' answers, without raising or lowering the bids.

The second group of scenarios offer a wider choice of options, some that might be more suitable to fringe areas around towns, such as protected springs and handpumps and other options involving a piped network that are more suited to core areas. These can be offered to different market segments (income groups). However, because there are more options on offer, it proves more difficult to compare options and their relative prices. In these surveys the respondent might be encouraged to select their preferred option before any prices are revealed, although the enumerator can point out the more expensive options. Alternatively, options are discussed one by one, and the respondent is asked their WTP a specific price for either one preferred option, or each option that they would like to use. The price can be raised or lowered if a bidding game is used.

2.4.4 Summary: Steps 3 and 4

In summary, certain criteria should be considered when designing the CV scenario:

Options: Are the options feasible within reasonable cost parameters? How easy will they be to maintain? How many options should be offered to respondents? Taking all these factors into account it is better to keep the number of options to between three and five. If there are only two options the comparative bidding techniques are more likely to produce accurate WTP values, but other feasible options may be ignored with only two options offered. If there are three or more options it is recommended that the respondent selects their preferred option based on some initial discussion of the likely price, which is followed by more in-depth split sample bidding solely on the selected options.

- **Developing more than one CV scenario:** Are there major disparities in income, housing tenure, or existing water supply services? Is it worth developing more than one CV scenario for different market segments?
- **Cultural and social factors:** Are there *cultural or social reasons* for selecting/not selecting options? How can we ensure all consumer groups are represented in the survey, including low-income groups, as well as women and men?
- **Institutional and political factors:** Are there *political reasons* for not selecting particular options? Who will manage the new system? Is the client interested in the respondent's own views on how the improved water supply system should be managed, or has management been pre-determined?
- **Payment vehicle:** Do you want to test the respondent's preferences for different payment methodologies, such as pay per jerry can vs pay per month, or pay a lump sum vs pay in instalments?
- **Is the payment vehicle realistic:** Is it worth offering the opportunity for households to pay off the capital cost price of a private connection in instalments if no credit is available either privately or through the water supply agency?
- **Which elicitation technique to use?** What level of statistical analysis is possible? Do you have a good statistician on the team, if so the referendum-style dichotomous choice questions can eliminate bias and provide accurate mean WTP values. If not it might be more appropriate to devise a bidding game with varied starting points. Simple cross-tabulations of responses will reveal if there is any bias in the responses.

2.5 Step 5 – Cost the options

2.5.1 What costs to include?

Many CV Surveys do not use the real costs of options, instead a large range of prices, based on, and above existing tariffs are used to elicit the WTP value. Some economists consider the primary purpose of the survey is to elicit maximum willingness to pay of users – independent of the real cost of supplying the improved service. The survey might involve referendum-style questions with a range of prices to ascertain mean willingness to pay for an option or water supply plan (see WSP, 2001).

The results of the survey provide project planners with an idea of how to set tariffs. But if mean willingness to pay is very small compared to the real cost of providing the hypothetical water supply improvement, project planners must hope that large-scale grant aid or government budget allowances are available to make up the short fall. If mean willingness to pay is much less than forecast operating and maintenance costs, it is unlikely that the water supply improvements can be built.

Once the options for the CV scenario are selected, it would be useful to estimate the cost of their provision and combine this with the CV scenario so that the WTP values elicited from respondents have a useful role in setting tariffs for the new scheme. This is an area where many errors are made, so it is important to devote time and energy in achieving reasonably accurate cost estimates. Large errors are known to have occurred, and can seriously effect the usefulness of the respondents, answers.

There are two important considerations when dealing with costing of options and running CV Surveys:-

- How is the real cost of providing the improved water supply service to be met? In particular, do you know whether capital costs will be paid for by an external organisation?

- Are realistic prices to be used in the CV Survey when WTP values are elicited, or are random prices to be assigned to different sub-groups in order to improve the statistical accuracy of the findings?

2.5.2 Will users pay for capital costs?

The existing willingness of central and local government to charge users for water, or to allow other organisations to charge users, must influence the design of the CV scenario. When the prices are set for the options, the intention is to base the prices around the estimated actual cost of providing the service **and** the range of prices that will realistically be charged in the future. It is necessary to include the real costs within the Contingent Valuation Scenario to find out if the respondents are prepared to pay those real self-sustaining prices. However, if it is clear that the full costs will not be passed onto the users, then it is important to include prices that reflect water tariffs that will be imposed in the future. Otherwise, the survey could create unnecessary concerns.

If the authorities in charge of water supply are currently reforming or privatising their water supply systems, they may not have clear policies on whether the state, or users, should pay capital costs for new infrastructure. Is there any point in working out the capital cost of upgrading a network when the authority in charge of cost recovery will not pass on this cost to the consumer, whether as an increased tariff or lump-sum charge? This depends on the specific situation.

Good cost recovery is reliant on supportive government policy, institutional structures, systems able to bill and collect tariffs, and systems being constructed to meet consumers' demand and WTP. Implementing a policy of cost recovery requires acceptance of payment principles and consequently behavioural change (Hazelton, 1997). Sometimes the authority might be considering an improved system and will be willing to contribute a certain percentage of the total costs, but is unsure of the ability of local people to pay. Generally, it can be assumed that regardless of national water policies, there is little money available to pay for the capital costs of upgrading schemes. Therefore, it may be better to make estimates of *all* costs of each technical option in order to ensure that a CV scenario could be used to work out accurate tariffs that will recover at least some proportion of total costs. However, this may vary from town to town, and a final decision will need to be made in the field with the other key stakeholders, once the position of the government, and the town water authority on tariffs has been assessed.

2.5.3 Should WTP prices be real tariffs, or statistical tests?

Many CV Surveys use large ranges of prices in the elicitation procedures. In Kathmandu households were asked to choose one of eight prices ranging from NPR (Nepalese rupees) 200 to NPR 2000. This was used to eliminate bias in a large city-wide programme. It was expected that 90-95 per cent of households would probably accept the lowest price of NPR 200 and 90-95 per cent of households would reject the high price of NPR 2000 per month. The proportion of 'yes' responses at particular prices was expected to vary according to the socio-economic characteristics of the respondents and would be clustered at the prices most accurately reflecting real maximum willingness to pay. The purpose of this discrete choice elicitation method was to improve the accuracy of the final econometric analysis and to ensure that the benefit estimation is robust. The price of NPR 200 did not reflect the tariff that was likely to be charged for an average household's monthly water use, it was simply the lowest value of eight randomly assigned prices for the service offered.

Does giving different respondents different prices spread confusion and raise expectations that the real costs of providing an improved waters supply are quite low? Experience of this approach is discussed in Box 8.

Box 8. Use of different price WTP questions in a Mozambique town

In a water supply CV Survey conducted in November 1994 (Whittington, 1997) in a small town in Mozambique, five different prices were randomly assigned to five sub-samples of respondents. In June 1995, the team returned to the town where the survey was conducted to brief a group of local government officials, including the District Administrator and community leaders, on the results of the CV Survey. After the formal briefing there was a lengthy group discussion about the policy implications of the findings, during which one elderly man, a neighbourhood leader, said that he had followed the implementation of the survey closely and talked to many respondents after their interviews and he generally agreed with the findings. However, he did not understand why different households were asked to pay different prices? Why should one household be charged more than another for the same water connection?

'Of course it was never our intention to leave the impression that different households be charged different prices for a water connection, but that seems likely to have been one outcome of our CV Survey. Our use of a referendum approach with different prices may well have increased public uncertainty and confusion about the costs of improved water services in this town' (Whittington, 1997).

CV researchers working in large urban areas might safely assume that there will be little chance that one respondent will talk with another. However, in small towns, villages and close urban neighbourhoods such an assumption might be wrong. In July 1995, a few hundred people were interviewed in three areas of Semarang, Indonesia, a city of 1.2 million people (Whittington et al., 1995). Each neighbourhood unit has an officially designated leader who had to be informed about the survey by higher level community leaders before the survey could take place. Once this was secured, the team of enumerators and a field supervisor were sent to the neighbourhood to interview all of the sample households in a short period of time, about two to three hours. In this way it was hoped that respondents would have little time to discuss the interview with other respondents before they were interviewed. However, in one community, the neighbourhood leader dropped in on an early interview unannounced, and heard the referendum price offered by the enumerator. This price was the highest of the four prices that were being used and the neighbourhood leader became concerned. He quickly spread the word throughout the neighbourhood that all respondents should answer 'no' to the valuation question. He felt that the improved water and sanitation programme offered in the CV Scenario was too expensive. His confusion was understandable because he believed that the high price that he heard was the *real* price that the respondent, and hence residents in his neighbourhood, would have to pay. The results from this community could not be used.

These examples demonstrate:

- how quickly information can spread in urban communities, particularly small urban communities such as the core area of small towns;
- how seriously some respondents may take the information presented to them and believe that the price they are asked to bid on is the real price that they will be expected to pay, if and when the project is implemented; and
- how easily a community can be confused when households are asked to choose from different prices and when other split sample experiments are used.

For small towns CV research is never hypothetical

CV researchers using split sample referendum-style approaches may say that this misinformation is the result of poor survey design; the language used in describing the CV scenario should ensure that the respondent knows that their decision is *hypothetical* and community leaders should be excluded from the interviews. However, as most researchers from developing countries will know, this is generally not possible or advised. Respondents are often told to 'imagine' that the new water supply service is not 'actually or necessarily going to be offered' (Whittington, 1997).

This nuance may be lost in translation, or not be conveyed accurately by the enumerator (who may not really understand it themselves). When local consultants conduct CV Surveys without assistance from international consultants this nuance is often not understood by the consultants carrying out the CV research, particularly when they know that a real project is under consideration and is not hypothetical at all.

Experience shows that in small towns, water supply managers often intuitively feel that the WTP prices elicited from respondents must reflect the financial reality of the whole project, i.e. they should be similar to the range of tariffs that would be charged to achieve the cost-recovery targets. Many of the CV Surveys conducted by the World Bank and others have focused on large cities where a programme of water supply improvement has not been agreed upon, where financing has not being sorted out, or the design of a suitable system even conceptualised. Therefore, the nature of the CV research is more experimental; the objective is to estimate the benefits of a broadly outlined project and learn how the benefits would change if different prices were charged.

When many CV Surveys are conducted, the researcher typically does not know the actual cost of the project, either because the cost analysis is being done simultaneously, or because there are several variants of the project, or different service levels being considered (Whittington, 1997). In small towns, whether under the auspices of a privatisation programme, new de-centralised local council agendas or centralised management by national governments, the CV Survey is more likely to be commissioned during a 'live' project, where engineers, government staff, NGOs or other donors have already considered what options could improve the town's water supply.

The project implementers will need to know what water supply options people want and can afford to pay for, and so are more likely to want feedback on whether a respondent is willing to pay an amount that will recover O&M costs or not. The economic theory of maximising WTP to assess the economic benefit of water to consumers is somewhat cast aside, and replaced by a more practical process of using household surveys to assess individual's preferred choice and willingness to pay for a range of realistically priced options.

If households cannot afford the basic O&M costs of a piped scheme, and this fact reveals itself during the survey, then the information is very useful and suggests to the project planners that a piped scheme is *not* financially viable and should not be designed, instead alternative and cheaper water supply sources need to be found. In some circumstances, it may materialise that households are willing to pay 80 per cent of the total O&M costs for the piped water, but then the funding agency and government will seriously need to consider whether they can fund 20 per cent of O&M continuously over the next 20 years.

Considering the above discussion, the natural conclusion for this guide, to develop a streamlined methodology for conducting CV Surveys in small towns, is to avoid using different starting prices with referendum-style questions that cannot be raised or lowered. It is advisable that prices elicited in the valuation section of the CV Survey reflect the real prices that would be charged, whether for capital and/or O&M costs of the various options offered.

As complex econometric analysis may not be used, the advantages of improved economic benefit estimation are outweighed by the disadvantages posed by respondents becoming confused and disillusioned with the process and the increased likelihood of misunderstanding by the CV practitioner, to the extent that the CV research may actually be less accurate.

2.5.4 How to calculate the cost of each option

If real prices are to be used during the elicitation section of the CV Survey, then appropriate methods must be used to calculate the cost of each option. These do not have to be very accurate, although if they draw on the project's official cost analysis they should be reasonably accurate. Box 9 highlights the problems that can emerge if care is not taken with cost estimates.

Box 9. Example of poor costing: Dar Es Salaam water demand assessment

When the prices were set for the 'bidding games' the intention was to base the prices around the real cost of providing the water supply and sanitation options. This is a difficult task, because the cost of provision will change according to the number of users, which the CVM is itself trying to establish. However, the engineers were more comfortable estimating high prices for private connections, which were considered more of a luxury for wealthier households, than they were for the community kiosks. An error was made in estimating the cost of providing a new deep borehole, with pump, pumping house, pipes to community kiosks, etc. Estimates increased from Sh2 million before the study, to Sh7 million after the study. This meant that the bidding game prices for community kiosks had been too low.

The lesson learnt from this error is that more effort should be made in the early stages to cost and verify feasible options. The consultant did not place enough emphasis on the importance of the costing exercise when discussing costs with local engineers and staff. When the analysis was completed, although 40 per cent of the sample had selected this option, the actual revenue that could be raised, based on the survey results, was insufficient to fund even 50 per-cent of the capital costs of kiosks without external support (Wedgwood, 2000).

If bidding games are to be used, a range of WTP values will be elicited from respondents, possibly with different starting points. At the middle of this range should be the real cost of the option per household.

As suggested above, project managers may not know whether capital costs are to be subsidised, and may wish to find out whether, and to what extent, respondents would be able to pay for the capital costs of their preferred options as well. In this case the range of WTP values might be quite large, or there might be separate questions about capital costs and O&M costs. In Dar es Salaam, respondents were asked about their WTP for the capital costs of a private connection if they had to pay a lump sum, or could pay in instalments. A second question was then asked about their WTP the monthly metered water bill. Therefore, the capital costs of the new piped scheme and O&M costs were calculated separately.

A number of methods can be used to estimate a cost for each option. These guidelines outline the two most commonly used methods: the Average Incremental Cost (AIC) method and the traditional full life-cycle costing per capita, termed Unit Cost Per Capita (UCPC) approach in this study. Both methods require analysis of a stream of future costs – however the AIC method estimates costs per volume of water supplied (or demanded) whereas UCPC calculates costs per person, or per household. The AIC method would usually only be used for the more expensive piped scheme options.

For both methods there are essentially three types of costs experienced over the life cycle of a water supply investment project. These are the:

- capital costs – these should either be financed through the use of loans and grant assistance and possibly also through up-front contributions from households;
- recurrent costs – often termed operation & maintenance (O&M) costs; and
- replacement costs – including the replacement cost of any hardware. The expected life of all capital cost components should be included in the life-cycle costing.

The cost of supply will include all these components, which will occur at different times throughout the project.

2.5.5 Capital costs

Capital costs should be divided into their main components, which will vary for each option and could include:

- hydro geological surveys and testing and information gathering from existing sources in the area;

- borehole siting, well digging, drilling and equipping, plus the cost of installing electric, mechanical or manual pumps;
- the construction of the concrete tank or reservoirs, pumping houses, etc;
- the piped network from the main water source to the reservoir, and from the reservoir to the water supply option;
- labour costs; and
- the cost of the individual components, (kiosks, taps, handpumps, soak pit, etc).

2.5.6 Operating and maintenance costs

These can be more complicated because local O&M costs on similar schemes may be too low because of inadequate funding and therefore do not provide an accurate guide. In many countries the ministry or department in charge of water supply is likely to have done some studies on typical O&M costs for different types of schemes. These can provide a useful guide, however care is needed in using these figures as they may have assumed high staffing levels or they may not have included all the cost components, which should include:

- staffing and administration costs, paying for the water operators, and expenses of the water committee or local authority;
- operation costs, mainly electricity, diesel, and fuel for pumping, but may also include chemicals;
- routine maintenance and repair, for which flat-rate figures can be estimated based on experience elsewhere; and
- meter reading, billing and customer services costs.

A common occurrence on small town water projects is that the scheme is constructed, then those responsible for O&M do not invest sufficient money in this important task, so water services eventually deteriorate. To increase the prospects of sustainable schemes, reasonably accurate O&M and depreciation cost estimates based on good O&M practice should inform future water tariff increases. It may also be necessary to explain to key stakeholders why the proposed O&M expenditures are necessary. Time and effort is therefore well spent on producing reasonably accurate cost estimates, so that people have some confidence in the validity of the estimates for future financial planning.

2.5.7 Replacement costs

The economic life of the different components should be estimated, including a factor for depreciation. Depreciation can be estimated in a number of ways. In financial accounting, straight-line depreciation is often used. If the expected life of an electric pump is five years, the cost of the investment could be divided by five and this value would be recognised as an expense or cost each year.

The cost allocated for a replacement part must be high enough to ensure that when major parts need to be replaced, the managing authority has enough funds to *immediately* provide a replacement. In small water supply schemes one common method for community-managed projects is to calculate annual investments that must be made in order to pay for the replacement at the predicted time. An example of this process – using *Annuity Factors* – is shown in the costing of a handpump in Section 2.7 on the Cost per capita approach.

2.5.8 Treatment of inflation and interest rates

It is recommended that *estimates* of future cost streams – whether capital costs, replacement costs or O&M costs used to make estimates of the likely cost of providing each option – are always in constant prices, which means that inflation is not included in the calculations for costing options. However, interest rates which reflect the opportunity cost of alternative investments should be considered important for working out how to cost the replacement of major components for the various options – this is discussed in Section 2.7.

Inflation does exist within the 'real' economy, therefore, those stakeholders who are responsible for increasing tariffs should take inflation into account as well as the tariff increases that are needed to meet expected O&M and depreciation costs.

Financial planning must allow for expected inflation. If the average price of goods and services is increasing by 5 per cent each year, the tariff that is eventually charged for the water supply options must also increase by a similar amount. Wages of staff, and the cost of contracted-in services, components and parts, etc. are likely to be increasing at 5 per cent annually, and without a matching increase, the tariffs will not be sustainable and recover O&M costs. This is further discussed in Section 5.1.3. The need to increase tariffs by inflation might be contentious and difficult for consumers who are not used to paying for water at all to understand. Section 5.4 of this document suggests methods for using the results of the CVM Survey as a tool to assist in negotiating with the community.

2.6 Average incremental cost

The key concepts in the assessment of all benefits and costs related to any development projects are related to the notions of opportunity costs, willingness to pay and willingness to accept. Willingness-to-pay values refer to the maximum amount that an individual is willing to pay for the product – in this case improved water supply offered through a variety of options.

WTP = Price + Consumer surplus

Consumer surplus is the excess that an individual is willing to pay for something over and above its price. The person does not actually pay the consumer surplus, and in effect the consumer surplus is a benefit to the consumer. In the case of non-market goods with no price, such as free water from a public well, all benefits received from using that source can be considered consumer surpluses.

Willingness-to-pay values are based on individual preferences, and the total value of any resource, including water supply, is the sum of the values of the different individual values involved in the use of the resource.

It is usual in environmental economics to use willingness-to-pay (WTP) values rather than willingness-to-accept values. It is often not clear when people have a right to claim compensation. It makes sense to estimate how much people are WTP for each potential use of the environment rather than to start with a difficult-to-develop preconception about how it should be used and to weight the valuation procedure accordingly.

A second foundation of all valuation is the notion of marginal cost, which is defined as:

Marginal costing is defined as the addition to the total cost as a result of producing one more unit of output, e.g. the cost of producing one more cubic metre of water, which in the future may involve purchasing bigger pumps or laying new water mains.

It is generally agreed that for economically efficient allocation of water, tariffs should be based on marginal costs to the extent that the marginal cost equals the marginal benefit. This is termed marginal costing. It is important to assume that the marginal cost has included all externalities, these are external costs which are often missed out. For road projects these might be the additional pollution caused by increases in vehicular use, or noise pollution. For water supply projects these might be the additional costs incurred to maintain the environment, or prevent water run-off from forming stagnant pools or affecting other properties.

If the marginal cost has included all externalities, it is called the marginal social cost and the optimum price for the waters supply options should occur when the marginal cost equals the marginal benefit. Unfortunately, marginal costing is difficult to implement in water supply projects (Franceys, 1994) because of 'lumpy' increases in investment that are needed for future capital cost components. An accepted approximation to marginal costing currently advocated by the World Bank and others is the Average Incremental Cost. The average incremental cost (AIC) is taken to be equal to the most economic output that exists when the long run marginal cost is equal to the long-run marginal revenue. The long-run marginal cost is the marginal cost over the whole life-cycle of the project, normally about 20 to 30 years. The AIC provides a smoothed-out long-run marginal cost calculated over the project life.

AIC is a forward-looking concept that effectively uses consumption as a proxy of benefit by calculating costs based on estimated consumption (Webster, 1999). The AIC is calculated by dividing the present value (PV) of the investment costs and operation and maintenance costs by the volume of water consumed each year – it is essentially a cost per volume, but considers future costs, including ongoing operating and maintenance and future volumes consumed.

$$\textbf{AIC} = \frac{\textbf{PV costs for 25 years (\$)}}{\textbf{PV of annual water demand for 25 years (m}^3\textbf{)}}$$

AIC calculations should be based on the future costs of the necessary investment and the recurrent operation and maintenance costs of the system. The average incremental costs will therefore represent the average, or long-run marginal costs over the entire life of the project, assumed here to be 25 years. No consideration needs to be made for inflation and exchange rate depreciation. To be able to use average incremental costs as the method for calculating the likely tariffs that would need to be charged to ensure sustainable cost recovery, the CV researcher, working closely with project engineers, should familiarise themselves with the concepts of *discounting* and *present values.* An example AIC calculation is set out in Section 2.6.4.

2.6.1 Discounting and using future costs

The AIC is a forward-looking method to calculate costs. Therefore, estimates are made of *future* capital and O&M costs and *future* volumes of water, which are likely to be consumed. The method assess costs over a 20 to 30 year period and so requires that a discount rate is used in order to work out the present value.

Discounting is a procedure used to account for the fact that economic resources have a 'time value': $10 paid today is worth more than $10 paid a year into the future, because received earlier it can be invested and thereby earn a return. For example $10 used today might buy five packs of sandwiches from the café, but next year $10 might buy only 4 packs. Conversely, $10 paid a year ago is worth more than $10 paid today, because received a year ago it could have been invested and might be worth $11 now.

Discounting is essentially the act of placing a lower value on future goods and services than on present goods and services. The value of $1 today is treated as being equal to the amount you would need to invest today to receive $1 in one year's time, or in two year's time, and so on. The discount factor is closely related to the real rate of interest in Britain and in many developing countries.

The value of $1 of water supplied from a piped network next year is put at:

$$\frac{1}{(1+r_1)}$$

where r_1 is the discount factor for year one. Therefore, if a discount rate of 5 per cent is used the value of $1 of water one year from now would be 95 cents. Remember percentages must be converted to decimals: therefore 5 per cent = 0.05, and 10 per cent = 0.1

$$\frac{1}{(1+0.05)} = 0.95 \text{ cents}$$

If a discount rate of 7 per cent is used the value of $1 of water in 10 years would be 50.08pence. This is because after 10 years the discount factor becomes:

$$\frac{1}{(1+0.07)^{10}}$$

The final formula for discounting is:

$$\frac{1}{(1+r)^t}$$

Where r equals the discount rate expressed in decimal and t equals the number of years.

Choice of discount rate

Many economists believe that the private opportunity cost of capital provides the best rate to use for discounting, because it best approximates the rate at which society actually trades off current and future consumption. The opportunity cost of capital to a given firm is simply the rate of return on the most valuable alternative project given up. However, evaluating large projects, which have broad impacts on society, the capital market is not always the best arbiter on which to make such a decision. Higher discount rates normally result from using the private opportunity cost of capital, which can 'discount away' some of the long-term environmental and social impacts or benefits of water projects. The Social Rate of Time Preference (SRTP) is based more on ethical considerations. Two key assumptions are built into the SRTP for calculating the discount rate (Word Commission on Dams, 1999).

- All else being equal, society values its ability to consume in the future as highly as it values current consumption; and

- There are practical limits to conducting transfers from present to future generations in order to make consumption equal for each generation; thus mitigation policies for avoiding losses of social goods are the only viable method to assure their availability in the future.

Under SRTP if there was no income growth, social discounting could be performed with a zero discount rate because each generation is assumed to be identical, and each values consumption equally. However, for small towns in developing countries it is likely that there is income growth and so it is probably more practical to base the discount rate on the opportunity cost of capital, or the official government interest rate in the country of research.

Therefore, it is recommended for small towns that CV designers base the elicitation of WTP values on the real financial cost of providing the improved water supply system(s). This amount is referred to as the 'present value' and forms the common basis on which costs and benefits occurring at different point may be compared to one another.

2.6.2 Present values

Present value is a very useful concept and is used in most forms of economic appraisal. Present values are used to work out the average incremental costs of water supply options. To work out the present value of costs, simply apply the discount rate to each year's total costs, (capital plus O&M plus replacement) as demonstrated in Table 4. A simple way to do this is to multiply each years' costs by a standard discount factor. The discount factor relates to the discount rate used; in Table 4 a discount rate of 8 per cent was used. The discount factors are available at the back of most standard financial textbooks – the researcher should ensure that the factor used correlates with the discount rate. The flow of costs are discounted over time and summed to produce one total present value of costs. Similarly, water consumption measured in a volumetric unit, such as cubic metres, is also discounted and summed using the same discount factor.

2.6.3 How to estimate future consumption

A paradox exists when costing options based on either the average incremental cost (AIC) or Unit Cost Per Capita Approach. The volume of water consumed can be very difficult to estimate, and to a certain extent requires prior knowledge of the proportion of the population utilising each new option. However, the whole point of the CV survey is to find out which water supply option consumers want, because only this information will allow for accurate estimates of the volume consumed, etc. The only solution is to make some estimates of the *likely* proportion of the community that will use each new water supply option. This may seem a 'top down' way to estimate costs, because the whole point of the demand assessment is to actually consult users about their preferences, not make assumptions on their behalf.

It is very common for engineers to refer to 'water demand' per cubic metre, this really means the *estimated* volume of water consumed. This still leads to confusion, especially when involved with a research project such as this, which uses 'demand assessment' techniques as one of its central tools. Estimates of future water consumption are *not* demand, because demand in this context also implies a choice of water supply option based on an individual's preferences and ability to pay.

2.6.4 Example of using AIC costing in Bushenyi, Uganda

To calculate the AIC a number of important assumptions must be made. These are demonstrated in Box 10, which used the costing of options in Bushenyi as the framework. In Bushenyi, five water supply options were offered to respondents including point sources (protected springs and handpumps) and connections to a piped scheme.

Box 10. AIC cost components – Bushenyi

Estimate of *likely future* consumption of the piped connection options, based on 24-hour supply to the town. In practice only house connections will have 24-hour supply; the water demand in all the other service levels is reduced to take this into account. Based on the survey by BERC (1999), the demand for alternate water sources was estimated. The BERC survey suggested that 6.5 per cent of households will use kiosks, 48.5 per cent yard taps, and 17 per cent private connections and 19 per cent would use point sources. This demand is assumed to remain in a constant proportion throughout the project period.

The estimated rehabilitation costs were prepared by the Directorate of Water Development to determine the additional funding required for the services.

The costs of construction of the water supply system were adjusted to take care of future depreciation of assets.

The standpost consumers will draw 20 litres per capita per day, yard tap users will draw 40 litres per capita per day, house connections will draw 80 litres per capita per day, and institutional water demand is assumed to be 50 litres per capita per day.

The unit operating cost of the system is equal to US$0.25 per m^3 which is the current value for the system if it produces 600,000 cubic metres of water (BERL, 2000).

This data was put into a simple spreadsheet to produce an average cost per cubic metre of water supplied. The AIC method can be used to calculate full costs, or, if capital costs are not included in the spreadsheet, the AIC is based solely on O&M and replacement costs.

The operation and maintenance costs have been assessed using the existing data from Bushenyi and other towns considered by Yepes (1996). Yepes found that the unit operating costs did not vary with the size of the town but more with the service level provided. It is therefore assumed in the calculation that the unit operating costs will remain constant even when the production is increased though this should reduce due to economies of scale. The unit operating costs are used to determine the cost of producing the water to meet the demand and are taken as US$0.25. Table 4 shows how the operation and maintenance costs are derived and how the present values of cost and production have been determined.

$$\text{Average incremental costs} = \frac{\text{Present value of costs}}{\text{Present value of production}}$$

$$= \frac{4{,}030{,}736}{4{,}630{,}837}$$

$$= \$0.87/\text{m}^3$$

Table 4. AIC cost calculations for Bushenyi

Cost of O&M of water per m³ in $0.25

Year	Population	Point sources 19% of consumption (m³)	Standpost 6.5% of consumption (m³)	Yardtaps for 48.5% of popn (m³)	House connection consumption 17% of popn. (m³)	Institutional consumption for 9% of popn. (m³)	Total annual demand (m³)	Present value of consumption (m³) = demand * discount factor	Annual costs in US$	Discount factor based on an 8% discount rate	Present value of costs = annual costs* discount factor
2001	23,875	90.7	11,329	169,059	118,516	39,215	338,118	289,868	84,529	0.8573	72,467
2002	24,592	93.4	11,669	174,136	122,075	40,392	348,272	276,458	87,068	0.7938	69,115
2003	25,329	96.3	12,019	179,355	125,733	41,603	358,709	263,651	3,998,557*	0.735	2,938,940*
2004	26,089	99.1	12,379	184,736	129,506	42,851	369,472	251,463	92,368	0.6806	62,866
2005	26,872	102.1	12,751	190,281	133,393	44,137	380,561	239,830	95,140	0.6302	59,957
2006	27,678	105.2	13,133	195,988	137,394	45,461	391,976	228,718	97,994	0.5835	57,179
2007	28,508	108.3	13,527	201,865	141,514	46,824	403,730	218,135	100,933	0.5403	54,534
2008	29,364	111.6	13,933	207,926	145,763	48,230	415,853	208,010	103,963	0.5002	52,002
2009	30,245	114.9	14,351	214,165	150,136	49,677	428,330	198,402	107,082	0.4632	49,601
2010	31,152	118.4	14,782	220,587	154,639	51,167	441,175	189,220	110,294	0.4289	47,305
2011	32,087	121.9	15,225	227,208	159,280	52,703	454,416	180,449	113,604	0.3971	45,112
2012	33,049	125.6	15,682	234,020	164,055	54,283	468,040	172,098	117,010	0.3677	43,025

Table 4. continued

Cost of O&M of water per m³ in $0.25

Year	Population	Point sources 19% of consumption (m^3)	Standpost 6.5% of consumption (m^3)	Yardtaps for 48.5% of popn (m^3)	House connection consump- tion 17% of popn. (m^3)	Institutional consumption for 9% of popn. (m^3)	Total annual demand (m^3)	Present value of consumption (m^3) = demand * discount factor	Annual costs in US$	Discount factor based on an 8% discount rate	Present value of costs = annual costs* discount factor
2013	34,041	129.4	16,152	241,044	168,980	55,912	482,089	164,151	120,522	0.3405	41,038
2014	35,062	133.2	16,637	248,274	174,048	57,589	496,548	156,512	124,137	0.3152	39,128
2015	36,114	137.2	17,136	255,723	179,270	59,317	511,446	149,291	127,862	0.2919	37,323
2016	37,197	141.3	17,650	263,392	184,646	61,096	526,784	142,390	131,696	0.2703	35,597
2017	38,313	145.6	18,180	271,294	190,186	62,929	542,589	135,756	135,647	0.2502	33,939
2018	39,462	150	18,725	279,430	195,889	64,816	558,861	129,488	139,715	0.2317	32,372
2019	40,646	154.5	19,287	287,814	201,767	66,761	575,629	123,472	143,907	0.2145	30,868
2020	41,459	157.5	19,672	293,571	205,802	68,096	587,142	116,665	146,786	0.1987	29,166
2021	42,288	160.7	20,066	299,441	209,918	69,458	598,883	110,135	149,721	0.1839	27,534
2022	43,134	163.9	20,467	305,432	214,117	70,848	610,864	104,030	152,716	0.1703	26,008
2023	43,997	167.2	20,877	311,543	218,401	72,265	623,086	98,261	155,771	0.1577	24,565

Table 4. continued

Cost of O&M of water per m³ in $0.25

Year	Population	Point sources 19% of consumption (m³)	Standpost 6.5% of consumption (m³)	Yardtaps for 48.5% of popn (m³)	House connection consump-tion 17% of popn. (m³)	Institutional consumption for 9% of popn. (m³)	Total annual demand (m³)	Present value of consumption (m³) = demand * discount factor	Annual costs in US$	Discount factor based on an 8% discount rate	Present value of costs = annual costs* discount factor
2024	44,877	170.5	21,294	317,774	222,769	73,710	635,548	92,790	158,887	0.146	23,198
2025	45,774	173.9	21,720	324,126	227,222	75,184	648,251	87,644	162,063	0.1352	21,911
				Total present value				**4,630,837**			**4,030,736**

The average incremental costs in the Bushenyi calculation of producing the water is US$0.87 (UShs 1,566/m^3) for recovery of operation and maintenance and replacement costs. This includes the $3,908,800 capital cost expenditure to rehabilitate the piped system in year three. The capital cost expenditure might take place in year one, or be spread over a number of years depending on how long the scheme would take to build. It was felt in Bushenyi that planning and collection of capital cost contributions would take up to two years and so the money would not be spent until year three – this is slightly artificial. However, in many projects, capital costs are assumed to be spent in the first year – the project is initiated and costs are incurred through community mobilisation programmes, etc. but the physical construction often takes more than one year before commencing. These prices were then used as the basis for the WTP values used to cost the piped water options in the survey.

The annual water production in 2001 is 338,108m^3 but increases proportionately with population size. It is interesting to note that in Bushenyi, the current tariff is $0.42 per cubic metre where connections are metered, which equals 48 per cent of the full cost-recovery tariff based on these AIC calculations.

2.6.5 Using a range of bidding prices

For the CV Survey, a wide range of bidding prices can be used for each option, in order to learn the *maximum* amount that households are willing and able to pay. The range should be flexible enough so that if the assumptions about number of users are wrong, this will not prevent a popular option from being implemented because the real cost of supply is much higher than suggested during the CV Survey. Box 11 demonstrates the range of prices used in the referendum-style bidding for Option 1 – protected spring in Bushenyi, Uganda.

Box 11. Question format for Option 1 – capital cost contribution in Bushenyi

As you know the local council does not have enough money to improve the springs in your area, therefore households will need to make a contribution. Everyone who contributes will be allowed to use the spring. How much are you prepared to contribute, in a one-off lump sum, to help with the construction of the spring? This price is per family.

1. sh1000 lump, if NO how much sh_______________
2. sh5,000 lump sum
3. sh10,000 lump sum
4. sh15,000
5. sh20,000, if YES what is the maximum amount sh_______________

For this survey, the enumerators started at either the lowest, middle or highest price, randomly assigned to each household. Respondents were given the opportunity to raise or lower their WTP values.

2.7 Cost per capita approach

The more traditional method involves estimating the current capital/installation cost of providing each option, plus allowance for operating and maintenance costs and depreciation of the capital assets and dividing by the number of people that will be using the system.

The present values of these costs are determined by discounting the cash flows at a rate equal to the opportunity cost of capital cost to the national economy – the discount rate. As discussed above, a decision needs to be made on the proportion of capital costs that users are likely to be expected to pay for. If a full piped network is to be provided free (initially at least), the capital costs paid for by the respondent might only be the price of the connection, plus a meter and tap. In some cases meters and taps are also provided free and the only cost to the respondent is a fixed 'connection fee'. If possible, most of the capital cost loan repayments should be met through the water charges.

The cost per capita approach is easy to apply for stand-alone sources such as protected springs or handpumps as demonstrated in the example of costing a handpump that follows.

Example of costing a handpump

When considering stand-alone water supply options such as handpumps, the main consideration when determining the O&M tariff is to incorporate future replacement costs. There are many ways of calculating capital replacement costs, some of which compensate for the time value of money. The value of money is related to interest rates in the local and international economy. The value of $1 today will purchase more goods than $1 will purchase in five year's time. Therefore, communities and project implementers are encouraged to think about how prices of local and imported components might change over their lifetime to ensure that O&M and replacement costs can be paid for in the future without sudden big increases in the cost of water, whether it is paid for by the jerry can or through monthly fixed fees.

It was advised in Section 2.5.8 that estimates of future costs used to calculate the option costs are always in constant prices. This means that inflation is not included in the calculations for costing options. However, interest rates, which reflect the opportunity cost of alternative investments, should be considered important for working out how to cost the replacement of major components for the various options.

In reality, inflation is accounted for because interest rates should include expected inflation if capital markets are working correctly. For example, suppose inflation was zero and to attract capital to your project you needed to pay 4 per cent interest on borrowings. (Here the interest rate is compensation for risk, i.e. it is not to cover inflation because there is none.) Now suppose you expect inflation to rise (you may see the prospect of energy costs rising or trade unions pushing wages up). Suppose you anticipate inflation will grow from zero to 5 per cent p.a. Now to attract capital you will need to pay not 4 per cent but 9 per cent (i.e. 4 per cent for the risk and 5 per cent for the loss of purchasing power caused by inflation.) Therefore the interest rate would become 9 per cent in this capital market (Barker, 2002).

Without considering the need for saving specific sums of money to replace major component parts, the sustainability of most water supply and sanitation projects is undermined. One way is to set aside equal amounts every year, taking into account interest rates. These amounts can form part of the O&M tariffs charged. This is known as *amortization*, and is based on an annuity factor (AF) which can normally be found in a cost table. Its value is a function of the expected lifespan of the equipment in years (n) and the interest rate (r) in the local economy.

$$\text{Annuity} = \frac{\text{Current price of replacement costs}}{\text{Annuity factor } (AF_{r,n})}$$

The formula for calculating annuity factors is a little complicated, but project implementers should not be put off by this. The annuity factors are generally found at the back of financing text books and involve simply reading off the table based on the number of years that the equipment is expected to last (n) and the interest rate (r). An example of such a table to calculate annuity factors is provided in Annex B.

Ideally, the annual amount paid each year (or saved in a communal/private scheme) should be slightly higher than the price divided by the number of years. This will ensure that the town, or those families using the handpump, have saved enough to compensate for future price changes of the required component.

Estimating the cost of a handpump can be relatively simple. The following example is based on the Finnish Nira handpump, used in many countries including Tanzania, from where the following data originates.[14] In 2000, the local cost of a Nira handpump in Tanzania was about US$625 (for a shallow well about 8 metres deep.) O&M costs are set out in Table 5, and average US$56 per year.

If the pump is well maintained, after 10 years its life can be extended by a further 10 years by replacing a number of critical components. These have a 2002 price of US$314. The amount that needs to be set aside each year to raise the equivalent amount that will be required to purchase the same component in 10 years time, can be calculated using an annuity factor.

Once again, an appropriate annuity factor can be looked up and used to calculate the annual amount which must be 'saved' or 'paid' by users. Reference is made to the annuity factor table in Annex B. In this case, assuming an interest rate of 5 per cent over a 10-year period, the annuity which should be set aside each year is US$40.60. The annuity factor does not include inflation, these prices are assumed to be constant.

[14] For further details see Quest Consult (2000).

$AF_{(5,10)} = 7.72$ (read off the annuity table)

$$\text{Annuity} = \frac{314}{7.72} = \text{US\$40.60 per year}$$

In addition, replacement costs for the handpump valued at $625 can be calculated, based on a 20-year life span. Again, applying an annuity factor to the present value of the handpump (US$625) results in an annual cost of US$50.20.

$AF_{(5,20)} = 12.46$ (read off the annuity table)

$$\text{Annuity} = \frac{625}{12.46} = \text{US\$50.20 per year}$$

Table 5 shows that in order to enjoy the benefits of the handpump in the future, its users should set aside almost US$150 a year for the first ten years. Assuming the pump is used by 30 families and a flat rate payment system, this is equivalent to an annual O&M tariff of approximately US$5 per household per year. This figure does not include the costs of tool replacement, every day caretaking and the administration of the cost recovery system itself.[15]

The resulting costs of the Nira handpump are summarised in Table 5.

[15] Household payments are modified by three factors – the distance to the source, the number of people in the household, and 'special' factors such as disability. Cross subsidies within the community are considered in detail in Section 5.1.

Table 5. Annual costs of a Nira handpump

Cost description	**Annual cost ($) with 5% interest (discount) rate**
O&M costs (recurrent) all years	56.00
10-year refit	40.60
20-year replacement	50.20
Total annual costs, years 1-10	**146.80**
Total annual costs, years 11-20	**106.20**

In many towns and communities, what happens in practice is that people wait until the handpump breaks down. At that stage, the community – or better-off households within it, may club together to pay for a repair. This could be termed 'reactive' cost recovery. Whichever cost recovery method is used, it is preferable that the community members are aware of the typical future costs, so that money will hopefully be set aside to meet expected large repair costs.

What happens if the interest rate or inflation changes?

Of course, the above calculations are based on forecasts of future inflation and interest rates in volatile economies and are often wrong. If inflation appears to be increasing within the national economy, and the community realise that they are not collecting enough money to recover future costs, a simple calculation of the future price of the pump could be conducted at any time during the repayment period, and this would tell the community how much extra they must collect. For example: [16]

Say inflation of 3 per cent over and above that included in the interest rate is anticipated. Over 20 years US$1 inflating at 3 per cent p.a. would have a nominal value of:

Inflation factor $= 1.8061 = (1 + 0.03)^{20}$ (Remember inflation is compound.)

So the pump with current price of $625 will, 20 years on, cost 625 x 1.8061 = US$1125. If you want to recover this from 'today's' customers you would need to collect an extra 1125 - 625 = US$500 over the 20-year period. (If inflation

[16] Example provided by Peter Barker, (Economist) 2002.

increased during the last five years you would only need to calculate $(1 + 0.03^5)$ to work out the inflation factor.)

You could collect this in many ways. The simplest would be:

$$\frac{500}{20} = \text{US\$25 per annum*}$$

*In fact this method would generate a little more than the expected replacement cost and so builds in a safety margin.

Therefore, in years 11-20, when the community is expected to collect only US$106.2 to pay for O&M and the new pump in year 20, the community should also collect an additional US$25 per annum to pay for the 3 per cent annual price rise which was not included in the original calculations.

These are only examples and serve to illustrate the many ways in which future costs can be included in the planning of community repayment schemes. The most important fact to remember is that all running, capital, and replacement costs should be included in any repayment scheme (unless the government/donor has paid the capital costs) and that prices do increase, exchange rates change, and interest rates are variable, so it is essential that repayment schemes build in a safety factor.

How to estimate the capital and O&M contributions for new water kiosks?

The development of appropriate option costs proves more problematic when attempting to estimate the contributions or tariffs required from *each household* towards the capital cost of a public kiosk, which is usually only one of many different water supply services connected to a piped network. This is particularly, true when the whole piped network needs to be rehabilitated. What proportion of the capital cost share to be paid for by users should be 'assigned' to the kiosk users compared to those households hoping to have private or shared connections?

Again, estimates of the total number of families likely to use each option must form the basis of the costing exercise. To calculate the cost per family, estimates of the proportion of people using each option need to be made. Simple weighted averages can be assigned to different options based on the estimates of the likely number of users – this technique was used in Bushenyi, Uganda, as demonstrated in Box 12.

Box 12. Unit costs per capita approach – Bushenyi

Capital Cost Contributions In Bushenyi, even though 6.5 per cent of the population were *assumed* to use the new kiosks for the AIC calculation, they will not consume 6.5 per centof water volumes because per capita consumption is much less from kiosks. Therefore, a ratio of consumption was worked out based on weighted averages. Kiosks were costed at 3.5 per cent of the total investment cost of US$3,909,880. It would cost US$131,005 to install kiosks in Bushenyi/Ishaka including a proportionate contribution to rehabilitate the piped network. 6.5 per cent of the population equals 301 families, therefore average capital cost contributions per family would need to be $435 to pay for the *full cost* of new kiosks. Similar calculations were made for shared yard taps and private connections.

O&M Cost Contributions Once the up-front capital costs have been calculated, the O&M costs were calculated using the cost of water per cubic metre. The main difference was the fact that the US$3,909,880 initial investment was removed from the cost stream – leaving just O&M and replacement costs. The operation and maintenance costs have been assessed using the existing data from Bushenyi and other towns considered by Yepes (1998).[17] If capital costs are not included in the calculation, the average incremental costs of supplying water from the rehabilitated piped system is US$0.23m^3 (UShs414/m^3.) – less than half the existing tariff for consumers using the existing piped network in Bushenyi.

The O&M costs of protected springs and handpumps were calculated by taking the net present value of all future estimated costs, including depreciation of assets and replacement costs. For example, in Year 7 it was assumed that US$2,000 would be needed to carry out major repairs of the borehole and to replace the handpump.

In summary, for the cost per capita approach the following costs need to be estimated and then divided by the estimated number of users:

- Capital costs of providing each new service. This can be dis-aggregated into units, i.e. Cost per stand post number of standposts needed + additional pipes.
- The re-payment costs of a loan if a government or donor grant is not used to pay for the capital costs.

[17] Yepes (1998) found that the unit operating costs did not vary with the size of the town but more with the service level provided. It is therefore assumed in the calculation that the unit operating costs will remain constant even when the production is increased though this should reduce due to economies of scale.

- The O&M cost of running the new service. For groundwater sources this should include the price of fuel for pumping, etc. and the costs of new parts.
- Replacement costs should be considered. If a cheap pipe will need repairs every two years this can be included on a simple spreadsheet. Similarly, pumps and meters often need replacing.
- Running costs also include institutional and management staff costs. New water supplies often require a system of bill issuing and collection. Meters might need to be read and bills calculated, which might require the purchase of new billing equipment.

2.8 Comparison of two costing techniques

The recent CV Survey in Bushenyi used both costing methods and experimented with different repayment scenarios. For the AIC calculation, all capital costs were included in the spreadsheet in Year 3 and no consideration was made for re-paying a loan. For the traditional approach, the capital and O&M costs were simply divided by the estimated number of users. The running costs were spread over 20 years with major rehabilitation and servicing costs in Years 7 and 14. It was assumed that users would pay the capital costs upfront and then O&M costs would be recovered through a tariff. The tariff is therefore much less for the unit cost per capita approach because capital costs have been taken out.

Table 6 below sets out the *full costs* of providing each option. Both AIC and unit costs per capita (UCPC) estimates are included in the table. The first two columns show the up-front capital cost contribution and monthly running costs for each household calculated using the UCPC approach. It is assumed that there are 5.1 people per household, (based on the results of the survey). Therefore, the unit cost per capita would be slightly more than one-fifth of the values given. The cost per household was used in the example because the AIC costs were calculated per household and so made comparisons between the two much simpler. The second column shows the required monthly payments assuming that lump sum capital cost payments have already been paid. The third column sets out the total monthly charge per household required to recover all O&M and capital costs over 25 years using the AIC approach.

Table 6. Cost of five water supply options using two costing methodologies

Description and costs per family	**Capital cost lump sum payment per family. Each family = 5.1 people. (USh and US$)**	**UCPC monthly payment (after capital costs) (USh and US$)**	**AIC (monthly full cost charge) (USh and US$)**	**AIC (additional connection fee) (USh and US$)**
Protected spring	120,000 ($66)	100 ($0.05)	750 ($0.41)	0
Boreholes fitted with handpumps, monthly fee for free use of the handpump	261,000 ($145)	650 ($0.36)	3,750 ($2)	0
Water kiosk within 50 metres of distribution network based on one jerry can per person per day	782,000 ($434)	1,240 ($0.68)	6,000 ($3.33)	0
Yard taps within 50 metres of distribution network based on 40 litres/capita per day	1,565,000 ($869)	2,480 ($1.37)	11,500 ($6.38)	25,000 ($14)
House connection within 50 metres of distribution network based on 80 litres/capita per day	3,130,000 ($1,738)	4,970 ($2.76)	22,500 ($12.5)	125,000 ($69)

Note: these capital cost lump sum contributions seem rather high, although they are unavoidable in some cases. Refer to Section 2.8.2 for a discussion of the merits and disadvantages of lump sum capital cost contributions.

For the protected spring, based on the UCPC approach, households could contribute USh120,000 (US$69) each up front and O&M costs would be minimal. Conversely, using the AIC approach set out in the third column, each household would need to pay USh750 per month (US$5 per year) but there would be no upfront capital cost contribution.

For the handpump option, according to the AIC calculation, households should contribute an annual payment of USh3,750 per month (US$23 per year). For the UCPC approach, each household would be required to make a lump sum payment of USh261,000 (US$145) and then monthly payments of just USh650 or US$0.37 per month.

For private house connections, using the UCPC estimates, each household would be required to pay over 3 million shillings (US$1740) as an up-front contribution plus USh2,760 per month running costs. This is obviously too high an up front contribution for the vast majority of households. The AIC approach would require a monthly payment of USh22,500; assuming each person in the household of five people consumed 80 litres per day.

2.8.1 Summary of two costing techniques

In summary, both approaches rely on discounting a stream of costs over the life of the project and on initial estimates of the proportion of people likely to use each option. That is unavoidable because the main objective of the exercise is to develop a realistic CV Scenario based on a *cost estimate per household or per person.*

The UCPC method has a number of advantages, particularly if the results are to be used to work out requirements for grant aid or loan assistance, or for open-market borrowing to fund the capital costs. The water authorities in small towns should not simply assume that they could charge the AIC per cubic metre of water consumed and hope to achieve financial sustainability over 20 years. To rehabilitate, or build, piped networks in the core areas will require up-front funding of some sort. A bank loan may have much higher interest rates than the discount rate used in the analysis. Getting a bank loan may be very difficult from risk-averse private banking institutions. Donors wishing to fund capital costs of new schemes will need to know the exact amount required in the first three years, not the long-term average cost of a cubic metre of water.

However, an advantage of AIC is that it is quite simple to calculate and it implicitly allows for cross-subsidisation. In our costing in Bushenyi, the unit cost of water was US$0.87 per m^3. This was the same for households using kiosks or private connections. Once the demand assessment has been completed, it is a relatively easy process to calculate equitable tariffs by increasing the unit cost of supply for private connections and reducing the unit cost for kiosk users. In addition, the AIC approach makes the best estimate of long-run marginal costs, which should ensure the most efficient level of water supply over time because it is the cost per unit of water supplied. Cross subsidies and how to set tariffs is addressed more fully in Section 5 of this guide.

2.8.2 Are capital cost contributions appropriate?

In situations where finding funds for new construction works is a problem, particularly for rural or small town water supplies, there are three main reasons why it can be useful to obtain capital cost contributions from households willing to participate, and these are:

- If only limited funds are available, the financial contributions from households in the community can help meet shortfalls in funding requirements.
- The cost contribution from households is a clear indication of their demand for the new services and encourages a sense of ownership of the new scheme.
- Such contributions encourage potential donors and government departments that the project is worthwhile and will be sustainably used. They are therefore more likely to fund the programme.

However, once the scheme is completed, problems can arise if new people move to the town and want a new private water connection but are unwilling to pay a large capital cost contribution for a scheme that may have been completed many years before. Indeed there is a tendency for people who have made a capital cost contribution for, say, a private connection, to think that they can have cheap water for evermore, and other people who did not contribute cannot have access to these services.

A better and more equitable way of funding construction is through increased water charges that can cover both capital loan repayments and O&M costs. So customers who use the services pay reasonable charges for those services, irrespective of when they arrive in the town.

If a proposed capital project cannot be funded without individual capital cost contributions from households, it is recommended that these contributions are kept to a minimum, leaving open the option that other people, who want a connection later, will be able to pay a contributions at that time.

2.9 Step 6 – Complete household survey and CVM questions

2.9.1 General requirements

Now that the CV scenario has been designed and options costed, completing the household survey and the contingent valuation section should be relatively simple.

The CVM questions should be designed to produce answers that are simple to understand. A common error for consultants seeking to use CVM to assess demand is to select too many options and devise too many payment scenarios (these issues were addressed in Steps 3-5).

Undertaking a large household survey involves a sequence of activities including: questionnaire and sample design, pre-testing, enumerator training, survey implementation, data entry, and data processing. There are a number of control procedures to improve the reliability of results: questionnaires can be carefully pre-tested; a selection of households can be revisited to verify the enumerators' work; double data entry and internal consistency checks can be used to check the data entry, etc. Some common problems that can occur when conducting household surveys are discussed briefly in Box 13.

Box 13. Common problems with household surveys

Large but poorly selected samples – Sampling procedures should be as rigid as circumstances allow, as it is better to have a smaller sample that is representative than a large sample which misses out key income groups.
Insufficient pre-testing and training – The team should work together closely for at least five days training, and spend two days pre-testing before regrouping to discuss relevant changes. A further 2 days training can be held to ensure that the survey forms are filled in correctly.
Too many questions – A very common error. The survey should focus on water and sanitation issues related to assessing the current situation and future demand for new services. *Questions that could not be analysed because of time and budgetary constraints should not be used.*

Two further measures can be taken to mitigate the problems associated with poorly written and managed CVMs:

- The enumerators (particularly those from the community), local community leaders, and other project stakeholders, including the client, should contribute to the design of as many questions as possible.
- The team should have no preconceived notion of what results are required, or expected. The questionnaire is simply a situational analysis of current water and environmental sanitation infrastructure and of future demand.

2.9.2 How to structure the questionnaire

The next three sections discuss the basic structure of the CV questionnaire.

- Section 1 – Introduction to survey; demographic and socio-economic data
- Section 2 – Existing water supply services
- Section 3 – WTP section

2.9.3 Section 1 – Demographic and socio-economic data

Introduction to survey

Before the interview begins, an introduction is required so that the respondent understands why they are being asked the questions and, more importantly, to emphasise that permission has been granted by a recognised authority. Respondents will be unwilling to answer any questions without feeling assured that 'official' permission has been granted.

For example, in Lugazi, Uganda the following introduction was used:

> *Hello, my name is______________ and I am working with Lugazi Water and Sanitation project on a study of Lugazi Town. We have spoken with your RC chairman, who has given us permission to talk with people in this RC about their current practices and needs for water and sanitation services. Your answers will be used to help provide better water and sanitation services to Lugazi and they will be kept completely confidential. (Whittington et al. 1994, p 73)*

Demographic and socio-economic data

This type of data is particularly important for large investment projects where econometric analysis is to be used to analyse the results. If econometric analysis is not going to be used (see Stage 10) the CV researcher should concentrate only on basic data. These questions are needed because they can be used to crosscheck the results of the CVM section for inconsistencies. In Kumasi, Ghana, the World Bank team discarded 2 per cent of all questionnaires because of obvious inconsistencies in the respondent's answers. For example, inconsistencies might be the respondent saying that they would contribute US$100 per annum to a scheme when their annual income was only US$10. The questions should focus on income, expenditure, household size, the employment of all members of the household, and educational attainment.

Many people undertaking household surveys ask too many questions, many of which provide 'interesting' data, that is not even tabulated or analysed. Always consider why a question is being asked and how the data is to be analysed. For a *streamlined* CV Survey, try and ask no more than 15 questions in Section 1.

Income data should be collected by asking the respondent the average income of their main wage earner *and* the type of employment and wages of *all* employed people in their family. Consequently, some families with three or four wage earners may have much higher weekly incomes compared to other families. Before the survey, the enumerators should have specific training in the use of various methods to find out accurate household income. This involves discussing in detail the types of work carried out by all members of the household, whether the household has a bank account, when salaries are paid, how many people went to school, what the fees were/are at the local secondary schools (which should be checked), etc.

Estimates of income and expenditure, as explained in these guidelines, are useful indicators of socio-economic status, and help the CVM practitioner to understand the results of the survey and determine their accuracy. Estimating income and expenditure is one of the most difficult parts of the survey and requires sensitivity on the part of the enumerator, and the ability to interpret fact from fiction. The enumerators should be able to build up realistic income and expenditure time lines for the respondents, but this will need to be practised during enumerator training. Participatory skills may be required for this section of the survey, not simply a question and answer format. It may be possible to undertake expenditure timelines, showing when the household has to make large payments, such as at the start of the school term for books and uniforms, or to purchase inputs for agricultural production such as seeds, fertiliser, tractor loans, hiring of labour, etc. Ordinary expenditure on food products, including staples and 'special' purchases of meat, etc. should be discussed. The house may have recently purchased a new roof, livestock, tractor, etc. which provides an indicator of surplus cash and/or labour.

Income and employment patterns vary enormously from person to person. Regular salaried employment is often reported in the core areas of small towns, but more often than not, employment will be seasonal. Therefore, the enumerator should try and understand how the money is earned, the number of months that money is earned (on average), and the number of months when no money is earned. Average annual incomes are therefore more reliable an estimate than monthly incomes which will vary continuously. Income might be earned through casual seasonal labour, through regular employment, through sales of crop surpluses (although many households store grain and rice as a buffer against external shocks), and through sale of livestock products, including milk and meat.

Often families receive transfers of funds from other relatives working in large cities or other countries, questions should be asked to ascertain the amount and regularity of such transfers. Sometimes they are very irregular, for specific medical or educational purposes.

An example of socio-economic questions including income, expenditure, household demographic data and questions discussing the existing water supply is included in Annex C.

Estimating wealth and vulnerability – the sustainable livelihood context
Recently, more emphasis has been placed on the need to understand whether a household has the *ability* to pay for improved water supplies. The use of tools developed within a sustainable livelihoods approach can help researchers to understand how a vulnerable household can cope with external shocks such a drought, loss of productive adults, etc. A DFID Knowledge and Research project (R8034)- *Building Sustainable Livelihoods for the Poor into Demand Responsive Approaches* has addressed these issues. In particular the research focused on the need to assess demand from a pro-poor perspective and understand water-livelihood linkages so that demand responsive approach can achieve increased poverty reduction, as well as lead to more sustainable water supply services.

New tools of poverty analysis are being developed to incorporate sustainable livelihoods and household economy approaches. These have the advantage of improving the project implementer's ability to understand the impact of water supply projects on poor and vulnerable households. An assessment of different wealth groups within the community forms an inherent part of these techniques, which could be incorporated into demand assessment techniques (including CVM) and improve the understanding of the impact of demand responsive approaches on the most vulnerable households.

2.9.4 Section 2 – Existing water supply

It is important that the survey establishes basic information on water consumption patterns in the target community. This will require, as a very minimum, information on water for drinking, washing, and cooking and seasonal variations in water use. More specific questions should be asked only where applicable. For example, if the respondent says that they never use water vendors, it is a waste of time to ask a question about how much they pay water vendors per jerry can.

A standard procedure is to determine the main water sources per season and then to ask specific questions about these. Demonstration questions are included on the next page. Depending on the nature of water-use patterns in the town, more specific questions might need to be asked about water consumption for livestock or for irrigating subsistence agriculture. Is it likely that building a new reservoir and piped water system will encourage farmers to water their livestock with water from the piped system, and how will this affect consumption of water? These kinds of question will be very useful for the engineers designing the water system. Where meter results are available, these can be used to crosscheck with people's stated water consumption from the piped water supply.

The full list of questions to determine a households' existing water supply, and their opinions on its reliability and quality, are set out in Annex C.

Private or shared connection

If the existing water supply is a private connection, or a shared connection to a piped water scheme the following questions might be asked:

15. Is the connection shared with other households?	0 – No – if no go to Question 17 1 – Yes
16. How many households share the connection?	_______number
17. How much did it cost to install the connection (Sh)? This includes the connection fee and any additional costs you had to pay for pipes, etc.	0 – no charge 1 – up to 10,000 2 – 10,000 to 50,000 3 – 50,001 to 75,000 4 – 75,001 to 100,000 5 – 100,001 to 150,000 6 – 150,001 to 200,000 7 – > 200,000________how much? 9 – Don't know
18. Do you sell water to neighbours, or other organisations or groups?	1 – Yes 2 – No – if no go to Question 19b)

continued .....

19a. How much do you sell water for?	1 – up to 10 per jerry can 2 – 10 to 25 per jerry can 3 – 26 to 50 per jerry can 4 – 51 to 75 per jerry can 5 – 76 to 100 per jerry can 6->100 how much? _________
19b. How many hours a day does the tap/well supply water (on average)?	1 – up to 2 hours 2 – 2 to 4 hours 3 – 4 to 6 hours 4 – 6 to 8 hours 5 – > 8 hours 6 – other_____________

Using communal sources – wells, springs, public taps, and handpumps

If the respondent's primary drinking water source is a combination of communal sources, springs, and rivers during the wet seasons and a handpump during the dry seasons the types of questions on the next page might be included.

20. How far is the water source from your home? (The enumerator often has to explain relative distances.)	0 – < 20m 1 – 20 to 99m 2 – 100 to 499m 3 – 500 to 999m 4 – 1 to 2km 5 – >2km
21. How long does it take to walk to the waterpoint and back again?	0 – up to 14 minutes 1 – 15 to 29 minutes 2 – 30 to 44 minutes 3 – 45 to 59 minutes 4 – 60 to 89 minutes (1 hour to 1 hour 29 minutes) 5 – 90 to 119 minutes (1 hour 30 minutes to 1 hour 59 minutes) 6 – >120 minutes (> 2 hours)
22. How long on average at peak time do you have to queue at the waterpoint?	0 – No queuing at all 1 – 10 minutes 2 – 20 minutes 3 – I always have to queue for 30 minutes 4 – I sometimes have to queue for _____ minutes (insert amount) but other times I don't have to queue at all.

Purchasing water from a vendor or neighbour

Many coping strategies involve purchasing water at some point during the year, particularly during the dry season when local springs and rivers have dried up. It is a useful crosscheck for the analysis of results if the survey data has determined the amount of 'cash' that is sometimes spent purchasing water. This is not to assume that the water is priced fairly, at an equitable price set in a perfect market. Often vendors or owners of private wells, etc. have a monopoly, or at least form a cartel to fix a higher price. If water is scarce people will be prepared to pay a high cost for water from vendors, as is illustrated in Box 14.

Box 14. The high price of water in Sudan

An influential study of the opportunity costs of scarce water supplies in two squatter communities on the outskirts of Khartoum was conducted in 1992. A random sample of 27 households were interviewed by local Arabic women to obtain information on water usage and income sources, including local beer brewing, livestock rearing, remittances from absent relatives, wage labour, etc. Fourteen of the households were then observed from 6am to 6pm for two days and interviewed about their use and storage of water. They were observed purchasing water from vendors, and using water for washing, watering livestock, and cooking. In Meyo, the 14 households spent an average of 16.5 per cent of their average income purchasing water. In Karton Kassala they spent 55 per cent of their average income purchasing water. However, the high price of water in Karton Kassala did not reduce average consumption. The price elasticity of demand is effectively zero; meaning that water was such an important asset that no matter how expensive, the women from Karton Kassala had to purchase a minimum amount. Clearly, there is a price threshold because households cannot spend more than their income. The study also suggested that the households in Karton Kassala are forced to trade off the other major household expenditure – food – against water, which contributed to severe malnutrition in the poorest households.

Source: Cairncross and Kinnear (1992)

Questions about expenditure on water provide useful information – including the following:

Water vending and cash purchases of water

23. How much do you pay during the rainy season?	Sh________ jerry can
24. How much do you pay in the dry season?	Sh________ jerry can
25. What do you think of the quality of the water that this supply delivers?	1 – Very clean, I know he/they get it from a good source. 2 – Quite clean, we don't need to boil it. 3 – Not very clean, we boil it for drinking. 4 – It varies, sometimes it is very dirty and we boil it, sometimes we think it is clean and do not boil it. 5 – It is very dirty.

Questions about health and disease episodes

Asking people about disease episodes can be particularly useful for CV Surveys related to environmental sanitation improvements. Hygiene questions including information on hand washing, children's defecation practices, etc. are very common in environmental health surveys. For a water supply CV Survey, these types of questions might not be necessary – and are probably better suited to a more participatory approach. Even if the survey data proved that 70 per cent of households washed their hands, how does this actually contribute to the final assessment of demand for water supply options, and the expressed willingness to pay for them?

Questions relating to health, hygiene, and disease episodes should really be addressed to female respondents only. As it is likely that at least 50 per cent of the sample will be males, this undermines further the value of these answers if only half the sample complete this section. There may be further problems because a male enumerator may not be able to discuss certain health issues with female respondents, but it is difficult to always ensure that female enumerators interview females. In Bushenyi, 'difficult' questions on hygiene, sanitation, defecation practices, etc. were not asked, instead the questions referred only to disease episodes. The enumerators found that male respondents knew equally well whether members of their family had contracted malaria in the last few months and so this gender issue was not so prominent.

If required at all, only simple questions to find out the overall incidence of disease episodes within the family should be used. The two questions set out on the next page basically sought information on serious illnesses contracted by any members of the family in the last two months. In Sub-Saharan Africa, where HIV/AIDS is a serious problem, teams of enumerators from both Tanzania and Uganda did not want to mention HIV/AIDS in this section because they felt the subject was still taboo in many towns and villages, and such questions might be offensive.

		Yes? Number?
27. What type of diseases have affected any members of your family over 12 years old in the last two months? **Insert number of people that were affected by each disease**	Diarrhoea	
	Blood or mucus in faeces	
	Vomiting	
	Malaria	
	Cholera	
	Typhoid	
	Other............	
		Yes? Number?
28. Have any of the children in the household who are under 12 had any of these conditions during the last two months? **Insert number of people affected by each disease.**	Diarrhoea	
	Blood or mucus in faeces	
	Vomiting	
	Malaria	
	Cholera	
	Typhoid	
	Other............	

2.9.5 Section 3 – Elicit willingness-to-pay values

The willingness-to-pay sections of the questionnaire should be drafted using the guidance given and building upon the agreed contingent valuation scenario, including feasible water supply options, payment modes, and a method for eliciting WTP values. An example of a complete set of WTP questions covering five water supply options are set out in Annex D. Normally, the WTP section is the final part of the interview, mostly because the WTP question may vary depending on the respondent's existing water supply, which will need to be determined first.

After the socio-economic and water supply questions, an introduction to the CV scenario can be drafted. An example is set out in Box 15. In towns where real projects are planned then the explanation in the CV scenario should be honest and provide as much information about the new scheme as possible. For example, in Tanzania, Water Aid were already working in certain wards on the outskirts of Dar es Salaam, therefore the CV scenario introduction set out in Box 15 was used.

Box 15. Introduction to CV scenario, Tanzania

I want to describe for you some kinds of improved water services that the Water Aid Community Managed Water and Sanitation Project is proposing for your street. I would then like to ask you a few questions about the level of service that your family would like if they were available in this street at higher prices than you are currently paying.

It is VERY IMPORTANT that you try and answer as honestly as possible, so that we can help the community design the best water and sanitation system. If you tell us a lower price than you can really afford, we may design a system that you do not want, that is too basic and cheap. In other words, it might be possible to have a higher level of service in this street.

On the other hand, if you give us a price that is very high, because you think we will provide the system anyway, we will design an expensive system that you cannot afford. The operating and maintenance costs will be too high and the scheme will fail after a very short time, and you will have to revert to your traditional services.

Also I would like you to remember and consider how much your family earns per month, and all the other things you have to pay for, such as school uniforms, food, transport costs etc.

Source: Wedgwood, A. (2000)

The Bushenyi CV Survey was used to research appropriate CV methodologies and so it was important to not raise expectations too much by being as honest as possible about the likelihood of the new scheme being implemented. This is reflected in the introduction statement in Box 16.

Box 16. Introduction to CV scenario, Bushenyi Uganda.

Enumerator please read out for all respondents before asking the WTP questions
I want to describe for you some kinds of improved water services that might be possible in Bushenyi. I would then like to ask you a few questions about the levels of service that your family would like if they were available in this area at different prices. We are aware that there are many problems with the existing system in Bushenyi because of lack of pressure as there is not enough water in the pipes. At the moment we are just researchers trying to assess what kind of water supply people would prefer, and how much different families are prepared to pay to contribute to the cost of providing improved services. We do not know whether the authorities will act upon the results of the study, although we do know that the DWD and local council are trying to improve the water supply situation in Bushenyi.

As you know, the local council at the moment cannot afford to operate and manage a reliable water supply system that provides continuous clean water. It is therefore important that users consider contributing something, which will be a percentage of the cost of improving the water supply service and for the running costs. Users able to contribute more money may be able to get a higher level of service.

It is VERY IMPORTANT that you try and answer as honestly as possible, so that we can help the community design the best water supply service. If you tell us a price that is a much lower price than you can really afford, a system may be designed that you do not want, that is too basic and cheap. In other words, it might be possible to have a higher level of service that you can use.

On the other hand, if you tell us that you would like to pay a very high price that you cannot really afford, because you think we will provide the system anyway, we will design an expensive system that you cannot afford. The operating and maintenance costs will be too high and the scheme will fail after a very short time, and you will have to revert to your traditional services.

Also I would like you to remember and consider how much your family earns per month, and all the other things you have to pay for, such as school fees and uniforms, food, transport costs, etc.

PLEASE JUST TRY TO ANSWER AS TRUTHFULLY AS POSSIBLE. I will describe five different water supply services to you and ask which you would like to use and how much you want and can afford to pay for each option. Now the cost of each option does vary so I will start off with a description of the cheapest option and move upwards. You may only want to select one option, or you might want to choose more than one option – this depends entirely on you.

Source: Wedgwood et al (2001)

It is important to note the various paragraphs in the opening statement, which seek to reduce the levels of strategic bias by emphasising the need for honesty and for the respondent to consider their own budget constraints.

Participation levels

After the opening statement, one idea is to try and understand whether the respondent would participate in meetings, workshops, and community discussions, which will likely form the next phase of the demand responsive approach to providing the new water supply system. The 'participation question' is only appropriate if the CV research is taking place because a 'live' project is planned in the town. If the CV Survey forms part of government research simply to assess people's WTP for water supply services without any plans to implement a project, this question would not be needed.

Box 17 shows the 'participation' question which was asked in Uganda immediately after the Introduction to the CV scenario (Box 16).

Box 17. Participation question example

Firstly , if an organisation was to work in this town to plan a new water supply system, would you participate and go to meetings and workshops to discuss your views and demands with them, and do you think you should pay at least something for an improved level of water supply service?

1 – Yes – I would be very interested and attend meetings and workshops to discuss water supply options and would consider paying for the better service.
2 – No – I wouldn't attend meetings although I will give money to get a new water system.
3 – No – I don't think we need any new water system. I am happy with my current water supply situation.
4 – I would not give any money because I do not believe that any improved system will be built.
5 – I will not give any money because I think that the government and council should provide free water.
6 – *Other reasons*_____________________________________?

If the respondent answers four or five do not continue the questionnaire but go to the next house. If respondent answers three probe further to assess the situation, but discontinue if unwilling to pay for improved water services.

If the respondent said that they thought the local council or government should provide free water and they should not pay anything, then the questionnaire should be discontinued, although the finding noted. Similarly, if the respondent's answer matched answer three or four in Box 17, it would be pointless to continue with the elicitation of bids because the respondent does not want to pay for water or believes that the government should provide and pay for all water.

Management/ institutional preferences

The client and other stakeholders may not be sure how the new water supply system is to be managed; they may be considering a number of possibilities. The questionnaire presents a good opportunity to consult townspeople, therefore an institutional management question may be included at the start of the WTP section. The respondent could be asked to vote for a new management system, for example it could be managed by *either* the utility or local council or private sector, etc. An example question is set out in Box 18.

Box 18. Management preference question asked in Bushenyi, Uganda

It may be possible for different organisations to manage the system, I will describe them for you. If you had a choice which of the following would you prefer to manage this new improved water supply service?

1 – A private operator. This would be based on a special management contract between the local council, the central government, and a private company. The assets will still be owned by the council and government. The private company will manage the system, maintain it, and collect the fees but the local council will have regulatory powers.

2 – A Water Users Association. This will be based on a committee of local people who will elect a supervisory body to manage the water system, collect revenues, and carry out repairs. The association will not make a profit and so the motivation for the association to carry out good repairs will depend on the quality of people in the association.

3 – The local council. They already manage the existing system.

4 – A central government department or the national water and sewerage company.

5 – A different organisation. Please describe your ideas ____________________________

Next, the options should be discussed and the WTP of respondents elicited through the various techniques discussed in Step 4.

An example of the questions used to elicit bids for a protected spring in a small town in Uganda are set out below.

Option 1- PROTECTED SPRING

Notes to enumerator: Do not show ANY prices, select a different starting point each time, and raise or lower the bid according to the answer. RECORD THE STARTING POINT WITH AN **S** AND THE FINAL BID WITH AN **F.**

QUESTION 1 – Would you use this option and are you willing to contribute a certain amount towards its construction or running costs?

Yes – I would like to use this option, and would be willing to contribute something towards its construction.

No – I would not use this option and would not like to pay anything for it.

Enumerator: If answer is No please go to next option.

QUESTION 2 – As you know the local council does not have enough money to improve the springs in your area, therefore households will need to make a contribution. Everyone who contributes will be allowed to use the spring. How much are you prepared to contribute, in a one-off lump sum to help with the construction of the spring? This price is per family?

1 – Sh1000 lump – If NO how much? Sh_______________
2 – Sh5,000 lump sum
3 – Sh10,000 lump sum
4 – Sh15,000
5 – Sh20,000 – If YES what is the maximum amount? Sh_______________

QUESTION 2b – What monthly fee, per family, are you prepared to pay towards general maintenance of the spring and pipes?

1 – Sh100
2 – Sh250
3 – Sh500
4 – Sh1,000
5 – Sh5,000 – If yes what is the maximum amount? Sh____________

Examples of all five options: springs, handpumps, water kiosks, shared yard taps, and private connections are included in Annex D.

The willingness-to-pay questions could also include a follow-up question to ask the respondent whether they expect that their household would increase or reduce their water use as a result of the new improved but higher priced water supply option. It would take considerable time during the interview to estimate accurately the quantity of water they are using now, or might use with the new option, especially when the existing supply is irregular or from many sources.

2.9.6 Enumerators' feedback

A space should always be left at the end of the questionnaire for comments from the enumerator. These can be very interesting, and can lead to certain answers, or the whole questionnaire being discarded.

Guidance should be given on the types of observations that are of interest to you during training, such as specific indicators of wealth and poverty, the size of the dwelling, the construction material, cleanliness, etc. Often the enumerators feel it is their duty to comment on whether they thought the respondent was answering truthfully. This can provide interesting data but also is highly subjective – so care should be taken.

In Box 19 is a list of comments made during the household survey in Bushenyi.

Box 19. End of interview comments by enumerators

Question 5. Expenditure was more than given income due to past savings.
Question 2. Respondent looks after her late brother's orphans
Respondent chose option 5 but could not afford any money.
Question 6A. Respondent is only willing to contribute in kind not in cash.
Question 4. Respondent uses Sh6000 yearly for transport to and from hospital for check-ups.
All the necessities are brought to the family by relatives.
Question 5. Observation showed that house was ramshackle.
Question 5. Expenditure was exaggerated, enumerator observed a poor household.

Chapter 3

How to manage a successful survey

3.1 Step 7 – Enumerator training and pilot testing

3.1.1 Select enumerators

CVM requires the use of intensive survey techniques, so it will be useful to select enumerators with at least some of the following attributes:

- Experience of carrying out in-depth, hour-long household surveys.
- Ability to carry out random sampling during their fieldwork and not simply visit households that appear friendly, or where the occupants are clearly home.
- Knowledge of the water and sanitation sector.
- Knowledge of the local language, culture, and customs.
- Senior members of the community where the CVM will be conducted. A small number of local people can be extremely useful on a team. Recent experience in Tanzania (Wedgwood, 2000) proved that with supportive training, local community members can help implement surveys. As team members they contribute extensive knowledge on the feasibility of particular options, whether there are taboos concerning particular water sources, suggestions for improvements to existing sources, local knowledge on current coping strategies, etc.
- The number of enumerators required will vary according to the sample size of the overall survey and how many days the survey will run for. It is better to recruit more enumerators than is necessary because some might drop out or not understand the process.

Often enumerators are social science graduate students from national universities. Many have worked on other surveys for other agencies. Enumerators will need to be paid at a local daily rate and if the town is some distance from their homes they will need living and accommodation expenses. These should be included in the overall budget of the CV Survey.

3.1.2 Classroom training

Training is ongoing, and although it may begin in Step 6, training continues once the draft questionnaire has been completed through to pilot testing. The training often helps to improve the CV questionnaire, because additional people are constantly reviewing the instrument.

The training should include:

- Understanding the basic objectives of the survey
- Understanding the Contingent Valuation Methodology
- Background to the water and sanitation sector
- Familiarisation of the questionnaire
- Training in conducting random sampling, emphasising the importance and methods for ensuring that the sample is as random as possible
- Role-playing survey techniques
- Pilot testing of the questionnaire
- Evaluation of the pilot testing, changes, and improvements to the questionnaire process

As mentioned, some of the enumerators might already have been involved with the work, helping develop some of the questions, assisting with translation, and ensuring that the questions will be understood by the targeted population.

A training plan should be developed and discussed with the enumerators during the first meeting. This can be very simple and the basic aim is to ensure that the enumerators are prepared for the wide range of tasks they will be expected to manage. Box 20 shows the training plan used in Bushenyi, Uganda.

Box 20. Enumerator training plan

Classroom·

- Introductions of survey goals
- Timetable for survey, workload, and expectations (At this stage enumerators that will not be available for the duration of the survey should inform the CV manager.)
- Review basic survey skills – who to interview, how not to introduce bias by prompting, etc
- Household survey, using codes, how to complete the boxes, understanding each question
- Techniques to collect accurate income and expenditure data
- Introduction to CVM concept
- Learning the four options from the option sheets, using the pictures, practice describing options
- Understanding the bidding process
- Role playing the introduction sheet – very important to understand how bias should be avoided through developing a realistic CV scenario
- Half-day role playing complete questionnaire
- Sampling techniques, use sketch of town to formulate a complete survey plan for the duration of the survey

Field training

- Pilot testing in the field
- Review completed questionnaires, discuss problems with the survey and sampling
- Revise questionnaire
- Photocopy questionnaire
- Select survey team leaders – explain role of team leaders
- Survey logistics

If split sample surveys are to be used the reasons why must be explained to the enumerators. Remember that the enumerators might also be confused by the different sets of prices.

At the start of the training it might be helpful to get the enumerators to sign an informal contract. This will set out their roles and obligations and the CV manager's role. For example, on three CV Surveys carried out in 1999–2000 in East Africa, at least two out of the eight enumerators arrived two hours late for the first training session. Often illness and poor public transport are to blame.

However, if the contract stipulates the times for classroom training, field training, and the hours of work for the survey, this makes everything transparent, and once the contract is signed lateness tends to become less of a problem.

Similarly, the contract should set out the enumerators' rates of pay and their expenses allowance.

Role playing forms an important part of the classroom training, particularly for the complicated bidding games and WTP sections of the questionnaire. Sample answers and roles can be written on small pieces of paper and randomly selected by the enumerators who then perform their roles with their neighbours.

At the end of the training periods, including the field training, an oral and written test should be set to ensure that the enumerators understand their roles and responsibilities and are fully familiar with the survey instrument. This can be a multiple-choice questionnaire and include a 15-minute interview with each individual enumerator.

Important instructions for the enumerators should be written up on a 'Survey Instruction Sheet'. An example instruction sheet used in Bushenyi is set out in Box 21.

Box 21. Survey instruction sheet for enumerators – Bushenyi example

- Visit a maximum of eight houses per day, up to six minimum.
- Please read the survey through three times, then practice it three times with your family and friends so that you get to know the different sections and can work efficiently. If you are taking more than one hour for the household survey and the WTP sections then try and speed up a little.
- Try to interview someone in the house who understands where they get the water supply from; this will normally be women of the household. However, because we will be asking income questions and dealing with financial issues, it would be better if you could speak to both *the male and female head* whereever possible.
- Begin with the household survey.
- You read out the questions on the left-hand side, you DO NOT have to read out all the intervals on the right-hand side. They are there to increase the speed of the survey and to help me with the analysis.
- If the person is having difficulty answering the question, or the question does not fit in one of the intervals, you can try and prompt them, but DO NOT lead them to give you an answer that might not be true.
- Put a circle around the number that the answer corresponds to. If the answer is not in an interval use the 'other' box to write the answer.
- After the household survey go to the WTP for water supply. (Remember to use the right survey for your street.)
- Remember the sampling procedure and do not simply question any household that is close by or where the owner is available.

WTP questionnaire

- First read out the general introduction to the WTP process.
- Second read out all the options and show all the pictures.
- Third ask the participation and management questions.
- Now go through each option. It is unlikely that respondents will want to choose and pay for all options, this will depend on their existing water supply system and the amount of money they can afford.
- Remember that each day you will need to do a different bidding model.
- There are two pilot days and seven survey days.

In addition, once the questionnaire has been completed (after the pilot testing) enumerators should be given a set of guidelines that include:

- Household questionnaire coding sheet
- Sketch map of the town with target sampling zones
- Pick up and drop off schedule for each day of the survey
- One main copy of the CV scenario script. To reduce photocopying this does not need to be included in the questionnaire.
- Survey instruction sheet

Translation

Once the enumerators have familiarised themselves with the questionnaire and understand every question, the next step might be to arrange a translation into the local language of the survey area. The enumerators should be fully conversant in the local language and so are the obvious choices for helping the field managers to translate the questionnaire. Indeed, translation often forms a useful part of the classroom training.

3.1.3 Sampling in the field

The first visit to the field with the enumerators should be spent ensuring that the sampling strategy makes sense. Up to now the enumerators and CV researcher might only have the sketch map of the town, and will need to walk and drive around to see how the town and fringe areas fit together. If the sketch map has been sub-divided into areas, these can be visited and the boundaries understood by the team. It is often better to have either an Enumerator 1 area, Enumerator 2 area, or a Day 1, Day 2 area, so that when the real survey takes place, enumerators know where they should be conducting interviews each day.

The sampling strategy should be tested with the field supervisor working closely with the team to ensure that the random sampling strategy is understood when in the field. The team should walk around the Day 1 or Enumerator 1 area together, and designate the 1st house in the area. This might not be the 1st house to be sampled, if it had been agreed (randomly) that the 5th house then 10th house, etc. must be sampled, then the 1st house is simply the basis for working this out. The starting point, or 1st house, needs to be agreed upon for all areas. It is likely that many of the areas will have some streets with obvious houses, and then many alleyways, open spaces, and side streets leading to other houses. The enumerator will count each house in a systematic way, and designate a route to be covered over the whole of the survey. This can be drawn on the sketch map.

3.1.4 Pilot testing

Pilot testing is an essential part of any household survey. Pilot testing is the rehearsal for the real thing: it allows the enumerators to practice the questionnaire with members of the public, rather than through stage-managed role playing; it enables the survey field manager to monitor the ability of the enumerators in the field through observing interviews.

The questionnaire and process should be discussed in detail:

Were any of the questions difficult for the respondents to understand?

Were the answers that used intervals missing some obvious ranges?

Were the CV prices reasonable or were the respondents only WTP the very lowest price or selecting the lowest option, if so why?

The answers may reflect poverty and low demand, which are valid research issues, or could point to poor survey design and misleading questions.

For streamlined CV Surveys in small towns, at least two days of pilot testing should still be completed. Larger surveys often undertake a week of testing. At the end of the pilot testing the CV field manager should expect to change the questionnaire. It is strongly recommended that the photocopying of the total required number of questionnaires is not done until pilot testing has been completed.

Pilot testing should also be considered an important part of enumerator training. The enumerators can improve their knowledge of the questionnaire in the 'real' environment, away from blackboards and role playing in the classroom. Persistent problems may emerge after a few interviews have been carried out which can be addressed during the follow-up meeting. It is advisable to hire a room in a local hotel for team meetings at the end of each day, although this might not always be possible. Team meetings can take place in cafes or in the reception area of the hotel where the enumerators are staying.

Each enumerator should conduct at least five questionnaires, and the field supervisor or CV researcher should be present to observe at least one of these. After the first two or three questionnaires have been completed the team should re-group and discuss any difficulties, or suggest changes to the questionnaire. In addition, after the field supervisor has observed an interview, time should immediately be set aside to discuss, in private, the way the interview was conducted, and any problems and suggestions for improvement.

The enumerators should conduct the pilot testing in one designated area. However, the pilot-tested questionnaires must not be part of the sample for the full study.

At the end of the first day the completed questionnaires should be carefully assessed. The understanding and capabilities of the enumerator can often be interpreted from how the questionnaires are filled out. It is a common experience at the end of the first day that every enumerator will have missed out questions, or at least forgotten to write in answers even though they were told those answers. They may have made a mistake recording the starting price asked, or the final price the respondent was WTP for their preferred option.

Feedback from the enumerators will inform everyone about difficult questions, as well as questions that have been poorly translated, or questions that the respondents simply do not understand. The team should discuss why the respondent could not answer these questions and what alternative question would convey the same, or similar meaning. If questions are being skipped this may be due to difficult or poor phrasing, not because the question has been misunderstood. It might be because of poor positioning in the interview schedule, or poorly worded instructions to the enumerator on the questionnaire. The pilot testing allows the CV supervisor to determine the adequacy of the enumerator's instructions. It will be possible to identify questions that make the respondent feel uncomfortable and to detect any tendency for the respondent's interest to be lost at certain junctures.

If questions are to be asked with intervals or ranges (closed questions), such as bands for income levels, etc., then it is often useful to ask open questions at the pilot-test stage to generate appropriate fixed choice intervals. If there are local people on the team, appropriate intervals may have already been included on the questionnaire. The pilot testing can then ensure that these intervals are correct and cover all reasonable answers that might be expected.

One of the most important lessons during the pre-testing is to insist that enumerators stick closely to the 'script', i.e. that they read out the main text, particularly when discussing the CV scenario, including the descriptions of the new options and the payment methods. This ensures that all respondents hear a consistent description and value the same improved service.

Focus groups

Focus group discussions can be used as a supplement to field pilot testing to further improve the quality of information provided. Focus groups are facilitated group meetings made up of selected individuals from the target population.

Participants can be split according to gender, age, or social class. This may happen automatically anyway if the focus group discussions are held in particular areas of the town. Participants can be selected according to their existing water supply use so that different parts of the household survey can be tested.

Sometimes participants are provided with a soft drink, and/or lunch. It has been known for participants to turn down the offer of a soft drink and take instead the equivalent cash sum, (Wedgwood, 2001)

The main purpose of the focus group discussion is to test the Contingent Valuation survey section of the questionnaire. The first discussion is often about the existing water supply, and people will happily talk about the problems they are having, the various sources, and the amount of money they pay vendors, the local council, etc. The options can be discussed, and the sketch diagrams shown to ensure that everyone understands the new options. The payment method and any bidding games should be tried with the group to ensure that they understand the elicitation technique. Some focus group discussions can provide useful information if water ladders, contingent ranking exercises, and pocket chart voting for options are conducted, (Coates et al 2001). However, the aim of this focus group discussion for WTP surveys is to test the survey instrument and make necessary changes before the main survey is carried out.

3.2 Step 8 – Implement survey

3.2.1 When to conduct the survey

The timing of the survey is likely to depend on the requirements of the client that has commissioned the work. If there is any flexibility, the survey manager should consider the impact on the survey whether it is done during the wet season or dry season. Will respondents have reduced demand during the wet season? Should the survey be conducted during the busy harvesting season?

The problem of non-responses should be borne in mind. Most surveys attract a certain amount of non-response, although in developing countries this tends to be a much smaller percentage. If the survey is timed badly, however, for example if it coincides with harvesting, or a busy festival, or period of political activity, more people are likely to be too busy to be interviewed.

3.2.2 Gender of respondent

Research has not yet established whether it is best to interview male and/or female respondents. In Dar es Salaam, Tanzania 53 per cent of respondents were female; in Kathmandu 63 per cent were male and 37 per cent female; in Lugazi, Uganda 48 per cent were female and 52 per cent male. A dilemma exists because in many households the male head of household has control of most of the finances and yet females and children in the house bear the burden of fetching water, and so know the economic (financial, time, and health) costs of their poor water supply.

In order to capture the effective demand of both men and women it is desirable that at least 50 per cent of participants in the survey are women. Where there are concerns about a potential low percentage of female participation, some strategies to consider are:

- At least 50 per cent of the enumerators should be women to make it easier to interview the senior female members of the households.
- Enumerators could interview both male and female members of the household simultaneously. However, in many cases this might not be possible because either the male, or female may be away at the time.
- Enumerators should conduct the survey when they think there is a good chance of women being at home.
- Ensure that the WTP and other survey results are discussed together with groups of women once the analysis has been completed.

3.2.3 Field manager's role

After the pilot-testing, it will be practical to select one or two 'enumerator team-leaders'. It might be beneficial to split the enumerators into two teams, particularly if two vehicles are available for dropping off the enumerators in the far reaches of the fringe areas. The team leaders can coordinate each day's activities with the survey manager, including where the survey will take place each day, pick-up and drop off times, etc. The team leaders can collect the questionnaires at the end of the day and carry out an initial check to ensure that they have been filled in correctly. It is always best to check the questionnaires each day, because if there are any errors or gaps, these are more easily rectified immediately. If there are consistent errors in the quality of filled-in questionnaires, the only course of action may be to dismiss the enumerator.

The field manager should act as the general coordinator working with the team leaders. Random checks on the enumerators, observing them during interviews, etc., are vital to maintain the quality of the survey.

Chapter 4

Data analysis and interpretation

Often, CVM consultants hand a CVM report in to their client and are not involved in the planning process. To ensure that this valuable demand-responsive data is used, more effort should be made with the presentation of the final report by linking the analysis of the CVM results with wider planning objectives. Project managers involved in water supply in small towns should consult with members of the CVM team before the final data analysis is undertaken. If necessary, they could make requests for additional analysis that might assist in formulating plans; for example more cost-recovery scenarios for the preferred options, further cross-tabulation of location/income data, etc. Step 9 outlines the types of simple analysis that can be undertaken and tests to improve the accuracy of the results. Step 10 provides guidance for CVM managers to improve the quality and usefulness of their outputs in influencing the financial sustainability of the future water supply system, particularly through the use of tariff models to recover specified costs. Finally, Step 11 suggests a number of ways for ensuring that the CVM report is used to influence the final policy decisions regarding the design, management, and financial sustainability of the new water supply system.

4.1 Step 9 – Data entry and analysis

4.1.1 Cleaning data

To reduce costs and time it should be possible to develop a table in Microsoft Excel and for one or two enumerators to carry out the data entry of the completed questionnaires. An example of a data entry table is presented in Annex E. The table is in Excel and each column represents a question from the questionnaire. Each horizontal line represents one completed questionnaire. All of the answers should be in some form of numerical code, although some words can be used for so called 'string' variables such as the names of diseases. Care must be taken to ensure that the numbers are entered in the same way and that spaces are not used for zeroes. If the answer is missing nothing should be entered into that particular box.

Data can be 'cleaned' to eliminate obvious examples of error, either on the part of the respondent answering deliberately untruthfully, or the enumerator recording the answers inaccurately. The easiest way to look for 'outliers' is to assess the raw data frequency distributions for obvious discrepancies. This might include households where the responses vary considerably from the mean. For example, a frequency distribution of household size suggested that one household had 112 members. This was an error in data entry, there were really 12 members. Other responses might be deliberately high or low, and should also be omitted from the analysis.

During the analysis of the Bushenyi CV Survey it became clear that a few errors had been made in the data entry. The most obvious examples are codes that should not exist. The frequency graph of electricity included four households with a Code 3, there were only two codes for this answer, either they had electricity (Code 1) or did not (Code 2). These results need to be removed from the system, or the original questionnaires need to be checked.

4.1.2 Is a CVM robust without econometric analysis?

Most of the literature reports that specialist consultants are required to ensure that results are reliable. The definition of specialist consultants varies, but is often taken to mean an economist, with previous experience and training in conducting similar surveys and analysing the results using an appropriate computer statistical package to check that results fall in line with rational behaviour. Undoubtedly, such a specialist will not be cheap, and most of these specialists are probably based in developed countries, in top-level university departments, consultancies, or at senior government level in developing countries.

When project planners read many of the CVM papers and reports that are now available, the basic concepts are simple, intuitively make sense, and appear to offer planners a solution to the provision of financially sustainable and demand-responsive water supply services. However, many CV reports also contain sophisticated statistical analysis, involving multiple regression called multi-variate analysis, Stewart Maximum Likelihood (for known WTP intervals), Ordinary Least Squares (for maximum bids), or random utility models (RUM) using probit and logit analysis (used for yes/no answers).

Most readers interested in the basic concepts of CVM do not understand these methods and might be put off further exploration into its use. More importantly, there are very few consultants in developing countries who are able to carry out such analysis. Statisticians from the country's main universities might have the necessary skills, but would be lacking in knowledge about the water sector, or about running household surveys with a strong poverty focus. There are no reasons why CVM should remain the exclusive domain of highly specialist consultants apart from this perceived need to carry out econometric tests on results. An important question for the analysis is 'Are these tests needed to ensure that the results are valid?'.

Examination of a number of CVM studies reveals that where the tests are carried out statistical significance varies enormously. Sometimes the education levels of respondents proved to be significant (Van Nostrans, 1997)[18]. Whilst other studies reported that *'more educated respondents generally bid more than less educated respondents, but this effect is statistically significant in only a few of the models and its magnitude is always small'* (Whittington et al., 1993). Because the impact of education proved small in one study and significant in the other, it had no impact whatsoever on how the results were written up and the suggestion from both reports was that all the results were valid and provided accurate demand assessment data.

Another problem that sociologists often refer to is the fact that statistics can always be shaped to fit any number of suitable assumptions. When interpreting the results of statistical analysis it is very easy to find an answer. For example if the co-efficients of the sex of the respondent are negative, implying that female WTP is lower than male, one interpretation could be that women are less likely to pay for water because they do not have access to finances and so are afraid to make higher bids (Wedgwood, 2000). Alternatively, if the co-efficient was positive, this would indicate that female WTP is higher than males. An easy interpretation is that because females do all the fetching and carrying, they are more aware of the potential benefits to them of an improved system. Either response makes sense, but neither has contributed to the main objective of the study, which is to assess feasible WTP for preferred options. Simple cross tabulation of responses will demonstrate whether female respondents' demand for particular options was higher than males.

If respondents with very low incomes constantly bid for very high-cost options, this might indicate that a certain amount of strategic bias has taken place. These kinds of inconsistencies can be revealed without econometric analyses; a simple check is to see whether household expenditure plus the WTP bid is greater than income.

---

[18] Van Nostrand (1997) indicated that education was statistically significant at the 5 per cent confidence level for certain options.

In conclusion it is suggested that the level and sophistication of analysis should depend on the size of the population being surveyed and the scale of the project. Surveys in large urban areas, capital and primary cities, or covering large populations and geographical areas in rural areas should usually carry out econometric analysis. If the CVM study is to be used for planning major infrastructure investments in large cities, it is reasonable to expect the consultants to conduct econometric tests in order to provide the government and donors' quantitative reassurance in the reliability of the results.

However, for small towns (and large villages, small groups of villages) with concentrated populations of between 5,000 to 50,000 people, CV surveys *without* econometric analysis are acceptable, so long as the sample size is 5 per cent of the total number of households and a rigorous sample, pre-test, and CV scenario has been designed.

Ministries in developing countries will be looking for value for money from WTP surveys, so the survey costs need to be minimised, bearing in mind the scale of potential capital investments that may be supported by the study. This is likely to mean that for small towns it is better to limit the inputs of expensive international consultants and thereby keep the survey costs to a reasonable level.

4.1.3 Checking the validity of results

The analysis of the CV results serves two purposes. First, the results need to be checked to ensure that they are plausible and credible before they are interpreted and developed into useful conclusions for policymakers and system designers. When analysing the results it is unlikely that all the responses will be accurate, or all inaccurate. It is more probable that some of the responses are accurate reflections of the households' willingness to pay for particular preferred options and others are not.

Debriefing questions

The debriefing questions asked at the end of the survey often provide vital information explaining why respondents behaved the way they did. Cultural, tribal, caste, and other social differences within the town might be explained in a few simple answers. The socio-cultural contexts to decision-making at the household level clearly impact upon the results. If these can be understood, this will allow for increased confidence in the credibility of the results. For example, all respondents might have opted for the most expensive of two options, even though through the analysis it looks as if half the town could not really afford it. The explanation could be simple strategic bias, or it could be that the first option involved building a reservoir over a local burial ground, or a belief that groundwater was dirty and so a borehole was unacceptable.

However, if there are no over-riding reasons, and respondents' answers are inconsistent with prior expectations, and the de-briefing questions do not show carefully considered answers, the credibility of the CV results are undermined.

Enumerator bias
It is normal when entering data to ensure that the enumerator carrying out each questionnaire is referenced on the spreadsheet (see Annex E). This is normally done with a code for each person. It is then possible to cross tabulate the responses for WTP with each enumerator. If one enumerator has consistently higher or lower valuation responses, this raises doubts about the reliability of the results. It is likely that the enumerator influenced the results in some way, either by encouraging the respondent to bid in a specific manner, or by not explaining the CV scenario in sufficient detail.

Time of interview check
A further check is to ensure that the respondent always writes down the time, in minutes, that the whole interview took. In Bushenyi, it was found that one enumerator consistently took less than half the time to complete the survey than the other six enumerators. This could be a sign that the enumerator rushed the interview, or didn't carry out all the surveys claimed, and wrote down false times without realising that an average of 25 minutes was not enough compared to his/her fellow enumerators. If this check raises some doubts, it will then be possible to further crosscheck the enumerators' results to see whether there are further inconsistencies with the responses. If necessary the enumerator's results may need to be discarded.

4.1.4 How to present socio-economic characteristics
Basic household information can be very important if the CV results are to be analysed statistically. Even if econometric analysis is not required, information on educational achievements, income, household size and employment patterns can be used to support and explain the results of the CV Survey, which might suggest preferences and WTP for particular options. According to economic theory, certain socio-economic characteristics should suggest higher WTP; these include higher incomes, more education, the existing price of water, etc. Similarly, it has been found that larger households, or households headed by a widow or grandparent with large numbers of children, normally affect the CV responses in a negative way, i.e. the higher the household size, the lower the WTP.

The aim of the streamlined approach to CV Surveys is to encourage a robust survey methodology, with realistic CV scenarios so that the results can be easily interpreted to produce useful design, implementation and policy recommendations. The World Bank Research Team carried out a range of statistical checks on the determinants of household demand for improved water services (Briscoe, 1993) which suggested that willingness to pay for improved water sources depends on a range of characteristics. The World Bank research offers some useful insights on the socio-economic characteristics that can be considered useful indicators of demand:

- Contrary to expectations, WTP for improved water services does not depend solely on income. Often the price elasticity of demand is low: for example a 10 per cent increase in household income may result in only a 1 per cent increase in the probability that a household would choose to use and pay for an improved water system.
- If the respondent has had five or more years of education, this increased the WTP for a private connection (from the 11 CV Surveys carried out) by 25 per cent. This is probably because the respondents realise that they have a higher opportunity cost for time spent collecting water than engaging in other tasks.
- The gender of the respondent proved to be statistically significant in the 11 surveys. However, the impact of gender was strongly dependent on the specific cultural context. In Tanzania and Haiti female respondents were WTP more for access to public taps than males; in Nigeria and India they were not WTP as much.
- If the perceived quality of a new water supply system is high, the WTP of households was always higher.
- Reliability was the most crucial determinant of demand. WTP and the number of households wishing to connect to a piped system was always higher if the respondent could be assured that the service would be more reliable than the existing supply.

These determinants of demand will vary according to the physical, cultural or social context of each individual town. They merely focus on the key socio-economic characteristics, which appeared to influence demand in the 11 CV Surveys undertaken by the World Bank Research Team. However, they do provide a useful focus for the analysis of the results of a streamlined CV Survey in small towns.

The simplest analysis involves examining descriptive statistics and frequency distributions of the socio-economic characteristics and existing water supply situation.

Simple frequency graphs

The graph below is an example of a simple raw data frequency graph. It summarises the education levels of the member of the household with the highest educational attainment (not simply the education level of the respondent) in Bushenyi, Uganda. (Wedgwood et al, 2001) Using SPSS or a similar statistical package, the codes represent each of the educational levels achieved and the graph is produced very quickly by the package. In this case, 34 per cent of respondents had finished primary school, whilst 19 per cent had no schooling at all, and 23 per cent had finished secondary school.

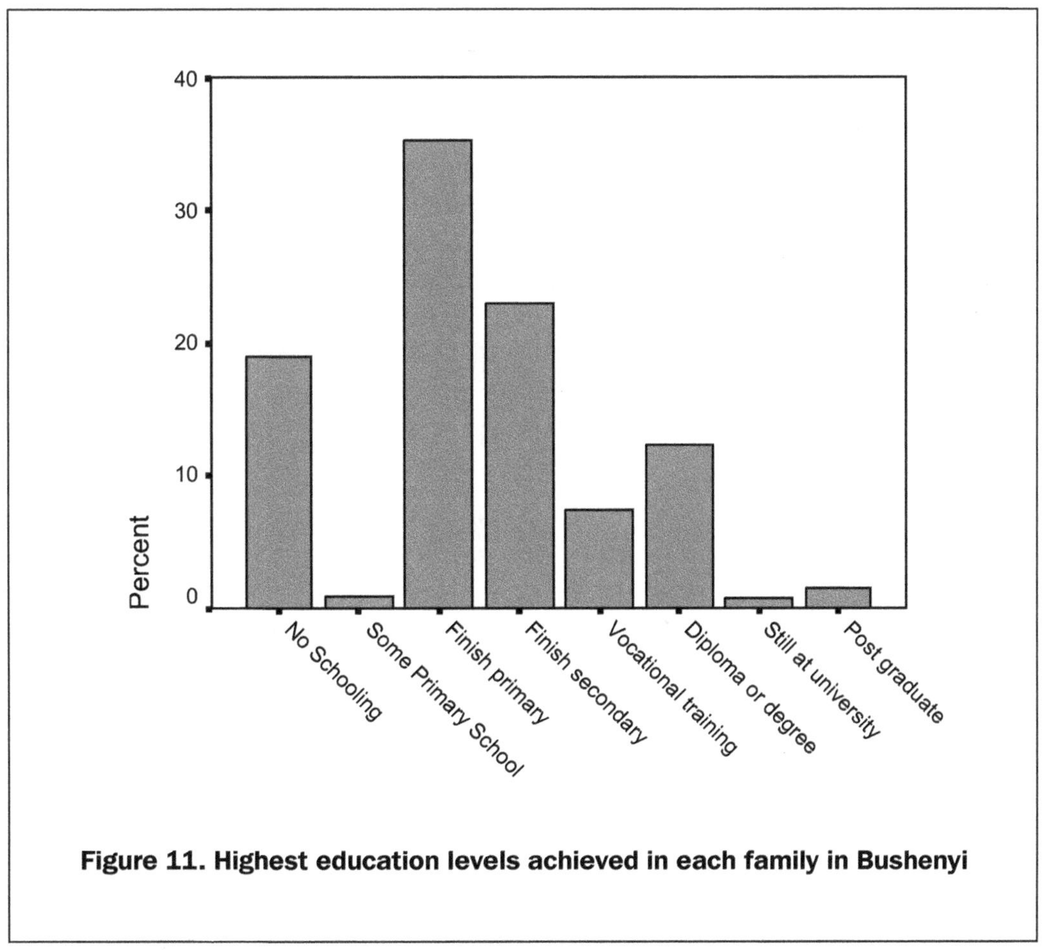

Figure 11. Highest education levels achieved in each family in Bushenyi

Source: Wedgwood et al, 2001.

The graph is very useful in representing a snapshot of education standards in the town. It is unlikely for the respondents to lie about educational attainment, and so the graph can be considered representative of the 422 households surveyed.

Income and employment

A similar frequency graph can produce information on employment types and income distributions within the town. The graph in Figure 12 summarises the main employment of the head of household in Bushenyi. In small towns employment patterns often mirror the geographical spread of households. There is a division between those living in the core areas relying on small businesses such as hotels, cafes, shops and transport and those living in the fringe areas relying predominantly on agriculture and some seasonal employment – possibly on the larger plantations.

More detailed social research could be undertaken on employment and incomes sources. Often complex coping strategies are pursued with individual household members carrying out a range of informal tasks to earn cash. Income varies enormously during the year – particularly for agricultural workers and farmers. Understanding the full household economy can be a time-consuming and difficult task in its own right. In the interests of expediency and practicality it is accepted that information obtained on the household's income, expenditure and employment patterns during the survey is likely to be incomplete and represent more of a snapshot of the households activities, and the town's economy, than an in-depth picture.[19]

---

[19] For a thorough analysis of household economies, particularly for rural households in famine and drought-prone regions where the impact of external shocks on income and access to food is most serious, see *The Household Economy Approach* Seaman, J et al., Save the Children 2000.

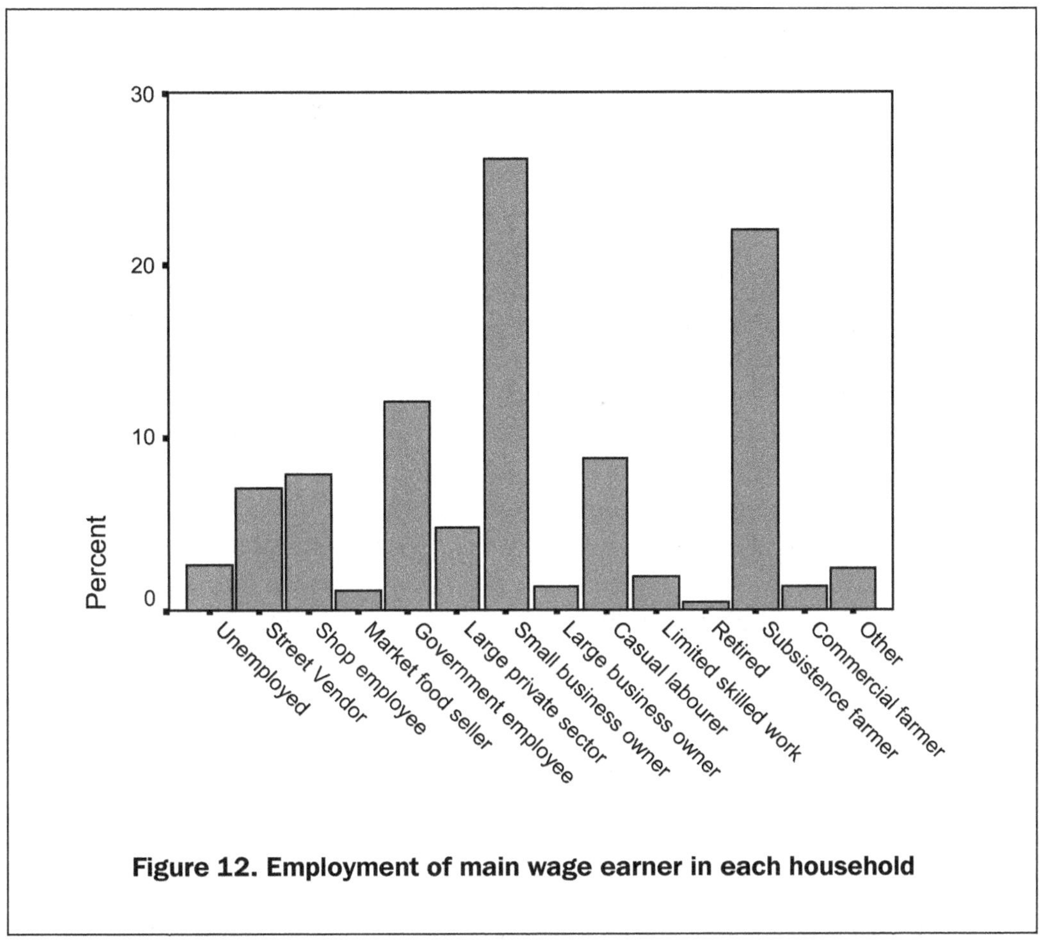

Figure 12. Employment of main wage earner in each household

Source: Bushenyi CVM Survey (Wedgwood et al, 2001)

The graph in Figure 13 summarises the *estimated* total income per family in Bushenyi. A useful check is to compare the mean and mode values of responses to the CV questions with other socio-economic questions, particularly, income and expenditure indicators. If a respondent agrees to pay over 50 per cent of their income on the new water supply offered this would call into question the accuracy of the data. (Although in some extreme cases people have been known to spend over 50 per cent of their income on water during droughts and very dry seasons) (Cairncross and Kennear, 1992). Other checks might involve comparing expenditure on the CV option with existing expenditure on food or education.

Therefore, in Bushenyi, the income data was cross-checked with the expenditure answers during data entry. If income was always lower than expenditure without a satisfactory explanation of the additional sources of income (absentee transfers, savings or pension) the results were discarded. The data shows large differences in wage earning capacity between households in the town. This is to be expected because the town is made up of a mixture of people living a predominantly rural subsistence life-style and others working in the coffee and milling factory, managing small businesses and benefiting from passing trade. 22 per cent of households earned between 800,000 and USh1 million (US$444 - $555). A further 19 per cent earned between USh1 to 2 million. Because of large income disparities, focusing solely on average incomes can be very misleading. At the very least, average incomes should be dis-aggregated into three or four separate wealth groups.

Given the strong relationship between location and income in small towns, income data that can be anchored to a particular location in the town should also be analysed. In Bushenyi, the results proved that there were massive income and aspirational disparities between households in the rural fringe areas and the core areas. This location/income analysis lends more credence to the reliability of the results. Bushenyi and Ishaka, like many small towns in Africa, are located on a major road. Much of the core's business revolves around passing trade and the processing plants for the local plantations. Consequently, incomes in the core area tend to be much higher. This fact is probably true for most small towns in Africa. Therefore, analysis of income differentials within the environs of small towns should play a central role in a demand-responsive approach towards the provision of *financially sustainable* water supply services in small towns. Table 7 summarises disparities between income levels in the core and fringe areas.

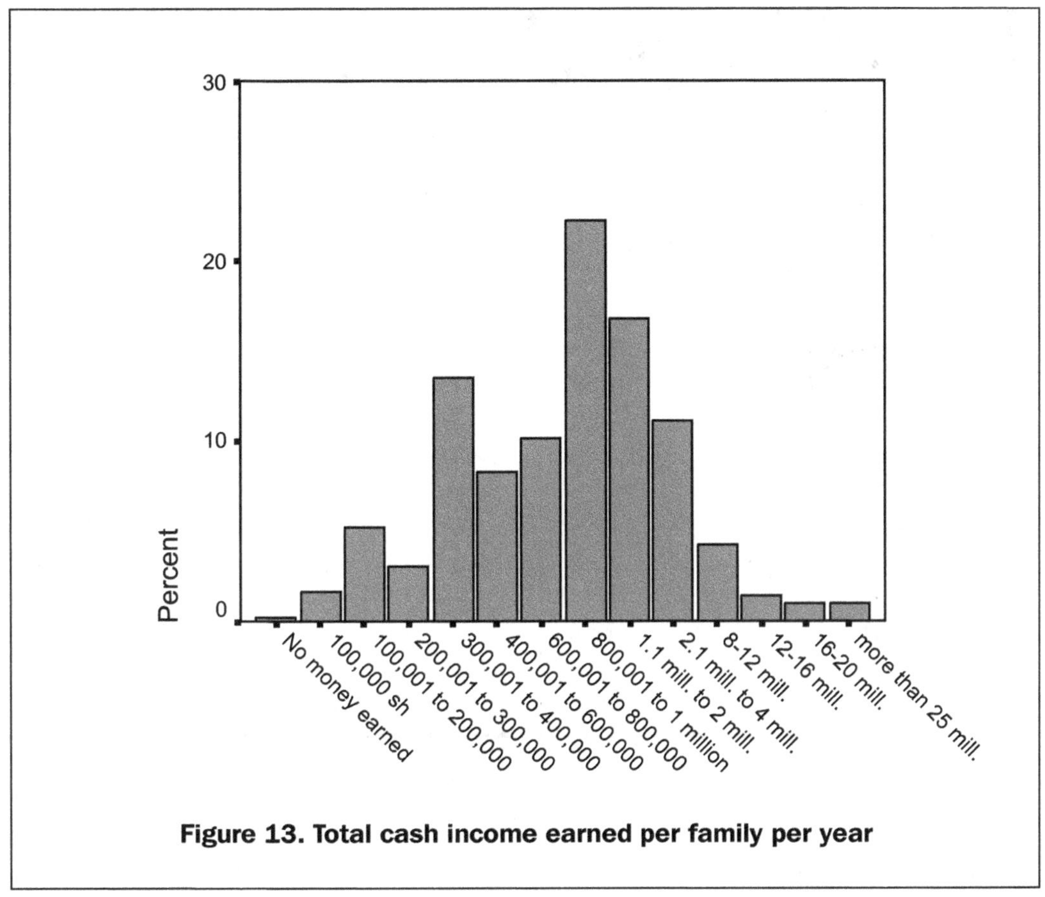

Figure 13. Total cash income earned per family per year

Source: Wedgwood et al, 2001.

With a few exceptions, households with higher incomes are more likely to be located in the core areas. For example, 50 per cent of households in Bushenyi core, and 47 per cent of households in Ishaka core have incomes above USh1.1 million per year. At the other end of the scale, 15 per cent of households in Bushenyi fringe and 18 per cent in Ishaka fringe have incomes of less than USh300,000 (US$166) per year. This compares with zero percentage of households in Bushenyi core and 1.6 per cent in Ishaka core. Table 7 shows the total household income spread between the core and fringe areas of Bushenyi and Ishaka, two towns located only 1km apart and managed by the same local council.

Table 7. Total household income by area – Bushenyi/Ishaka CV Survey

Income per year per household/family (USh)	Core Bushenyi	Fringe Bushenyi	Core Ishaka	Fringe Ishaka	Average figure
No money earned	1.6%				0.2%
100,000		3.5%		2.3%	1.7%
100,001 to 200,000		5.3%	0.8%	11.7%	5.2%
200,001 to 300,000		6.2%	0.8%	3.9%	3.1%
300,001 to 400,000	6.5%	17.7%	6.7%	19.5%	13.5%
400,001 to 600,000	4.8%	12.4%	5.0%	9.4%	8.3%
600,001 to 800,000	8.1%	13.3%	8.4%	10.2%	10.2%
800,001 to 1 million	27.4%	12.4%	31.1%	20.3%	22.3%
1.1 to 2 million	21.0%	15.9%	20.2%	12.5%	16.8%
2.1 to 4 million	19.4%	10.6%	16.0%	3.1%	11.1%
8 to 12 million	4.8%	0.9%	8.4%	3.1%	4.3%
12 to 16 million	1.6%	1.8%	0.8%	1.6%	1.4%
16 to 20 million	3.2%		1.7%		0.9%
More than 25 million	1.6%			2.3%	0.9%
	100.0%	100.0%	100.0%	100.0%	100.0%

The table shows that incomes were higher in both core areas, easily expressed in terms of the proportion of households with incomes above USh1 million.

This simple analysis has not assessed the exact statistical correlation between WTP and incomes, educational attainment, household size, etc. However, if this income data is then compared with demand for the five water supply options offered, it is easy to see that if households in the fringe/lower income areas were acting rationally, according to economic theory, they should express demand for the less expensive options compared to households in the core/higher income areas.

Table 8 represents the corollary to Table 7 by demonstrating that demand for different options varies considerably between locations and is based on rational economic decision-making by respondents. Higher income households living in the core areas were two to three times more likely to select private connections as their preferred option. Similarly, respondents in the core areas were twice as likely to select public kiosks. The one anomaly is in the fringe area of Bushenyi, where 53 per cent of respondents selected, and were willing to pay for the shared yard tap. Although 80 per cent of these households were only able to afford the minimum price of USh25,000, which would just cover the connection cost, but would not pay for any of the pipes and fittings.

So additional capital loan funding would be required if it were decided to extend the pipe network to the Bushenyi fringe area. The likely revenue from water charges from shared connections in the fringe area could be compared to the likely capital and O&M costs of extending the pipe network. This would require further liaison between the CV researchers and the engineers, to determine the viability of laying water pipes in the fringe areas. A compromise solution of only partially extending the network into the fringe areas may be the best economic option.

Table 8. First choice option selected by location, Bushenyi CVM Survey

Option	Core Bushenyi	Fringe Bushenyi	Core Ishaka	Fringe Ishaka	Average figure
1. Protected spring	29.5%	25.5%	22.6%	43.2%	30.5%
2. Handpumps	4.5%	.9%	2.8%	9.9%	4.6%
3. Public water kiosks	9.1%	5.7%	24.5%	12.6%	13.6%
4. Shared yard taps	29.5%	53.8%	29.2%	27.9%	36.0%
5. Private connections	27.3%	14.2%	20.8%	6.3%	15.3%
Total %	100.0%	100.0%	100.0%	100.0%	100.0%

Analysis of the raw data provides enough relevant information to understand the socio-economic characteristics of different income groups in the town. Other checks for data consistency might include examining the water-vending situation in the small town. If good quality vended water is available but a household does not buy it, but then expresses willingness to pay more from a public kiosk, this suggests certain inconsistencies with either the way the questions were presented or the responses. If the vended water is of poor quality or prohibitively expensive then this check does not apply.

4.2 Survey management and participation issues

One of the first questions in the CV Survey should attempt to understand levels of institutional bias that might exist in the town by asking respondents whether they would be willing to participate in any meetings concerning their towns' water supply. It is also worthwhile determining whether they feel that it is reasonable for them to be asked to pay something for an improved supply. In highly politicised areas, particularly where the state water authorities have failed to provide regular water supplies but made many promises, there may be an entrenched belief that it is the state's duty to provide free/cheap supplies. In these areas WTP for new water services will be lower than expected.

In Bushenyi, a 'willingness to participate' question demonstrated that over 85 per cent of respondents expressed their willingness to pay something towards an improved scheme, and to participate in community consultations and meetings to discuss the best scheme for the community. 34 households (8 per cent) of the total said that they were happy with their existing supply, five respondents believed that nothing new would ever be built anyway because of past broken promises so they were unwilling to express any willingness to pay, and 11 households (2.6 per cent) said that the government should provide free water. Therefore, 367 households (87 per cent) were asked further questions on their willingness to pay for their preferred option.

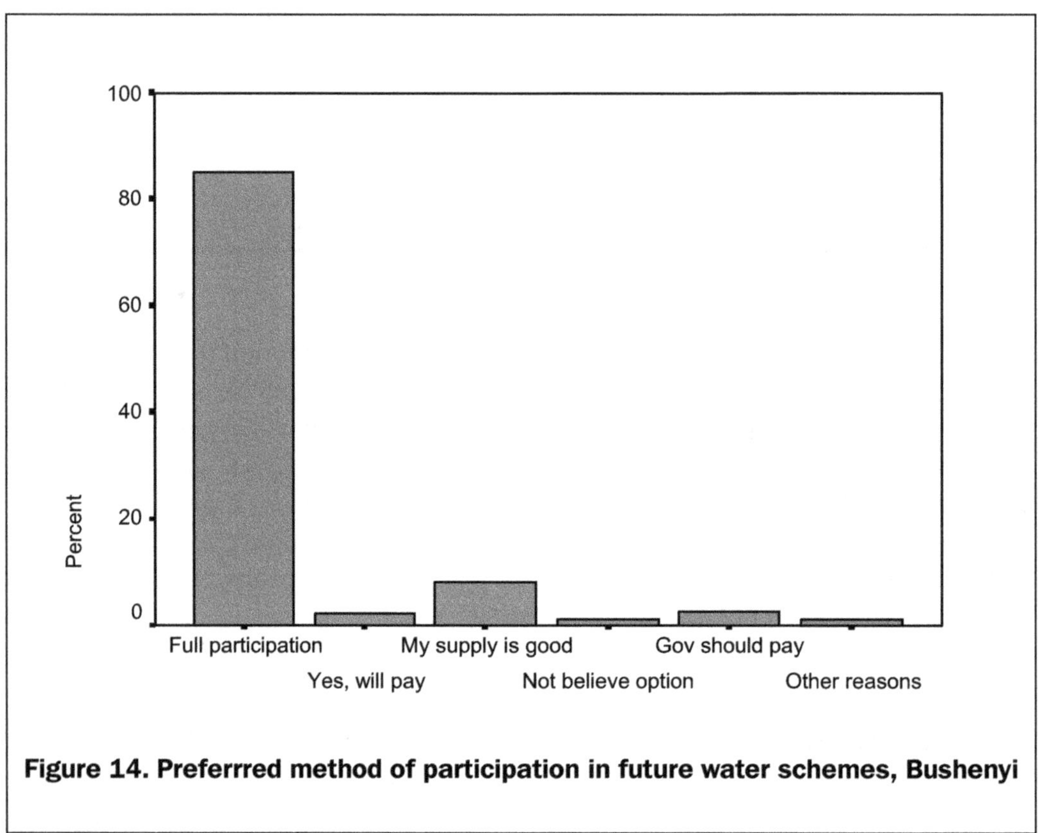

Figure 14. Preferrred method of participation in future water schemes, Bushenyi

Source: Wedgwood et al, 2001.

The management of the new scheme might be built into the CV scenario, i.e. each option actually has a specified management plan. This was the case in Dar es Salaam where Water Aid were already working with community water committees and none of the options involved piped water schemes. The CV scenario included questions such as;

'Your water committee wishes to construct more community kiosks. How much would be you willing to contribute towards the construction cost?'

However, in Bushenyi the town's existing water supply scheme was a mixture of local council controlled (unreliable) piped networks, private vendors and wells and public springs. The Government of Uganda is pursuing a decentralised, flexible policy and allows the private sector, water user associations, local councils or state authorities to manage small towns' water supplies. Therefore, it was reasonable to ask respondents their own views on water supply management. The questions had been pre-tested with a small focus group to make certain that they were comprehensible. The graph in Figure 15 summarises respondent's preferences for management of the improved water supply system. The results are interesting: 19 per cent selected a private operator and 38 per cent preferred a water user association.

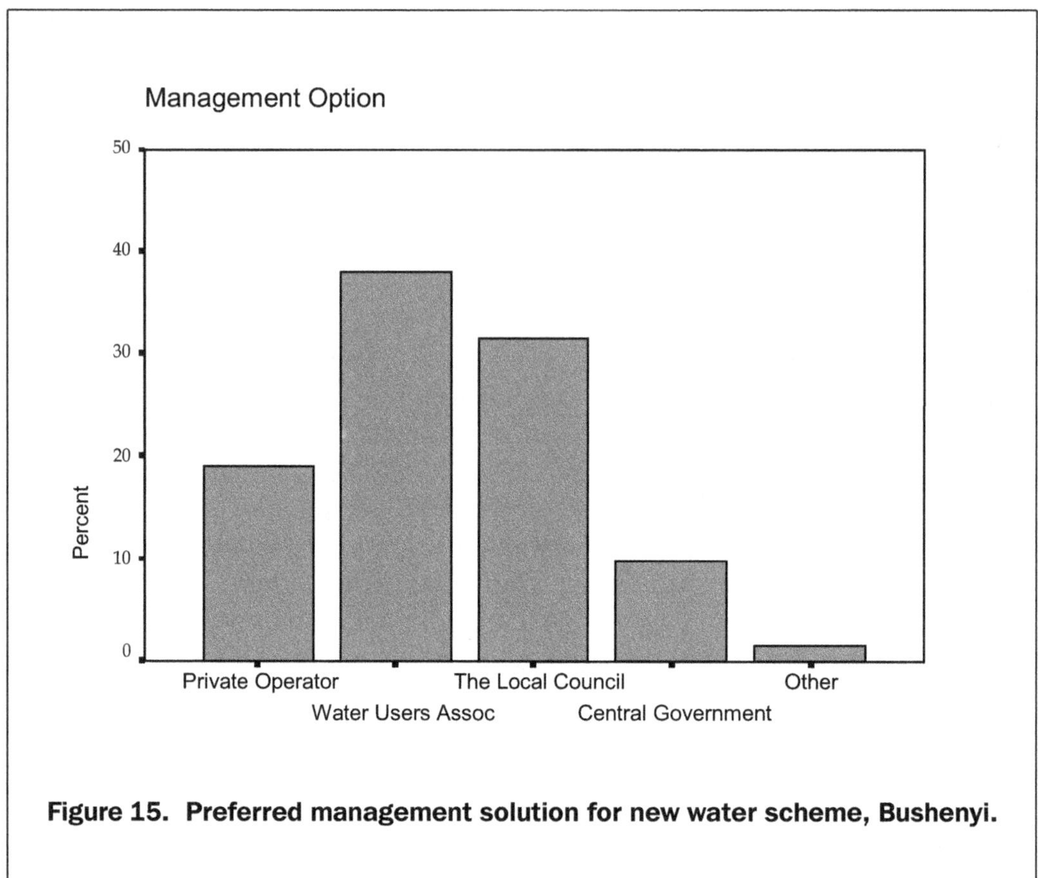

Figure 15. Preferred management solution for new water scheme, Bushenyi.

These results have serious implications for the design of a demand-responsive sustainable water supply service in Bushenyi. Too often, CV Surveys focus on statistics and produce complicated revenue graphs without considering the implications of other key findings. The majority of respondents selected a water user association to manage the scheme. However, evidence from other small towns in Uganda (Wobulenzi is a prime example) suggest that water user associations are not always appropriate management models, particularly in spread out communities using more than one water supply service.

The policy of the Directorate of Water Development (DWD) in the Ugandan government (in 2002) is that private operators under Management contracts provide the most suitable management option for small town water supplies that are not managed by the National Water and Sewerage Corporation. It is clear from these results that the DWD and other stakeholders would need to promote the private operator option in Bushenyi, if they are to have the support of most of the residents in that town.

4.2.1 Interpreting demand

Normally, the CV scenario includes a choice of payment method, i.e. whether to pay per jerry can, per month, in instalments, etc. In Lugazi, although over 60 per cent of those selecting the public kiosks preferred to pay per month, the report recommended that the kiosks should charge per jerry can. This was based not only on the results of the survey, but also on the experiences and perceptions of the CVM team who had spent over two weeks in the town.

The team were aware of the local political situation, the likely problems that might emerge for water user groups managing the popular and crowded water points, and the (non) acceptability of preventing people from using kiosks if they had not paid their monthly fee. Therefore, the CVM researcher must not assume that the survey results are the only source of useful information. Having spent two to three weeks in the town, the CVM researcher will have gained many constructive insights that staff in central/local government would find useful.

The first important analysis of demand is to tabulate the percentage of respondents that selected each option as a first choice. If there is very low demand for a specific option there is little requirement for further analysis of this option.

It is essential that the CVM researcher continually interpret the data for the design engineers. If 70 per cent of households selected a private connection and 30 per cent hand-pumps this might present an interesting dilemma. Should the design engineer consider a mixture of point sources and a piped network? Or is further consultation required with the community to understand why some households do not want to use a piped network? Households in the fringe may have selected handpumps, which might prove a more cost effective solution than investing in a large piped network. Therefore, the location of households is as important as the options chosen and should be clearly presented in the final report.

Table 9 summarises the option choice in Dar es Salaam: 54 per cent preferred community kiosks and 43 per cent private connections.

Table 9. Water supply option selected in Dar es Salaam

	Frequency	Valid Percentage
New community kiosks	222	54.7
Private connection	177	43.6
Do not want any new water system	7	1.7
TOTAL	406	100.0
Do not know / refused to answer	14	
	420	

Source: Wedgwood, A. Assessment of Demand, Dar es Salaam. 2000

The pie chart Figure 16 summarises demand for five options in Bushenyi. The numbers on the chart refer to the technical options listed in Table 8. Option 1 (protected springs), and Option 4 (shared yard taps) were the most popular choices. Option 2 (handpumps) was surprisingly unpopular – although a technically viable option for the fringe areas around the town. This may be due to problems previously experienced with the maintenance of handpumps.

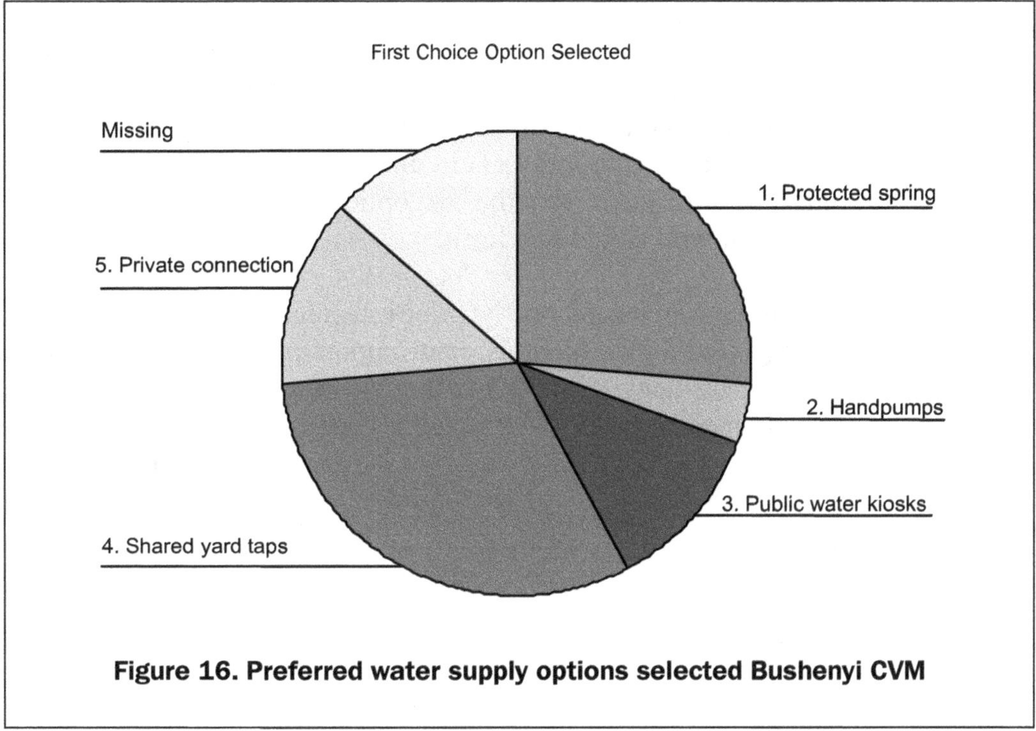

Figure 16. Preferred water supply options selected Bushenyi CVM

Source: Wedgwood et al, 2001.

The most important results are simple tables and graphs showing the households' WTP for different options at particular prices. These can be converted into cumulative frequency graphs to show the expected revenue that could be raised, based solely on the results of the survey. These graphs and tables are particularly useful to feed into a tariff model. Standard tables can show the percentage of respondents that preferred different options. The next task is to analyse in more detail the different monthly fees/ up-front contributions/ prices per jerry can that households stated they would be WTP for each option. Based on the preferences demonstrated in the Bushenyi pie chart, the consultant decided to concentrate the more in-depth analysis on protected springs and shared yard taps.

Price effect

Depending on the type of CV bidding procedure used, an examination of the raw data should reveal a certain price effect. A table or graph of the percentage of people willing to pay for an option at each randomly assigned price should show less demand for the options at the very highest price. The highest price is normally set to choke off demand; it should be an 'unreasonably' high price for households to accept. If the survey has been poorly designed, or options priced inaccurately, then demand for the greatest price offered might be high, but still be a legitimate representation of willingness to pay for that particular option. It could however mean that respondents agreed to pay high prices because of strategic bias, that is they believed that in the end the government or council would pay for the option anyway. Alternatively, maybe rumours had circulated that people should say they are WTP the highest price to ensure that the best option is built, without considering the consequences of who would pay for it.

The graph below (Figure 17) shows how the price effect has choked off demand at the highest price suggested for the monthly contribution towards the maintenance of protected springs in Bushenyi. This shows that the range of bidding prices are correct and that the highest average WTP value has been captured in the survey.

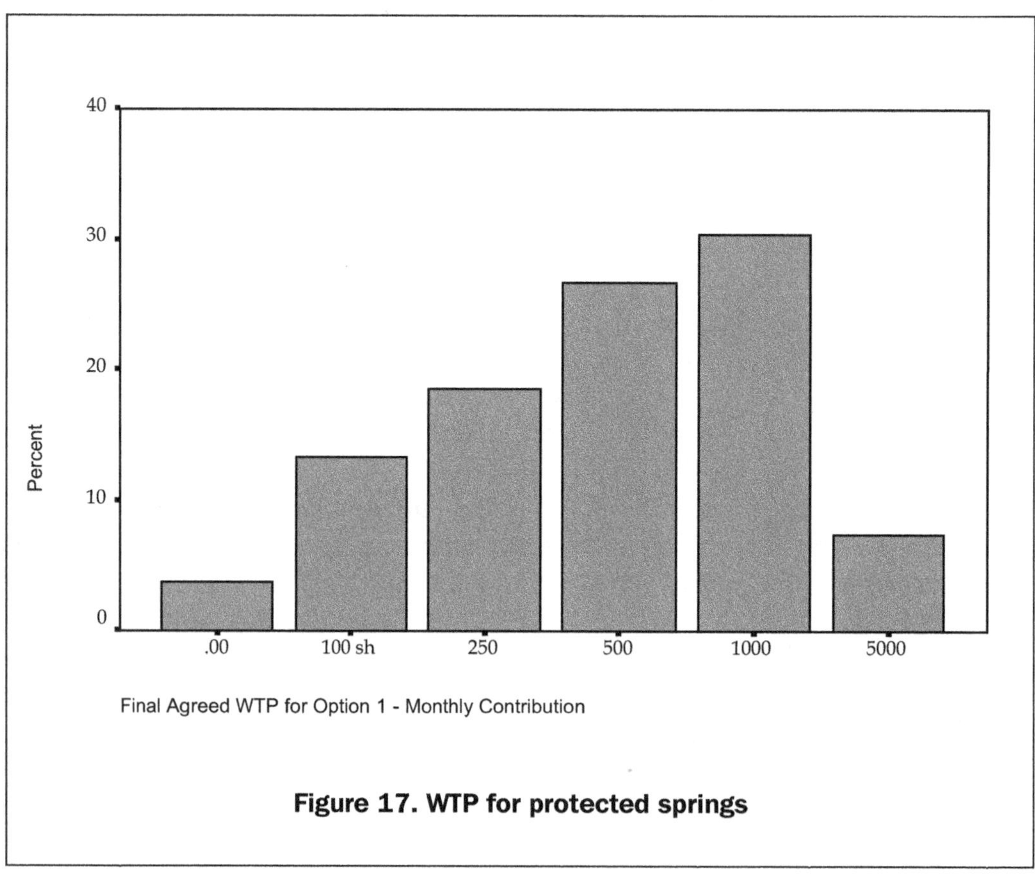

Figure 17. WTP for protected springs

Source: Wedgwood et al, 2001.

If respondents always answered at the low end of the price distribution, this might indicate another form of bias in the answers. It could mean that the enumerators did not explain the options clearly and that households did not believe that they would ever be built. Respondents may not have understood the options, or not understood the means of payment, and so only accepted the lowest price. Or it could simply mean that the respondents were rejecting the CV scenario for other cultural, social, or political reasons that the enumerators did not understand.

Chapter 5

Policy and financial implications

Chapter 5 of these guidance notes is concerned with how to use the WTP and consumer survey results effectively, in order to inform investment planning and tariff setting, the revision of technical design options, and the design of future institutional arrangements for managing water services.

If the results are carefully analysed and presented – including the WTP for preferred service options for the different consumer groups – then suitable investment scenario(s) or options can be developed by using and adapting a financial model. This will increase the prospect for achieving viable investment plans for proposed future small town water services.

A key stage that is often neglected is the dissemination of the results and consultation with key stakeholders such as government and the small town community. To use the survey results effectively it is often necessary to influence policy and seek agreement about preferred service options and future tariff levels. Strategies for doing this are outlined in the following sections.

5.1 Step 10 – Using CVM results to develop tariffs

The CVM data generated provides a good basis for developing water revenue and expenditure projections for a town. This is because there are reliable estimates of the amount of money that households are prepared to pay for the range of interventions offered. These in turn can be incorporated into appropriate tariffs, or financial sustainability models, possibly containing a range of scenarios to make a realistic plan for investment decision-making for the town. Section 1.4 outlines at what stage the WTP survey results are incorporated into a typical investment planning process.

Many factors need to be considered when setting tariffs. It should be stressed that various types of tariffs can be used to collect revenue, and to deliver subsidies to specific groups within the town. Knowing the WTP of the respondents provides useful information, but the analysis must be supported by in-depth knowledge of the local and national policy on water charging, subsidies, and financing of small town water supply.

The implications of imposing significantly higher water tariffs on the poorest members of the community must be considered. Opportunities for cross subsidy can be also explored and the emphasis must be on developing a water-pricing system that is understood by the community and the water supply authorities. The tariff and billing system should be easy to manage and flexible enough to cope when more people connect to more expensive service options, or join the new scheme.

5.1.1 Commonly used tariffs

A tariff is normally a set of procedural rules used to determine the conditions of service and the types and levels of charges for water users in various categories. For example, a monthly bill may be comprised of two parts: one part based on the volume of water used and the second based on factors other than water use. It is possible that one of these components will be zero and the water bill will be determined solely by the other (Boland and Whittington, 1997). For example, a water bill could be based on the value of the property on which the connection to the town's distribution network is located. Alternatively, a water bill could be determined by multiplying the volume of water used in the billing period (if a meter is used) by a per unit price. An example of a two-part tariff would be a fixed charge per month plus an amount equivalent to the volume consumed times a per unit charge.

Water tariffs in small towns may need to be restructured and increased in order to ensure the financial sustainability of a new scheme. This may be difficult politically, but the results of the CVM study or other demand assessment research should be used to support the increase. The re-structuring of tariff structures may be assisted by new national-level legislation and administered by a national body, or decentralisation may have devolved more powers to the town council.

Water agencies, town councils or private sector managers should consider the proper design for the tariff before the new water supply scheme is commissioned. New tariff structures will need to be agreed by key stakeholders including local authorities, the user population, the relevant government departments or regulators and possibly lending institutions.

What are the main purposes of the tariff?

- Adequate cost recovery is often the primary purpose of a tariff. A decision needs to be made on the level of cost recovery. Should the tariff recover capital costs, or just the marginal operating costs? Where will the initial financing come from to pay for the capital costs?
- Economic efficiency can be achieved by setting all prices equal to their relevant marginal costs (refer to Section 2.6 for a definition of marginal costs). This will insure that users receive the largest aggregate benefits (Boland and Whittington 1997).
- Equity usually means that users pay amounts which are proportionate to the costs they impose on the utility. This implies that equals are treated equally. Fairness is often used interchangeably with equity but is a more subjective notion. Some may think that it is fair to charge all customers the same unit price whilst others think that fairness requires subsidies to some customers. A marginal-cost based tariff is expected to be equitable but not always fair (Boland and Whittington, 1997).
- Cross subsidisation is a term related to fairness but often explicitly incorporated into tariff design. It is assumed that tariffs in developing countries should be used to redistribute income from richer household to poorer households. The idea behind increasing block tariffs (discussed later) is that the first block is priced below the marginal cost and subsequent blocks are priced slightly above marginal costs. This should mean that large volume water users subsidise small users.

Policy and institutional factors also play an important role in the type of tariff that should be set and the cost-recovery levels which are targeted. Table 10 presents some of the key issues that should be considered.

Table 10. Key issues for setting tariffs

Issue	Potential impact on tariff policy
National policy priorities	National or state policy might impact on tariff setting. For example, if government policy is to move towards full cost recovery, including capital costs, this should impact on tariff increases.
Cross subsidisation of poorer communities	If one aim is to improve equity, tariffs can be set at different levels for different user groups. This could be done by volume of use, or by type of user (commercial, business, etc.).
Consideration of the cost of water supply	A key decision is to determine whether tariffs should aim to cover only the operational costs of a water supply system, or to include capital costs and provision for future expansion.
Willingness to pay of communities	This is an important factor and is becoming increasingly accepted as a key element of tariff setting. Tariffs can be raised for those individuals / communities who are willing to pay more for water supply.
Willingness to charge	Policymakers/politicians may often be unwilling to increase water charges because they perceive that tariff increases are likely to be unpopular with the public. Orientation of policymakers is often required to demonstrate the benefits to all stakeholders of generating adequate funds through increased tariff levels.

A simple set of principles have been proposed to improve tariff-setting methodologies. These principles, often called CAFES, are described in Box 22, and it is suggested that policy makers need to consider all these factors in agreeing future tariff structures.

Box 22. Tariffs and CAFES principles

Tariffs should adhere to 'CAFES':

- *Conserving* – The structure of tariffs should influence consumption to the extent that consumers will purchase enough of the service without being wasteful.
- *Adequate* – The funds generated must be sufficient to enable financial commitments to be met and some contribution to be made to future investment.
- *Fair* – The tariff charges must be allocated between consumer groups in a fair and equitable manner paying particular regard to the needs of the poorer members of the community.
- *Enforceable* – It must be possible to charge and collect the tariffs that fall due.
- *Simple* – The tariff should be simple to administer and easy for consumers to understand.

Source: Franceys (1994) adapted by K. Sansom

Types of tariff

The literature discusses a range of tariffs used in the water sector (Katko, 1991):

- Flat rates: tariffs does not change with consumption
- Uniform rate: tariffs increase uniformly with respect to consumption
- Decreasing block tariffs: tariffs decline in steps as consumption increases, reflecting the economies of scale that might exist in terms of the cost of supply
- Increasing block tariffs: tariffs increase incrementally as consumption increases
- Lifeline tariffs: essentially part of the increasing block tariffs, but the first X litres of consumption are either free or very cheap

Uniform tariffs, when the price increases in a straight line according to the amount of water used, are often difficult to manage and price. For a small town water supply authority a different price would be applied to each cubic metre, or part-metre of water consumed. The tariff would be easier for users to understand and a different structure would need to be applied to public taps.

Lifeline tariffs and increasing block tariffs are often the tariff structure 'of choice' in developing countries, but have recently been criticised because they tend to discriminate against poor users of shared connections (Boland and

Whittington, 1997). With increasing block tariffs, the water user is charged a unit price for the first units abstracted, up to a specified amount, which defines the end of the first block. Above this amount the user is charged a higher price for the second block of units, and so on until the highest block is reached.

In order to design an increasing block or lifeline tariff one must decide on three things: the number of blocks, the volume of water use associated with each block, and the price to be charged per unit of water within each block.

Increasing block tariffs (IBTs) and lifeline tariffs are commonly used in developing countries, particularly urban areas. Several arguments suggest that they promote equity because they force richer households to cross-subsidise poorer households because wealthy households will use more water than poor households. The higher rates paid by industrial and commercial customers allows the water utility to cross-subsidise poor customers, and if the price of the highest blocks is high, it can discourage wasteful use of water and thus promote water conservation.

In practice, however, the IBTs used in most cities give households with private connections much more water than the internationally cited standards for basic water needs. The internationally cited standard is usually in the range of 20-30 litres per capita per day. It is often difficult for politicians to restrict the size of the initial block, because a large block directly benefits not only the poor but also the middle- and upper-income households. Therefore initial blocks may work out to be many times more than 20-30 litres per capita per day. IBTs do not adjust the size of the initial block for the number of members of a household, therefore households with more members, which tend to be the poorest, are penalised.

IBTs also tend to benefit households with private connections, compared to households sharing a connection, or those using public taps and purchasing water by the jerry can. In the latter case, consumption at the tap is so heavy that the water will soon be charged at the higher blocks and poor users are in effect paying more per unit of water than small middle-class households with a private connection.

Box 23 gives an example of increasing block tariffs used in Sri Lanka's Small Towns Programme. The Sri Lanka Community Water Supply and Sanitation Project (Small Towns Component) serves three districts with a total population of around 55,000. Tariffs are set based on specific operating costs plus a profit margin. The following rates are applied:

Box 23. Sri Lanka tariff example

Residential Tariff – volumes of water consumed per month

0 – 10 m^3
Rs 2.50 / m^3

11 – 20 m^3
Rs 3.00 / m^3

>20 m^3
Rs 7.00 / m^3

Commercial
Rs 26.00 / m^3

Tariff review and revision is the responsibility of consumers associations along with the local authority. The National Water Supply and Drainage Board provides a facilitating role through solicited technical advice.

In Sri Lanka, each household can consume 10,000 litres per month at the cheapest tariff level. With an average family of five, that equates to 66 litres per capita per day, double the WHO recommended basic needs volume of water. For small families with fewer children, consumption would have to be much higher per person before the higher tariff was reached.

An additional problem that occurs with increasing block tariffs – as is shown in the Sri Lanka example in Box 23 – is that it acts as a disincentive for the on-selling of water to neighbours. Where on-selling is likely or offers good potential to increase water sales and usage, it is often better to have one flat tariff rate per m^3 at a level that is sufficiently high to cover planned costs.

5.1.2 Cross-subsidisation

As a general rule, the case for a subsidy to be built into the tariff structure – a water subsidy – is something that needs to be assessed rather than assumed. The results of the CVM Survey will provide useful information for the financial planner in determining appropriate subsidies – if necessary. It is not always the case that water services are unaffordable to low-income households, nor that subsidising water consumption is the best way of improving public health amongst the poor (Foster et al, 2000).

A research programme was carried out in Panama in 1998 based on a Contingent Valuation Survey and complementary information from the 1997 Living and Standards Measurement Study (LSMS) and the customer database for Panama's national water utility IDAAN (Instituto de Acueductos y Alcantarillados Nacional). The CVM was used to find out how many people are excluded from receiving water and sewerage services because they genuinely cannot afford them. It sought to establish the maximum amount that households were willing to pay to consume a typical volume of piped water and to obtain a connection to the sewerage network. The willingness-to-pay results were compared to existing tariffs to provide an indication of affordability. The main premise was that subsidies were only justified if willingness-to-pay values fell short of the true economic cost of providing the piped water supply.

The results of the survey showed that while the current cost for water is US$0.21 per cubic metre, poorer consumers would still be willing to pay up to US$0.46 per cubic metre. This implies that the price of potable water would have to rise substantially before it became unaffordable to low-income households – and that there is room to increase investment and raise tariffs. A policy of cross subsidisation might not be the most economically efficient use of resources, instead IDAAN should concentrate on improving the reliability and area covered of the existing network by raising tariffs up to, but not above, US$0.46 per cubic metre.

If the results of the CVM Survey show that a reasonable percentage of respondents are only able to afford the cheapest options at the minimum prices, or cannot afford any options at all, the need for some form of cross subsidisation may be accepted in the small town sitiaution. This will depend on the CVM results – if more than 5 per cent of respondents are clearly unable to afford the prices for any of the options discussed in the survey, a case should be made for considering some form of subsidy. However, this will vary from survey to survey and depend on the cost and types of water supply options offered. In Bushenyi, less than 1 per cent of respondents said they could not afford protected springs.

If subsidies are considered – how might they best be achieved?

Simple forms of cross subsidisation in the community can be achieved through a variety of mechanisms, although many schemes are difficult to implement and manage. The simplest methods include:

(a) Higher income groups pay a larger up-front capital cost contribution.

(b) Low service-level options such as springs, dug wells, and handpumps receive a higher capital subsidy from governments or donors, than better service options such as private connections on piped supplies.

(c) Households that are able to afford private connections (considered a higher level option) pay more per unit of water than those using public connections (although if the public connections are kiosks with attendants, they will of course pay more per container).

(d) Poorer households receive agreed volumes of free water and do not pay any capital costs towards new schemes.

(e) Poorer households pay reduced water charges for all options, including a reduced rate for piped water and water by the jerry can.

Clearly, many of these methods overlap and some methods are much easier to administer than others. Options (a) and (b) are likely to be easier to manage than the other options. Local communities may of course come up with their own solutions for cross subsidisation, so this is an issue worth discussing with the community once the WTP results are documented and disseminated.

Eligibility criteria and subsidies

Under the direct subsidy approach, governments pay part of the water bill of poor households that meet specified eligibility criteria. This direct subsidy is sent straight to the household – because all households have a piped connection. This approach was first used in water sector reforms in Chile in the early 1990s (Foster et al, 2000). This method requires an assessment of income levels and eligibility before it can be successfully implemented. This is often the most difficult aspect of implementing a subsidy programme. The intended beneficiaries of subsidy schemes are invariably those living below the poverty line, usually expressed as an annual threshold for per capita income or expenditure. In practice, it is very difficult to measure income levels directly and therefore to determine whether a particular household should benefit from the subsidy (Foster et al., 2000).

It is necessary to develop eligibility criteria that can be measured objectively and observed easily and are difficult to falsify or misrepresent. Eligibility criteria can be either zonal (locational) – based on the characteristics of the area where the household lives – or individual – based on the characteristics of the household itself. The main issue is the extent to which the criteria can simply and accurately identify the target group.

There are two forms of targeting error (Foster et al, 2000): errors of exclusion and errors of inclusion. Errors of exclusion are when members of the target group are not captured by the eligibility criteria and hence fail to receive the subsidy. Errors of inclusion, are when people outside the target group receive the subsidy by somehow managing to comply with the eligibility criteria.

As a criterion, zone of residence has the advantage of being easier to observe and administer and relatively hard to falsify. However, the extent to which it correlates with the underlying measure of poverty depends on the size of the zones and the extent to which poverty is geographically situated. For small towns, the obvious split would be to charge different prices for those living in a designated core area compared to those living in the fringe areas. Errors of inclusion and exclusion would occur because there are some rich farmers living in the fringe areas and some poor households living in high-density core settlements.

It is much harder, costly, and resource intensive to obtain reliable information on individual household income and expenditure in order to assess eligibility for individual subsidies. In Panama, an extensive search for eligibility criteria indicators was conducted by making cross-tabulations between possible indicators and poverty levels using data from the LSMS survey. The most successful proxy variables were:

- poor-quality floor materials;
- lack of telephone connection;
- primary-educated head of household; and
- toilet facilities located outside house.

These variables are specific to urban residents in Panama. It is easy to see why they would not necessarily be suitable for small towns' inhabitants in low-income countries.

Because every community is different, a simpler approach would be for the town council or water committee to give discretionary subsides to poor families based on their knowledge of the families coping strategies and living conditions. To make this as transparent as possible it is better if this is decided by formal town council meetings.

Subsidies applied per option

A more practical way to levy a subsidy would be to price water supply options so that higher level options subsidise lower level options. The eligibility criteria would be self selective – any household that values water from a private connection sufficiently, and is hence able and willing to pay for that connection, could be charged a slightly higher fee per unit of water than households using public connections. Section 2.6 – 2.8 of this guide discusses costing water supply systems using the average incremental costs method. This produces an average cost per unit of water. In small towns with piped schemes, cross subsidisation is possible because the water authority can vary the amount charged per unit of water between options. If the average incremental cost of water from the piped scheme is \$1 per m^3, a small surcharge could be applied to water bills where households have a private connection.

Simple calculations on the number and proportion of households with private connections and their expected consumption would reveal the surplus cash available. The surplus cash could then be used to reduce the tariffs charged per jerry can at the public kiosks. This method avoids the need to carry out zonal or individual assessments of poverty, and is much easier to manage and calculate.

It should, however, be noted that water kiosks are often an expensive option because the person who sells the water needs to be paid for their time. Shared connections offer a cheaper option if they are feasible, with householders onselling water to their neighbours. For this option it is not necessary to pay somebody to sell water all day and shared connections can act as competition to the water kiosks and hence keep prices at reasonable levels.

In very small towns, particularly those completely reliant on limited groundwater sources, the cross subsidisation of running costs can be difficult to implement. For example, in programmes with only one option that 80 per cent of the town select, and can afford, what criteria should be used to determine which are the poorest households – if any – requiring subsidies? Would the community water committee, local council, or water authority manage means testing? These questions are not easily answered, and there are examples of cross subsidisation within communities, but they are quite rare. More often than not, schemes requiring a joining fee or upfront initial contribution provide simple cross subsidies by allowing the poorest households, widows, old people without dependents, etc. to pay reduced, or no fees. If there are on-going tariffs, such as a price per jerry can, or monthly fee, it can be difficult to manage the distribution of free or subsidised water.

It would be easiest to subsidise a particular basic water supply option and to charge more for higher level options. But if the town water supply only includes basic options then this will not be possible and a subsidy based on discretionary concessions for certain poor families may need to be developed. This is best determined at the local level.

Basic rules for tariff setting

The types of tariffs to be used depend very much on the institutions managing the water supply system. If the CVM report is to make recommendations on the types and levels of appropriate tariffs, *the types of tariffs and subsidies that are advocated must reflect national policy guidelines.*

In addition to the 'CAFES' principles for setting tariffs in Box 22, other factors to consider when designing tariffs include:

- *Public acceptability.* A successful tariff should not be the focus of a lot of public criticism of the water supply agency. It is therefore important to promote the need for tariff increases and the WTP results can be used to build consensus.
- *Political acceptability.* Similarly, the tariff designed for use in small towns must be acceptable to local and national political leaders, otherwise there is the risk of external political interference and the failure of the system. Often the 'willingness to charge' issue is as important as 'willingness to pay'. Politicians need to be involved and consulted as part of the consensus building for water charge increases.
- *Incremental price changes.* In order to work towards full cost recovery covering O&M, depreciation, loan repayment and future expansion costs, tariff changes may need to be incremental over a number of years.

5.1.3 Inflation and index linking tariffs

The discussion in Section 2.5.8 and 2.7 focused on costing options in order to provide reasonable ranges of prices to ask respondents' their WTP for various options in the willingness-to-pay sections of the questionnaire. It is recommended that constant prices be used when working out the present values of costs, but that interest rates are taken into account to enable an appropriate annuity factor to be used for costing the replacement costs of major components.

However, when working out the appropriate tariff and designing tariff models it is suggested that constant prices are used both for the costs and revenue streams, but that the final tariff values are then index linked to account for increasing costs. This essentially means that inflation is considered within the model. Unlike economic analysis, financial analysis involves real cash flows from consumers to service providers – for accounts to balance each year it is likely that the consumers, payments must increase to match the increased costs associated with providing the service.

As was stated in Section 2.7, inflation does exist within the 'real' economy, wages increase, and the costs of local or imported pipes, tools, and office stationery will all increase. It is therefore necessary to increase future tariffs by the annual rate of inflation plus any other increases associated with moving towards full cost recovery.

Most countries produce a range of indexes to assess levels of price increases and decreases in the regional and national economy; these might focus on agricultural prices, manufacturing outputs, and wage rises, etc. The tariff increase should reflect the price changes relating to the supply of the improved water supply. This is most likely to be the retail price index or the government's official inflation rate.

The need to increase tariffs by inflation might be contentious and difficult to understand for consumers who are not used to paying for water. Section 5.5 of this document suggests methods for using the results of the CVM Survey as a tool to assist in negotiating with the community. It is during this process that the reasons for tariff increases need to be fully explained, to ensure that consumers are not taken by surprise after the first year when tariffs are likely to increase year on year to ensure adequate cost recovery.

5.1.4 Designing a financial model

The objective of developing a tariff/financial model is to consider the appropriate tariff levels that will maximise revenues, based on service options that users prefer and are willing to pay for. Due allowance can of course be made for acceptable increases in tariff rates of over the coming years. The output from the financial model is the preferred investment scenario(s) that will include projected income and expenditure over the coming 10 to 20 years, based on preferred service options for each consumer group. An example financial model based on an Excel spreadsheet is included in Annex F. The following sections provide advice on developing such a model.

Revise option costs

The CVM results provide an estimate of the revenue that can be raised, but an equally important question for the tariff model is to determine what costs need to be recovered to ensure adequate cost recovery?

It may turn out that the amount of revenue that users stated they would be willing to pay for various water supply options exceeds the marginal cost of supply, (either with, or without capital costs). Alternatively, forecast revenues may fall short of expected costs. The only way to determine how forecast revenues and costs balance out is to design *and cost* the improved water system based on the findings of the CVM Survey.

The water supply options priced for the CVM Survey estimated the proportion of the population likely to use each option. Once the results of the demand assessment have been evaluated it will be possible to use more accurate estimates of likely use patterns based on the survey results. Therefore, in order to develop a tariff model, the first task will be to revise the investment costs required to implement the preferred options. Options with low demand should be 'discarded' and only the most popular options included in the tariff model.

A recent study in Ghana (WSP Small Towns Water Supply System Tariff Design 2000) involved field visits and a preliminary analysis of data gathered in eight small towns which produced a table showing the actual cost of maintenance and repair in small towns in the Central Region of Ghana. The towns' main water sources are boreholes, with a mixture of electric and mechanical pumping. Water supply services are mixed, including some private connections, public kiosks (taps), and vendors. Table 11 summarises each cost component as a proportion of the total running costs.

Table 11. Ghana – comparison of O&M costs in small towns

Costs in percentages	Afrowood Study[20]	Burgeap Study[21]	Seven villages	Assin Praso	Average
Energy	15%	9%	8%	11%	10.75%
Repairs and maintenance	34%	10%	29%	30%	25.75%
Salaries of staff and vendors	42%	53%	38%	44%	44.25%
Administration costs including board sitting allowances	3% (excluding sitting allowance)	20%	17%	15%	17% (excluding Afrowood)
Travel and transport costs	5%	9%	7%	1%	22%

Source: WSP (2000) Small Towns Water Supply System Tariff Design. Field Report.

What is most interesting about Table 11 is the wide variations in certain cost components, particularly repairs and maintenance and travel and transport costs. The main lesson to be learnt here is that it is difficult to take examples of costs in small towns and transfer them to other small towns, even if the water supply sources and services are similar.

The data also indicated the theoretical water sales required to break even. Sales ranged from 4 to 34 litres per person per day between different towns.

Recovery of capital costs

Many tariff models only consider recovering the running costs of a water supply system. However, if only limited or no government grants are available, and the water authorities believe that the townspeople must contribute towards the capital costs, it will be necessary to build a capital cost element into the model. This can be in the form of a loan, financed at varying interest rates. Capital costs also vary enormously between locations, as demonstrated in Table 12.

[20] Source: Afrowood Consulting

[21] Source: Burgeap Consulting Engineers

Table 12. Capital costs for small towns water supply programme – Uganda

Town	Pipe line laid (m)	House connections	Revised contract sum (UG sh)	Price (US$)	Price per metre of pipe (US$)
Luwero	18,000	250	1,173,000,000	651,667	36
Lugazi	19,000	120	1,597,000,000	887,222	47
Busia	28,000	150	1,634,000,000	907,778	32
Malaba	10,000	52	416,000,000	231,111	23
Kalisizo	6,500	183	503,000,000	279,444	43
Lyantonde	22,000	180	2,364,000,000	1,313,333	60
Ntungamo	16,500	115	449,000,000	249,444	15
Rukungiri	12,000	144	732,000,000	406,667	34

Source: Govt. of Uganda, 2001

The price per metre of pipe laid emphasises how construction prices can vary. These are for the capital works in small towns in Uganda. All of the schemes involved established a piped network with private connections and kiosks. In Lyantonde the price per metre of pipe laid was four times greater than in Ntungamo. The average price per metre of pipe was US$36.

For many piped schemes, individual households are asked to pay for the additional pipes and connection fittings required to connect their house to the mains pipe. If this is the case it is essential that householders are made aware of the likely cost to them. A menu of prices based on average distances of the mains pipe from the tap location could be set out on a sheet to provide a broadly accurate cost.

A recent ADB scheme in Sri Lanka[22] required households to pay for the pipe and tap (but not the metre) and to provide all labour. Neither the water committee of the CBO managing the project nor individual households had any idea of the likely costs involved, even though the mains pipes, tank, and pump house had already been built. The next step was for individual households to purchase the additional pipes and tap and make the connection to the mains pipe. Many

[22] ADB-Assisted Third Water Supply and Sanitation Project. National Water Supply and Drainage Board. Sri Lanka. Hambantota District 2002. Consultant's observations during May 2002 field visit.

households had already built a trench in anticipation of laying their own pipe and connecting to the mains pipe – but were still unaware of the costs involved. Estimates of the likely costs to be incurred by individual households made during household interviews ranged from Rs.500 to Rs.3,000. It was clear that some low-income households would not be able to afford Rs.3,000 and little consideration had been made for small-scale loans. Poorer households were not cross-subsidised within the scheme. It is important, therefore, for project managers to be transparent about likely connection and capital cost contributions by households as early as possible in the project development.

A cost model example from Dar es Salaam is set out in Box 24 and Tables 13 and 14 summarise a cost model set up to establish the most appropriate tariffs required to recover running and capital costs using both loans with commercial interest rates and direct grant aid.

Box 24. Dar es Salaam cost model

Cost model
In Dar es Salaam, a cost model was developed based on the results of a CVM Survey to assess demand for either public kiosks or private connections in four communities. The communities varied in size and density, so the costs of rehabilitation also varied. To develop the model the consultant first estimated the cost of providing boreholes, piped connections, and public kiosks to the various communities. Depreciation was estimated using a factor to calculate the annual investments that must be made in order to pay for the replacement in the future. The factor used was higher than would actually be needed if the water committee could guarantee returns on money saved at the interest rate of 8 per cent. This factor was risk averse by assuming that very little interest would accrue on any savings, thus ensuring that the water committees had enough money to replace and repair their major capital assets when necessary.

If the tariff for *both* community kiosk users and private connections is TSh1 per litre the internal rates of return (IRR) are positive, as set out in Table 13. In addition, three quarters of households are assumed to contribute TSh1000 per adult towards the installation of new kiosks and 25 per cent contribute TSh100,000 towards the borehole fund for improved pipe connections. These proportions were based on the exact results from the Contingent Valuation Survey.

Two funding scenarios are explored in Table 13:

- grant aid to pay for the difference between up-front contributions made by the individual households and the total capital costs; and
- a loan from a private lending institution with an annual interest rate of 25 per cent.

The results were very positive. Considering the high expenditure involved in setting up the piped network, and the high interest rate, the positive results for loan financing are surprising and could have major policy implications for water committees, CBOs or private companies considering offering mixed service levels in these slum communities in Dar es Salaam.

Break-even tariffs
Table 14 shows the tariff required for both community kiosks and private connections in order to recover all capital, O&M, and depreciation. Three cost options were tested:

- a 25 per cent interest on a loan towards the capital costs;
- grant aid to pay for the capital costs;and
- a 5 per cent interest loan – drawn from a revolving fund.

The price per jerry can varies considerably according to the population served and the number of boreholes, etc. There are certain fixed costs such as the drilling and servicing of boreholes, etc. which cannot be avoided; these reduce the unit cost of supply in Yombo Mwinyi and Keko Mwanga B. If a loan/revolving fund of 5 per cent were used to pay for all capital costs, this would be re-paid within three to five years. As is the case in many developing countries, the price paid by consumers connected to the cities' piped system is much less than this. The tariffs in this model are more equitable, because households using the public kiosks do not cross-subsidise richer households with private connections.

Table 13. Rates of return for private connections and kiosks in Dar es Salaam

Community	IRR grant aid	NPV grant aid (Tanzania shillings (TSh))	IRR loan finance at 25 per cent interest	NPV Loan Finance (TSh)
Zamcargo	54%	57,905,256	12%	8,905,494
Yombo Mwinyi	139%	494,230,631	81%	429,055,659
Keko Mwanga B	86%	494,230,631	38%	137,285,691
Kibonde Maji B	56%	145,556,116	24%	79,671,498

Note: Assuming a tariff of TSh1 per litre, (refer to box 24).

Source: Wedgwood and WaterAid, 2000

Put into perspective, householders are already paying TSh1 per litre for water from the community kiosks and often pay up to TSh5 per litre for vended water – therefore these tariffs are not unreasonable for a more reliable and closer source. Currently, 25 per cent of households use vended water, at a much higher cost, at some point during the year.

Table 14. Private connections and kiosks (break-even tariff) in Dar es Salaam

Community price per jerry can (20 litres)	Grant aid (TSh)	25 per cent loan finance (TSh)	5 per cent revolving fund (TSh)	Number of years to pay 5 per cent loan
Zamcargo	12	17	16	5
Yombo Mwinyi	8	12	11	3
Keko Mwanga B	9	15	13	4
Kibonde Maji B	11	17	16	4

Note: figures are in Tanzanian shillings per 20-litre jerry can.

Source: Wedgwood and WaterAid, 2000

Table 14 demonstrates that even without grant aid assistance, the break-even tariff to provide water to these communities would be less than the current average tariff of TSh20 per 20-litre jerry can.

Example of tariff calculation based on the costs of water supply

Table 15 is a summary of simple tariff calculations based on three scenarios: O&M costs only, O&M plus capital costs, and a third scenario that includes depreciation. The annual operating cost of providing water in a small town in Ghana is US$30,000 per year. This is based on a supply and demand for 6 million litres of water. The capital cost of the infrastructure needed to provide the water is US$300,000. The infrastructure has an expected life of 25 years. The water provider expects a profit of 10 per cent per annum.

Table 15. Calculation of tariff levels based on costs

Method	Estimated costs	Tariff level (per litre)
Operational cost	$30,000	0.50 cents
Operational plus capital cost	($30,000 + $(300,000 /25))	0.70 cents
Operational plus capital cost plus profit element	($30,000 + $(300,000 /25)) * 1.10	0.77 cents

Source: M. Thomson and Sansom, K.R., 2002

Note: the calculation of capital costs assumes straight-line depreciation

Revenue factor

A parallel step in determining the types and level of tariffs would be to work out how much revenue could reasonably be generated from the town if the selected options were provided at optimum tariff levels based on the willingness-to-pay results.

The revenue factor is a useful calculation obtained by multiplying the cumulative frequency of willingness-to-pay ranges by the price interval, divided by 100.

Revenue factor = cumulative frequency * (price/100)

The higher the revenue factor, the more revenue will be generated if the price corresponding to that revenue factor is charged. Table 16 summarises a break-down of WTP for handpumps obtained during a Contingent Valuation Survey of demand for new water supply services in Busia, a small town in Uganda. The table is very easy to construct and from this a graph can be drawn to show the total revenue that could be generated for each particular option, based on the stated WTP of respondents.

For example, in Table 16 the highest revenue factor is 26.3, which corresponds to a price of USh50 per jerry can. Even though only 35.9 per cent of respondents were WTP the equivalent of USh50 per jerry can from their metered yard tap, if this price was set as the tariff in Busia, 52.5 per cent of all respondents have stated that they are WTP at *least* USh50 per jerry can. The maximum amount of revenue could be raised if metered yard taps were provided in the town.

For the simplest tariff model the revenue factor can be used to guide the setting of tariffs, although the revenue raised may still not be sufficient to recover costs, so further financial appraisal would still be required. In this example, 47.5 per cent of respondents stated that they were not willing, and/or unable to pay the equivalent of USh50 per jerry can for their metered yard tap's supply.

Table 16. WTP for metered yard taps – using the revenue factor

Price per jerry can	Frequency (%)	Cumulative (%)	Revenue factor
200	0.9	1.4	2.8
150	1.8	3.2	4.8
100	13.7	16.9	16.9
50	**35.9**	**52.5**	**26.3 (highest)**
30	4.6	57.1	17.3
25	11.6	68.7	17.1
20	6.1	74.8	15
15	0.3	75.1	11.3
10	2.7	77.8	7.8
5	0.6	78.4	3.9

Source: Van Nostrand and Associated Consulting Engineers 1997

It may of course be necessary to set the tariff at less than USh50 per jerry can, initially at least, in order to address 'willingness-to-charge' concerns. A related issue to consider is whether there are nearby alternative water sources for people who cannot pay the USh50 per jerry can.

In determining tariff policies and levels, judgements need to be made on the following issues:

- How to meet all costs for sustainable and adequate services. A financial model (which is discussed below) can assist with this together with sensitivity analyses using different tariff levels.
- What are appropriate tariff levels over the coming years for the preferred options, based on tariff calculations and on the WTP results.

Care is needed to ensure that all consumer groups (including the poor) will have viable water supply options available that they can afford. If it is not possible to have full cost recovery and provide a range of service options to meet the needs and spending power of each consumer group, then subsidies from government or cross subsidies from other users should be considered.

Revenue sources

The revenue sources in the financial model may include:

- future user payments for water service options based on tariff calculations and the revenue factor calculations discussed earlier;
- government loans towards capital costs;
- government grants towards capital costs;
- community capital contributions;
- government subsidies for O&M (that will hopefully be decreasing);
- municipal subsidies for O&M;
- capital cost contribution from donors; and
- private finance assistance.

A dynamic financial model should consist of tariffs over a 10-20 year cycle. Population growth estimates should be based on the data obtained during the survey. At a very minimum, a tariff model for the preferred options should be able to recover all O&M costs plus depreciation of all assets (a 'replacement fund' to finance future repairs).

A financial model using a standard spreadsheet programme such as Excel should be able to test the financial viability of a range of tariffs and costs. Each run of the model can be based on a range of assumptions, for example costs can be much higher, tariffs lowered, the percentage split of users varied, etc. *The model should be user friendly*, not only accessible to economists or finance staff. The revenue streams should be based on the household sizes obtained during the survey and on any other data, including estimated consumption of water.

5.2 Example small town financial sustainability model

5.2.1 High- and low-cost investment scenarios

A financial sustainability analysis model for Bushenyi in Uganda is set out in Annex F. It contains two investment scenarios: the 'high cost' scenario is based on the results of the Contingent Valuation Survey which was carried out in June 2001. The number of households selecting the four preferred options and their mean WTP was used in the model. Handpumps were not included as an option because the survey suggested that they were very unpopular. Previous experience with handpumps breaking down meant that most households considered them an unreliable water source.

In addition, the data for 'existing water use in the core area' was taken from the results of the CVM Survey in Bushenyi. The 'target water use patterns from WTP survey' were also taken from the CVM Survey and are based on respondents' willingness to pay and choice preferred option. This model separates out core and fringe areas; more sophisticated models could disaggregate the data into varying income groups. This might prove useful if there is a willingness by the authority to charge higher rates to higher income households, with the aim of cross-subsidisation within the community.

The low-cost scenario ignores the high demand for private connections in the fringe areas and instead provides more protected springs and kiosks to the fringe areas; the piped system only covers the core areas, which reduces the capital costs significantly.

Both models include existing and projected use of service options, projected costs, and revenues, leading to the projected deficit/surplus each year over the 25-year period. The model is very useful because it enables sensitivity analyses, varying subsidy and tariff levels, and changes in the percentage of households using each option now and the target percentage using the option in the future. The model can inform key policy decisions on matters such as which are the preferred service options and what should be the subsidy and tariff levels over time.

Estimates are made of average consumption per person according to the water supply option used. The most interesting aspect of this model is the 'percentage change in use' columns. The values can be varied by the model user to show the growth, or decline, in the number of households using each option. The model aims to represent the difficult transition period between the existing water supply system and the changes in water supply use once the system has been rehabilitated and extended.

In many small towns the main pipes and water tanks/reservoirs are built in the first stages of a rehabilitation programme and then smaller pipes and house connections are built when funds/labour/user contributions are available. This on-going process can take a number of years. Individual sections of the model show:

- the percentage of the population in the fringe and core areas using each option. The percentages in Year 1 represent existing water-use patterns;
- the actual number of people using each option. These change each year according to the growth/decline rates applied at the beginning of the model;
- the physical number of options within the fringe and core areas. The number of people using each option is used to calculate the actual number of protected springs, public kiosks, and house connections that exist in Year 1 and will exist in the future;
- the costs of providing and maintaining the new and existing options, based on the Government of Uganda/World Bank investment analysis; and
- tariffs for each option with the amount of revenue that will be raised each year.

The total costs and revenues can be compared to show how a change in the tariff rates, or changes in the number of households connecting to the piped scheme, affects cost recovery.

The shaded boxes can also be changed to examine cost recovery according to:

- the amount of grant aid provided; and/or
- the interest rate for a commercial loan can be changed to show the levels of debt servicing and cost recovery if no grant aid is available.

5.2.2 Example high-cost scenario

The model user can change all of the numbers shaded in the first part of the spreadsheet in Annex F.

Table 17 summarises existing water use in the core and fringe areas and target water-use patterns which should be achieved over the next few years. The rate of change from the existing water use to the target water use is summarised in a separate column and can be changed by the user to slow down the process if it is felt that construction would be delayed or a longer transition period required.

In the high-cost scenario the piped scheme would be built in the fringe areas as well as the core areas and meet the expressed demand from the survey. 41 per cent of the fringe area prefer protected springs and 9 per cent would use kiosks, this compares to 30 per cent of the core area who would use springs and 15 per cent who would use kiosks. The number of households wishing to use kiosks is higher in the core areas because of the shorter distances involved to the nearest kiosks.

Table 17. Water use and target use percentages – high-cost scenario

Option	Existing water use		Target water use patterns from WTP survey	
	Core area	Fringe area	Core area	Fringe area
Protected springs	49	72	30	41
Public kiosks	4	1	15	9
Shared yard taps	12	2	30	40
Private connections	14	2	25	10
Other (vending, unprotected springs)	21	23	0	0
Total	**100**	**100**	**100**	**100**

In Table 18, the first column indicates the average volume of water that is consumed per person per day for each option. The second and third columns show the rate of change from existing water supply use to the improved water supply options each year.

The final columns indicate the tariffs that will be charged in the first year once project options are built, and the final column shows the percentage increase in tariffs per year. For protected springs the tariff is a monthly fee per family, for kiosks it is the price per jerry can, and for the piped connections it is the price per cubic metre. These tariff rates can be changed by the model user to quickly gauge the financial surplus/deficit that accrues over time. This would help in decision-making on the proportion of capital costs that need subsidies through direct grant aid and the proportion that can be repaid over time.

Table 18. Tariffs charged for water options – high-cost scenario, Bushenyi

Option	Volume of water consumed pcpd (litres)	% change in use CORE per year	% change in use FRINGE per year	Tariffs in year 1 (USh)	Tariffs % annual increase
Protected springs	20	-10	-10	750	1
Public kiosks	20	20	25	50	2
Shared yard taps	50	20	50	1,250	3
Private connections	80	20	25	1,750	3
Other (vending, unprotected springs)	20				

Source: Wedgwood et al, 2001.

Table 19 summarises the capital costs and percentage of grant aid provided. The model assumes that the grant aid is received in Year 1 and the loan is used to pay the remaining deficit, in this case 10 per cent of the total capital costs. Again the percentage of grant aid and interest rates can be varied.

Table 19. Capital costs and percentage grant aid

High-cost investment scenario	
Piped scheme capital costs US$	3,909,880
Protected springs capital costs US$	147,618
Percentage grant aid	90
O&M Cost of water production / m^3 (US$)	0.5
Loan (interest at %)	**5**

Operating and maintenance costs are included in the calculations of the model: for the piped scheme they are based on a cost of water production per cubic metre, and for the protected springs are based on the World Bank Investment Analysis for Uganda. Operating and maintenance revenues match the number of households using the new water supplies and so grow until the target water-use patterns have been achieved.

Once all of the costs and tariffs are input, the model works out the expected revenue or surplus each year. Based on the figures in Tables 17, 18, and 19 the water managing authority would take until Year 8 to pay off the outstanding loan of 10 per cent of all capital costs whilst continuing to expand the water system according to user demand. The first five years' cash-flow are summarised in Table 20. The second row demonstrates the revenue that would accrue from operating and maintenance tariffs if 90 per cent of the capital costs were paid for either by a donor or central government and no interest was charged for the remaining deficit.

Table 20. First five years high-cost scenario (90% grant aid and 5% interest)

Year	1	2	3	4	5
TOTAL REVENUE FROM TARIFFS (US$)	71,101	91,523	118,267	153,443	185,850
Surplus/deficit with zero interest rates and 90% grant aid	**-394,029**	**-374,733**	**-343,173**	**-293,130**	**-225,544**
Outstanding loan (with grant aid)	405,750	394,029	394,435	382,596	351,683
Debt servicing		19,701	19,722	19,130	17,584
O&M expenditure	59,380	72,228	86,706	103,401	118,264
Revenue	**71,101**	**91,523**	**118,267**	**153,443**	**185,850**
Surplus/deficit with loan repayments and grant aid	**-394,029**	**-394,435**	**-382,596**	**-351,683**	**-301,681**

5.2.3 Example low-cost scenario

The low-cost investment scenario is exactly the same, and involves simply changing the proportion of households using each option. As summarised in Table 21, in this scenario the piped scheme is not extended to the fringe areas, consequently a much smaller percentage of the town's population use the piped schemes, and the capital costs are reduced significantly.

Table 21. Low-cost investment scenario – percentage use of options

Option	Existing water use (Core area)	Existing water use (Fringe area)	Low-cost investment target use patterns (Core area)	Low-cost investment target use patterns (Fringe area)
Protected springs	49	72	35	60
Public kiosks	4	1	30	30
Shared yard taps	12	2	15	5
Private connections	14	2	20	5
Other (vending, unprotected springs)	21	23	0	0
Total	100	100	100	100

The tariffs remain the same as in the high-cost investment scenario but capital costs are significantly reduced to US$1,500,000. Other costs are set out in Table 22. Under this scenario, it would still take six years to repay the loan of 10 per cent of capital costs. The capital costs for constructing protected springs are higher, and more people are using protected springs and kiosks. The tariffs charged for protected springs only cover their O&M, therefore very little surplus cash is fed back into paying off the loan. If the tariffs for protected springs were raised their capital costs could be paid off more quickly.

Table 22. Low-cost investment scenario summary

Low-cost scenario	
Piped scheme capital costs US$	1,500,000
Protected springs capital costs US$	201,553
Percentage grant aid	90
O&M cost of water production / m^3 (US$)	0.5
Loan (interest at %)	5

Table 23 summarises the scenarios described earlier and two further scenarios, with higher capital costs and less grant aid. Tariffs have also been changed.

Under Scenario 2 the capital costs are higher and the proportion of grant aid less. Tariffs are also slightly less. In Scenario 2 the higher costs are significant when coupled with the smaller amount of grant aid. Tariffs do not compensate adequately and even with more efficient operating costs of US$0.4 per cubic metre, it would take 15 years to repay the outstanding debt of the high-cost scheme.

For Scenario 3 capital costs are significantly reduced and the proportion of grant aid is 95 per cent. However, tariffs are raised to cover operating and maintenance costs and to repay the remaining loan very quickly. This scenario might be a more realistic representation of a private sector water manager seeking to invest in small towns water supplies – the lower capital cost investment might make the scheme more attractive to a private sector operator. In Scenario 3 tariffs are higher in Year 1 and rise at approximately 1-3 per cent per annum. For the low-cost scenario, the loan is repaid in three years and by Year 10, without further capital investment, the scheme would generate profits of US$108,000 per annum. It is assumed that further investment in upgrading the system would be undertaken by the water authority – the model could be expanded to include re-investment of surplus profits to upgrade the piped scheme, explore future groundwater and surface water supplies, and make environmental improvements in the town.

Table 23. Summary of Investment Scenarios – varying costs and tariff rates

	High-cost scenario 1	Low-cost scenario 1	High-cost scenario 2 (private sector)	Low-cost scenario 2 (private sector)	High-cost Scenario 3	Low-cost Scenario 3
Capital cost of piped scheme	$3.9 million	$1.5 million	$6 million	$2 million	$4 million	$1.8 million
% grant aid	90%	90%	70%	80%	95%	95%
Interest rate for outstanding loan	5%	5%	3%	3%	3%	3%
Protected spring tariff per month (Sh)	750	750	700	600	750	650
Kiosk tariffs per jerry can (Year 1) (Sh)	50	50	50	40	50	40
Private connection tariff per m³ (Sh)	1750	1750	1500	1250	1750	1500
Cost of water production per m³ (piped scheme) (Sh)	$0.5	$0.5	$0.4	$0.4	$0.4	$0.4
Year in which loan paid off	8	6	15	12	4	3

Many different scenarios could be run. For example, tariffs can be based on ability and willingness to pay and the water supply system designed to match ability to pay and demand for the various water supply options.

Alternatively, a scheme can be designed without any prior knowledge of ability to pay or demand for different options and tariffs based solely on the costs of supply. This is not recommended because the scheme may not match users, water requirements, they may not be willing or able to pay the tariffs, and the scheme may be over-designed and under-used, leading to poor O&M and a rapidly deteriorating system.

5.2.4 Raising tariffs in the future

In practice, if there is a strategy to increase tariff levels over time, the following points need to be considered carefully:

- Estimate the demand for water at different tariff levels – lower tariffs can be expected to generate more demand. However, demand will not generally vary by as much as a rise in tariffs once customers become used to paying for water.
- Ensure that the total amount of revenue generated will be enough to cover the operational and/or capital costs of providing water – ideally there should be enough to cover both of these elements so that the provision of water is financially sustainable.
- Keep the community informed of tariff increases and the reasons why – CVM can be used as a negotiating tool with the community – see Section 5.4.

An example of tariff increases over time is shown in Box 25.

Box 25. Example of increasing tariffs over time – Guinea

Guinea entered into a lease contract for water services to its towns and cities in 1989. The government was committed to cost recovery for the services, but wanted to avoid a major tariff shock at the beginning of the contract. So, for the first six years of the contract, an International Development Association credit subsidised a declining share of the private operator's verified supply costs while the water tariff was raised until it covered costs.

Before the reform, households paid US$0.12 per m^3 for water, rising to US$0.83 by 1996. The arrangement jump-started the move toward full cost recovery and more sustainable water services, giving credibility to reform in a region and during a time when there was very little experience of the private provision of water services. It also set a time limit on subsidy commitments.

Source: Easing tariff increases – financing the transition to cost-covering water tariffs in Guinea, Locussol, A. and Brook-Cowen, P. 1999

5.3 Step 11 – Ensuring that WTP studies inform policy and practice

5.3.1 An overview

Water supply planning in small towns is made more complicated because policy decisions regarding one aspect of the system affect the operation and use of the whole system or other water supply sources. The demand for different options is interrelated: if people continue to use point sources, the piped system may be under used; conversely, if more people use private connections than was anticipated, the system may be unable to cope with demand.

The number of households using a piped system is a crucial planning parameter, therefore, the results of an accurate CVM should also make the results explicit and simple to understand for non-economists who will be expected to use these results in designing and planning a new system. This last point is perhaps the most important aspect of successful demand-responsive planning. In the past, many CVM Surveys have been reduced to academic exercises with reports gathering dust on the shelves of water supply ministry offices. Therefore the results must be explained clearly, in simple and plain language.

Most water supply planners are not familiar with the terms, or do not understand the significance of the results of the economic verification tests, so it is important to focus only on the valuable information generated and how it can be used. A consultant, research institute, or government department conducting a CVM Survey should always consider:

- What information would the water supply planners want to find out from the WTP and consumer survey?
- What will help them improve the sustainability and effectiveness of this water supply system?

It is, therefore, important to consult the project planners about the valuable data that you can provide and what information they would like, before the WTP survey reports are finalised. In order to produce draft outputs to support project development and influence policy in a streamlined manner, it is suggested that two key reports are produced:

(a) a draft WTP and consumer survey report; and
(b) a draft investment planning report for the small town water services.

Report (a) will enable the project team to assess the willingness-to-pay results and to provide data so that the financial model can be developed. Report (b) will include the financial projections and tariff levels based on the preferred investment scenarios. It may also include the revised outline technical designs, the preferred service option for each consumer group and the institutional implications. Producing two reports has a number of advantages – it allows the CVM work to be published quickly and inform other project partners, and it allows the investment planning and sensitivity analysis with the financial model to be participatory and considered.

The final draft of report (b) should preferably be produced after consultations with key stakeholders including government and the community.

5.3.2 Stage 1 – Draft WTP and consumer survey report

When government departments, municipalities, water authorities, etc. are contemplating new town water supply projects to improve services, there are a number of important issues to consider. To develop the financial projections and revise the project design it is very useful to know:

- the number of households that want to use each water supply option;
- estimates of the likely consumption of water for each of these options;
- how much people are willing and able to pay for their preferred option;
- the preferred method of paying for the improved water supply system;
- how respondents think the water supply system should be managed;
- what scheme options are preferred by the various consumer groups in the community, and for what reasons;
- whether are higher income groups are able to pay more and do they want higher level options? and
- the likely tariffs that must be charged to cover O&M, O&M plus replacement costs, and full costs.

This information should arise from the survey, or be calculated during the analysis of the CVM questionnaire. To improve the presentation of results and the accuracy of the survey the following factors should be considered:

- The CVM report can be used to provide information to project engineers on the kinds of technical options that households prefer. Such information should be presented to engineers and project designers in simple tables.

- CVM can provide reasonably accurate information on the amount of money people are willing to pay for their selected option. To increase the likelihood of this information being used, the team should ensure that the technical options are costed accurately.

- During the CVM Survey, socio-economic data is collected. This will provide information on relative incomes, wealth gaps, and poverty in the target community. It may be possible for the data to be used in other ways, possibly for databases managed by the local authorities, or to assist other schemes and projects.

Once the draft 'Willingness to pay and consumer survey' report has been completed and disseminated, it is possible for the project planners and key decision-makers to develop the financial model and preferred investment scenario(s).

5.3.3 Stage 2 – Investment planning report

When the data is being analysed using the financial model, it is important to consider the total amount of revenue that might be raised and a range of tariffs that could feasibly be charged, and what that would mean in terms of cost recovery. Such data should be presented clearly, so that managing authorities can work out whether subsidies are required, and at what level. Annex F and Section 5.2 provide examples of how to present the data. Some key considerations in developing the investment scenarios include:

- If many respondents want a piped system, or more sophisticated water supply services, and can afford to pay enough to recover O&M costs and only a proportion of capital costs, can the project team and government department obtain additional financing for the capital costs?
- Most governments are looking to reduce subsidies for water services in small towns. What are reasonable targets for subsidy reductions, assuming they will have to be gradually reduced over a number years?
- Will the users be prepared to pay water charges that will cover all costs including O&M, debt servicing, and depreciation for the proposed scheme option? If not what proportion of the costs can they pay?

- If respondents prefer a mixture of point sources and piped connections, will this be viable or will further community consultation be required?

Once the preferred investment scenario(s) have been developed and agreed amongst the project team, the draft 'investment planning' report can be compiled. It should include the preferred service option for each consumer group, the financial projections, projected deficits and surpluses, as well as the proposed tariff levels and any subsides.

The report would also benefit from the inclusion of the revised outline technical designs and an outline project implementation plan including any phasing. The proposed changes for the future management of water services could also be included.

The draft 'investment planning' report can then be used for consultation with key stakeholders, including community groups. After conducting the WTP survey there is little point in embarking on consultations with the community until the financial projections and draft investment plans have been completed, because people will want to know which options are being offered where at what prices, in order for then to give useful feedback.

5.3.4 Dissemination and advocacy to influence policy

WTP survey recommendations have not always been able to influence policy in the past. This is likely to be because:

- the results are not clearly presented in the survey report;
- one report on one town is not likely to influence the most senior decision makers; and
- there may not be government staff who are able/willing to promote the recommendations.

To address these concerns the following strategies are suggested:

- Pay particular attention in the report drafting to the presentation of the results, the recommendations, and their implications. Highlight key results and proposals in the executive summary.

- Government departments should be encouraged to commission their own WTP surveys, rather than donors taking the initiative. This should generate a better sense of ownership in the survey outputs. Hopefully these WTP guidelines and other work will enable local in-country consultants to undertake the surveys and hence make the consultant costs more affordable.

- Where possible, produce overview reports that collate WTP survey results and investment planning proposals from a number of towns. Such reports are more likely to influence senior policymakers than a report for one town.

- Develop a report dissemination strategy with follow up promotion work that is more likely to reach and influence senior policymakers, who make key decisions on the allocation of funds in the sector.

An example of CVM results influencing policy and designs in Lugazi in Uganda is discussed in Box 26.

Box 26. CVM results used to influence policy and designs in Lugazi

Planning and design for Lugazi town was carried out by ACE consultants. The senior engineer confirmed that they had considered the findings of the CVM report in their design, in particular, the summary of the CVM report, which stated:

'even though only a minority of households will initially demand private connections, the water authority should focus its attention on providing these households service because they are the key to revolutionising the water delivery system of the community'(Whittington 1998)

In particular, instead of building a large number of kiosks, the design team decided to construct only five kiosks in busy, public places. Instead, more priority was given to the promotion of private house connections. The water supply system was completed in August 2000, and by April 2001 there were 130 private house connections, with a waiting list of 500 households, 329 of which had paid the USh50,000 connection fee up front. The Lugazi CVM report included a detailed and easy-to-read section aimed at both local managers and DWD policymakers. This included a section titled '*Water Policy Mistakes to Avoid in Lugazi*'. The consulting engineers said that they found this section very useful and although exact cause and effect cannot be assumed, it is interesting to note that all eight water policy 'mistakes to avoid' highlighted in the conclusion have been addressed in Lugazi. For example, the report recommended that both private and public taps should be metered. This is now the case. The report suggested that vendors should be allowed to use the public taps, and that vending should be allowed to continue because vendors do provide a valuable service and reduce the burden for fringe dwellers of queuing and walking long distances to fetch water. Vendors are still active in Lugazi, particularly selling to households located in the fringe areas. The final recommendation was to ensure that the demand for public taps is not over-estimated and the system over-designed.

Examination of consumption patterns in Lugazi suggests that the predictions made in the 1994 CVM report (Whittington et al. 1994) were accurate. Demand for private connections is higher than was first anticipated by project designers before the CVM was commissioned. On-selling of water is occurring, to the extent that seven private connections sell more water than three of the kiosks.

5.4 WTP results and implications for technical options

The technical designs, in terms of which service options will be offered in which areas of the town, may need to be reviewed in the light of the WTP and consumer survey results, as well as the financial projections. Some key considerations are discussed in the following sections.

5.4.1 Towns without pipe networks and expensive technologies

There are many examples of towns and large villages that have had piped water systems with costly pumping and treatment arrangements, but they have fallen into disrepair. In such cases the people of the towns usually resort to using other supply options such as wells and handpumps, and may suffer water shortages. One of the key reasons for scheme failure is often that inadequate attention has been paid to who would pay for the O&M of the scheme and how it would be effectively managed.

The WTP survey results when combined with the financial projections provide unique data to support the key decision: if or when to introduce piped schemes and other expensive technologies in the small town. The financial model clearly sets out all the anticipated revenues, expenditures, and deficits over the coming 10 to 20 years. If reliable funding of the projected deficit cannot be found, then serious consideration should be given to using cheaper alternative options and technologies, and delaying the investment in the more expensive technologies.

As a town grows and becomes more prosperous over the years, the capacity and willingness to pay for more convenient but expensive solutions will increase. So where there is insufficient demand for the sustainable management of a new scheme in 2002, for example there may be adequate demand in 2007. So it is beneficial to do repeat WTP studies to capture such changes in demand.

The results from the WTP survey provide objective data on where new piped water distribution pipes should be laid and the likely number of people seeking private connections. Such information increases the chance of a viable scheme and also enables those people who want to reduce political administration and move towards more commercial and customer-orientated management.

5.4.2 Towns with limited piped networks

A common situation for water supply coverage in small towns is that some or most of the residents in the core or central area have pipelines that are nearby, while people in the fringe areas have to rely on alternative sources of water. As the town grows and increasing numbers of people want more convenient piped water services, the demand for an expanded piped water system increases.

Proposals for an improved water system are usually developed and costed, which may include an expanded pipe network, plus increased bulk water supply capacity. In some cases it may be necessary to consider new water sources that can involve significant extra capital and running costs. Key questions to consider before approval of funding is given include:

To where and how far should the pipe network be extended?
If the pipe network is extended to areas where people have low willingness-to-pay levels, or where the housing density is very low in fringe areas, there may be problems with the viability of the overall scheme. As the WTP survey will have area-based results, this information can be used, in conjunction with technical information and participatory planning, to determine where and how far to extend the pipelines.

To what extent should the bulk water supply capacity be increased?
The willingness-to-pay survey will provide valuable information on the likely take up in each area of the town of both new pipe connections and the various service options. This can be used to inform the short to medium-term water supply requirements together with future population projections. Some element of spare capacity for future expansion will be required.

Should other alternative sources be developed further?
Where the WTP survey results and participatory planning with communities reveal that there is a demand for technical options other than pipe supplies, developing these options should be considered. This can be done as an alternative to a pipe distribution system, or two or more options could be pursued if they are feasible and there is sufficient demand.

5.5 Community negotiations for investment planning

5.5.1 Consultation outputs

CVM is a very useful tool for policymakers and implementers because the WTP results can be used for negotiations with community groups and other stakeholders to justify water tariff increases linked to service improvements. Because there are few examples of CVM being used in actual project design, the most common criticism is that users may not pay the proposed tariffs even though they might have *said* they would during the survey. However, the WTP results from a thorough survey provide a valuable basis to begin negotiations on investment decisions with key stakeholders, including community groups.

It is worth reminding ourselves of the quote in Section 1.3.3 from the summary statement of the 'Small towns water supply and sanitation conference, held in Addis Ababa on 11–15 June 2002 which states that:

'The Contingent Valuation Methodology allows planners to assess the ***willingness to pay*** *and provides the necessary basis for projecting sales and revenues. This information is essential to support community participation and enable "informed choice" at the household level as well as for the community as a whole. WTP surveys provide the parameters to underpin financial models needed to evaluate expansion plans and to set tariffs.'*

In small towns, there is considerable merit in undertaking a process of consultation between local government, water supply managers (whether public or private), and community groups. This would entail the discussion of the WTP results and their implications, as well as the conclusions from the financial analyses. These negotiations should lead to an informed agreement on aspects such as the following:

(a) preferred service options to be available for each main consumer group;

(b) proposed future tariff levels and structures for each service option;

(c) proposed connection charges and rules for the use of each service option;

(d) project implementation plan including any phasing (subject to the agreement of the project financiers); and

(e) future management plans for water and sanitation services.

Whether the proposed project goes ahead will of course depend on the final decisions by the financiers for the capital funds such as government, donors, and lending institutions. But if those financiers know that the aspects listed above in (a) to (e) have been developed and agreed based upon reliable information with good prospects of leading to sustainable schemes, they are more likely to approve funding. The funding agencies may not require the agreement of all the aspects (a) to (e) before approving the project, this depend on their own fund disbursement policies. But an early agreement of these issues will improve prospects for effective implementation.

5.5.2 Consultation processes

Once the WTP and consumer survey results have been analysed and reported, the preferred investment scenarios and any subsidies should be determined and agreed by the project team and government, using the financial model, in readiness for the consultation process. It may also be necessary to amend the technical designs in the light of the preferred investment options.

A capable consultation team needs to be formed that will hopefully include:

- an engineer who was involved with the design options;
- a senior member of the WTP survey team;
- a manager from the organisation that manages water services (who wants to demonstrate that existing and potential customers are valued and they want to deliver reliable services);
- a capable facilitator who will manage the consultation process; and
- a representative of the local council or water committee.

To aid informed decision-making an effective consultation process is likely to include the following two phases and activities:

Presentation and discussion phase

1) Preparation of clear plans of the town showing the existing and proposed main pipelines and water points for the preferred investment option(s) for presentation to community groups and other stakeholders.
2) Dissemination and presentation of the WTP results, the proposed service options, tariff levels, etc. that arise out of the preferred investment scenario(s) to the community through council committees and through focus group discussions with community groups.
3) Key informants from the project team will need to explain carefully the WTP results and the proposed options and tariffs to each meeting or focus group.
4) In arranging focus group discussions it is important that key consumer groups such as core and fringe area residents, low-income areas, commercial users, and women and men, are adequately represented.
5) Sufficient time should be allowed for community members to understand the issues, raise questions, and give feedback. This may entail at least two meetings with each group.

Feedback and negotiation phase

6) The feedback from the meetings needs to be carefully documented.
7) Depending on that feedback the consultation team will need to respond. If, for example, residents in the fringe area ask for more of a pipe distribution network to serve more houses in their area, it would be necessary to explain the cost and tariff implications of doing this.
8) After carefully explaining the need for tariff increases for the proposed piped systems, if there is a clear reluctance to agree to future tariff increases, it would be necessary to consider cheaper investment options with less expensive service options.
9) A suitable forum for agreeing the final preferred investment plan and service options would be the town council or water committee, taking into account the comments from the various focus groups and the project team.

This is an iterative process that can increase the prospects of sustainable services. This process would serve a number of purposes:

- Discussions about preferred options for each consumer group and future water tariffs can be more meaningful and useful because they would be based on very good data on consumer demand and feasible investment plans.
- The community members would understand that they had been part of the decision-making process and that the new project and tariffs had not been imposed by distant engineers and accountants in central government ministries.
- To develop confidence in the WTP survey, the community can be reminded that X% (the number interviewed) had indeed expressed a willingness to pay the suggested tariffs to receive the improved water supply system. The sampling strategy and professionalism of the survey technique can be demonstrated to increase consumers' confidence in the findings.
- There would be an increased likelihood of the community accepting tariff increases to ensure the financial sustainability of the new water supply system with such a consultation process.

Many methods have been suggested in these guidelines to increase the accuracy of the WTP survey process and the likelihood that respondents answer truthfully, with carefully considered choices, selecting options that they would like to use and pay for. The CVM report is not the final step, but part of the overall consultation process. The report may not only be a useful tool for policymakers, design engineers and water authorities – it can be used as a means of negotiating with the community.

5.6 Influencing finance policy and 'willingness to charge'

One aspect that a CVM Durvey does not measure is the 'willingness to charge' higher water tariffs of municipal and government authorities. However, a well-presented WTP survey can be used by able advocates to justify water tariff increases linked to service improvements. When politicians and other key decision-makers are presented with the WTP survey results, the report recommendations are likely to be regarded as worth pursuing, particularly if those decision-makers have to make difficult choices over the allocation of funds.

Advocacy of the report's findings may be required particularly where the implementation of the proposals requires some change of attitudes by key stakeholders. To address these issues the following strategies can be considered:

- Where possible, produce overview reports that collate WTP survey results and proposals from a number of towns. Such reports are more likely to influence senior policymakers than a report for one town.
- The key findings from the survey can also be put into a summary form that is more easily understood by busy policymakers.
- Opportunities should also be taken to present key information at meetings and workshops, so as to maximise the potential for supporting policy reform and the selection of sustainable service options.

It is therefore necessary to allow for sufficient funds in budgets for the 'advocacy phase' of the WTP survey and investment planning report dissemination.

5.7 Implications for institutional arrangements

Any substantial changes in the management of small town water services (i.e. O&M, cost recovery, new connections, customer services, etc.), are likely to be brought about by new government policies. For example, the introduction of private sector operators is best brought about by government creating an enabling environment and supporting the development of well-designed contracts.

Further advice on private sector participation using Service and Management contracts is contained in Volumes 1 (Guidance Notes) and Volume 2 (Case studies and contract analysis) of *Contracting Out Water and Sanitation Services* (Sansom et al., 2003 (a) and (b).

However, the WTP and consumer survey results and the subsequent investment planning provide valuable information to determine appropriate future management arrangements for water and sanitation services. The institutional implications of typical results for three small towns are as follows:

Small town A:
The WTP results reveal that there is insufficient demand and WTP for a new piped water system for a viable scheme to be developed. The residents are willing to pay for a variety of point sources such as handpumps and protected springs.

Institutional implications: Until there is a sufficient demand for a piped system, it is best to develop capacity in the sustainable management of groundwater point sources. This could include encouraging the local private sector to undertake O&M of the handpumps, etc., which may entail 'area-based contracts' so that there are sufficient economies of scale to attract capable contractors.

For smaller towns with mainly rural characteristics that have community management through water committees, the development of the capacity of these committees may be necessary and this should be included in the scheme proposal.

Small town B:
The WTP results reveal that the core area of the town is WTP for a limited expansion of the water distribution system, whereas the fringe area residents have limited willingness and ability to pay for a viable piped system in their vicinity. So springs, dug wells and handpumps are the most viable options in the short to medium term in the fringe areas.

Institutional implications: The institutional capacity to manage an expanded piped distribution system in a commercial and consumer orientated manner needs to be developed. This may involve recruitment to a local council of people with the right skills, or by utilising the private sector. In both cases the question needs to be asked:

'Are there sufficient economies of scale to attract and pay for staff with the required skills?'

It may be necessary to aggregate small town water services for a number of towns to be managed by one organisation. This could be undertaken by, for example, a private operator under a management contract for a number of towns, or by a regional water company or a co-operative managing water services for those towns that are part of that co-operative.

The level of professional support to develop the required capacities and new approaches will also need to be considered at an early stage of project development. As more water is supplied to the town, the capacity for dealing with sullage drainage and sewage disposal needs to be developed by local service providers.

Small town C:
For a fast-growing small town the WTP results reveal that most of the town residents are WTP for individual or shared pipe connections. A large new piped system for the town appears viable.

Institutional implications: The same institutional implications as Small town B are relevant here. The planned substantial expansion in the piped system indicates a need for an appropriate increase in the service management capacity. In addition the introduction of new systems becomes more viable for a larger number of customers. Better systems for computerised billing, financial management, meter reading, O&M, and new connections should be considered.

The WTP and consumer survey results provide an early indication of the need for enhanced future management arrangements that are necessary to provide adequate, reliable, and sustainable water services. Developing capacities to achieve these changes needs to be incorporated in new project plans.

Further guidance on how to improve the management of small town water and sanitation services are increasingly available on the websites of key institutions such as WEDC, WSP, World Bank, IRC and EHP, as research outputs in this area are published.

Bibliography

Altaf, M Anjum, Haroon Jamal and Dale Whittington (1992) Willingness to Pay for Water in Rural Punjab, Pakistan. UNDP/World Bank Water and Sanitation Program Report Series 4. Washington D.C.

Altaf, A. and Hughes, J. (1994) 'Measuring the Demand For Improved Urban Sanitation Services: Results of a CV Study in Ouagadougou, Burkina Faso', *Urban Studies*, 31 (10)

Arrow, K. and Solow, K. (1993) *A Report of the NOAA Panel on CVM,* USA

Bohm R.A. *et al.* (1993) 'Sustainability of Potable Water Services in the Philippines', *Water Resources Research*, 29 (7)

Boland, J. and Whittington, D. (1997) *The Political Economy of Increasing Block Tariffs in Developing Countries.* IDRC, Ottawa Canada. www.eepsea.org/publications/specialp2/ACF33E.html. See also Dinar, A. (2000) *The Political Economy of Water Pricing*

Briscoe J.and World Bank Water Demand Research Team (1993) 'The Demand for Water in Rural Areas', *The World Bank Research Observer*, 8

Business & Economic Research Company Ltd. (2000) *Setting up three management systems for 3 Urban Water Supplies and Sewerage Services*, Business and Economic Research Company Ltd., Uganda

Cairncross, S. and Kinnear, J. (1992) '*Elasticity of Demand For Water In Khartoum, Sudan*', *Soc Sci Medical*, 34 (2):p.183

Chambers, R. (1997) *Whose Reality Counts?* p.93, IT Publishing, London

Coates, S., Sansom, K. and Kayaga, S. (2001) *'PREPP – improving utility watsan services to low income consumers'* WEDC Conference, Zambia.

Consult 4 Ltd (2001) *Reform of the Uganda Water Sector: The Wurban Water Supply and Sanitation Sub-Sector. Sector Reform Paper – Final Report* For the Minstiry of Water, Lands and Environment, Uganda. In association with Palmer Development Group, Ernst and Young South Africa and Sunshine Projects Ltd. Uganda.

Cummings R.G Brookshire, d and Schulze, W (eds) ., (1986) Valuing Environmental Goods: An Assessment of the Contingent Valuation Method. Rowmand And Allanheld, Totowa. NJ

Cummings, R.G. (1986) 'Valuing Environmental Goods: An Assessment of the Contingent Valuation Method', in: Brookshire and Schulze, W.D. (Eds.)

Deverill, P., Bibby, S., Wedgwood, A and Smout, I. (2000) *Designing Water and Sanitation Projects to Meet Demand,* WEDC, Loughborough University.

DFID, (1998),*Draft Guidance Notes for DFID Economists on Demand Assessment in the Water and Sanitation Sector,* DFID, London

Dinar, A, (ed.) (2000) *The Political Economy of Water Pricing.* Oxford University Press, Oxford.

DWD (1996) *Project proposal for funding by Directorate of Water Development,* Ministry of Natural Resources, Kampala, Uganda.

DWD (1999) *Unpublished investment proposal to the World Bank for funding, Kampala, Uganda.*

Eyatu O.J. (2000) *'Management models for Small Town water schemes in Uganda'* Unpublished research project report, WEDC, Loughborough University.

Foster, V., Gomez-Lobo, A. and Halpern, J. (2000) *Designing Direct Subsidies For the Poor – A Water and Sanitation Case Study.* Public Policy For the Private Sector Note No 211. June 2000. The World Bank Group, Private Sector and Infrastructure Network.

Franceys, R. (1994) *Management of Water Utilities in Low Income Countries: India and Uganda.* Institutional Development Series, WEDC, Loughborough University, UK.

Garn M.,(1998) '*Managing Water As an Economic Good'.* Presented at the UNDP-World Bank conference on Community Water Supply.

Government of Uganda, (2001), *Small Towns Water and Sanitation Programme*, progress report, Uganda

Griffin C. and Briscoe, J., et al. (1995) '*Contingent Valuation and Actual Behaviour: Predicting Connection to New Water Systems in the State of Kerala, India*', World Bank Economic Review, 9 (3)

GTZ (2000) *Ghana, Small Towns Water Supply System Tariff Design,* WSP Nicholas Pilgrim RODECO.

Hazelton, D. (1997) '*Sustainable Piped Water Supply in Rural Uganda'* Unpublished M.Sc. research project. WEDC, Loughborough University, UK.

Katko, T. (1991) *Paying for Water in Developing Countries*, Tampere University of Technology. Working paper No 74, Finland.

Locussol, A. and Brook-Cowan, P.(1999) *Easing tariff increases – financing the transition to cost-covering water tariffs in Guinea,* World Bank, Washington DC, USA

Markandya, A. (1997) *Ganges Action Plan – CVM For River Water Quality of the Ganges River,* Report for Government of India and DFID.

McGranahan, G., Leitmann, J. and Surjadi, C. (1997) '*Understanding Environmental Problems in Disadvantaged Neighbourhoods', Urban Environment Series Report No 3,* SEI, Stockholm.

Moriarty, P.B., Patricot, G., Bastemeijer, T., Smet, J. and Van der Voorden, C. (2001) *Between Urban and Rural: Towards Sustainable Management of Water Supply Systems in Small Towns in Africa.* IRC International Water and Sanitation Centre, The Netherlands.

Nicol, A., *Adopting a Sustainable Livelihoods Approach to Water Projects: Implications for Policy and Practice,* ODI Working Paper 133, London.

Njiru, C. and Sansom, K.R., (2001) '*Strategic marketing plan for water services in Mombassa and coastal region of Kenya',* WEDC, Loughborough University, UK.

NOAA (1993) *Natural Resource Damage Assessments Under the Oil Pollution Act of 1990 – The Use of CVM.* NOAA, USA

Pearce, D. (ed.) (1981) *The MacMillan Dictionary of Modern Economics.* MacMillan Press, London.

Pearce, D. and Moran (1994) *The Economic Value of Biodiversity,* IUCN and Earthscan, London.

Public-Private Infrastructure Advisory Facility and the Water and Sanitation Program (2002). *New Designs for Water and Sanitation Transactions – making private sector participation work for the poor.* Washington DC.

Quest Consult (2000) *Mtwara CDS Programme: An Assessment of the Implementation of Demand Responsive Approaches in the Community Developmebt Support Programme*. Final Report. Concern Worldwide, Dar es Salaam. April 2002.

Revels C., (2002) *Business planning for small town water supply,* paper presented at the Addis Ababa Conference on Water Supply and Sanitation (WSS) Services for Small Towns and Multi-Village Schemes, Ethiopia, Water and Sanitation Program, World Bank.

Sansom, K., Coates, S., Njiru, C. and Francys, R. (2000) *Strategic Marketing To Improve Water Utility Finances and Services to Poor Urban Water Consumers.* WEDC discussion paper. June 2000.

Sansom K.R., Franceys R.W.A.F., Morales-Reyes J. and Njiru C., (2002a) '*Contracting out water and sanitation services –Volume 1 - Guidance notes for Service and Management contracts in developing countries',* WEDC, UK.

Sansom K.R., Franceys R.W.A.F., Morales-Reyes J., Njiru C., (2002)b) *'Contracting out water and sanitation services – Volume 2 - Case studies and analysis of Service and Management contracts in developing countries'*, WEDC, UK.

Seaman, J., Clarke, P., Boudreau, T. and Holt, J. (2000) *The Household Economy Approach: A Resource Manual For Practitioners.* Save The Children Development Manual No 6.

Thomson M., and Sansom K.R., (2002), *'Finance policy for small towns'*, unpublished research notes, WEDC, Loughborough University, UK

Vaidya, C. (1995) *Study on Willingness to Pay for Water and Sanitation Services. Case Study of Baroda.* Submitted to HUDCO, New Delhi.

Van Nostrand, J. and Associated Consulting Engineers Uganda (1997a) *Socio-Economic and Willingness to Pay Study Busia.* Prepared for the Republic of Uganda Ministry of Natural Resources: Directorate of Water Development. Small Towns Water and Sanitation Programme. Phase II a WSP Programme.

Van Nostrand, J. and Associated Consulting Engineers Uganda (1997b) *Socio-Economic and Willingness to Pay Study Malaba.* Prepared to the Republic of Uganda Ministry of Natural Resources: Directorate of Water Development. Small Towns Water and Sanitation Programme. Phase II of a WSP Programme.

Van Nostrand, J. and Associated Consulting Engineers Uganda (1997c) *Socio-Economic and Willingness to Pay Study Luwero.* Prepared to the Republic of Uganda Ministry of Natural Resources: Directorate of Water Development. Small Towns Water and Sanitation Programme. Phase II of a WSP Programme.

Webster, B. (1999) *Effective Demand For Rural Water Supply in South Africa.* Ed by Ian Smout. WEDC, Loughborough University, UK.

Wedgwood, A. (1997) *An evaluation of the use of CVM for Gomti River Pollution Control Project*, DFID

Wedgwood A. (1998) *Use of Willingness to Pay Techniques for the Economic Analysis of Water and Sanitation Projects*, UNDP World Bank WSP. Conference Paper.

Wedgwood, A. (2000) *Rapid Appraisal Using CVM and other Demand Assessment Techniques*. Dar Es Salaam Conference on Comparative *Techniques to Assist in the Design of New Projects*, DFID/UNICEF.

Wedgwood, A. and WaterAid, (2000), *Dar es Salaam Community Managed Water and Sanitation Programme – Demand Assessment in Four Street Communities,* unpublished document, Tanzania

Wedgwood, A., Oriono, J.E. and Sansom K.R., (2001) *Testing Contingent Valuation Techniques for Small Towns. A Case Study of Bushenyi, Uganda*, DFID KaR Programme.

Wedgwood, A., Markandya, A. and Taylor, T. (1998) *An Assessment of the characteristics of demand in Maharashtra Rural Water Supply and Sanitation Project. Benefit Transfer Model.*

Wedgwood, A. (Poole) and Sengupta, A.K. (1997) *Proceedings, Workshop on Willingness to Pay for Drinking Water Supply and Sanitation*, UNDP World Bank Water and Sanitation Programe and DFID.

WELL (1998), *DFID Guidance Manual on Water Supply and Sanitation Programmes,* WEDC, Loughborough University, UK

White, J. (1997) *Evaluation Synthesis of Rural Water and Sanitation Projects.* Evaluation Department of DFID. EV Report 596

Whittington D, Briscoe J Mu, X and Barron, W. (1990) *Estimating the Willingness to Pay for Water Services in Developing Countries: A Case Study of the Contingent Valuation Method in Southern Haiti*. Economic Development and Cultural Change 38, no 2. 293-311.

Whittington, D., Okorafor, A ., Okore, A. and McPhail, A. (1990). *Strategy for Cost Recovery in the Rural Water Sector: A Case Study of Nsukka District, Anambra State. Nigeria.*

Whittington, D., *et al*. (1993) 'Household Demand For Improved Sanitation Services in Kumasi, Ghana. A Contingent Valuation Study', *Water Resources Research*, 29

Whittington, D., McClelland, E. and Davis J, (1994) *A Rapid Appraisal of Household Demand For Improved Water and Sanitation Services in Lugazi.* Prepared for the Min. of Natural Resources August 1994.

Whittington, D., Davis, J., Miarsono, H. and Pollard, R. (1995) *Urban Sewer Planning In Developing Countries and the "Neighbourhood Deal": A Case Study of Semanrang, Indonesisa.* Report to the World Bank

Whittington, D. (1997) 'Administering Contingent Valuation Surveys in Developing Countries'. World Development 1997

Whittington, D., McClelland, E. and Davis J. (1998) 'Implementing and Demand Driven Approach to Community Water Supply Planning: A Case Study of Lugazi', Uganda. *Water International*, 23: 134-45

World Bank (1998) *Proceedings of the Community Water Supply and Sanitation Conference*, Washington DC, 5-8 May, 1998.

World Bank Water Demand Research Team (1993) 'The Demand for Water in Rural Areas', *The World Bank Research Observer,* 8: 47-70

World Commission on Dams (1999) Thematic III Financial, Economic and Distributional Analysis –Version 1 July 1999.

WSP (2001) authors including Dale Whittington, Subhrednu Pattanayak, Jui-Chen Yang, and staff of Tribhuvan University Central Department of Population Studies, Kathmandu, Nepal. *'Willingness to Pay For Improved Water Supply In Kathmandu Valley, Nepal',* For WSP South Asia.

WSP (1999) UNDP Water and Sanitation Programme South Asia. Field Note. *Willing to Pay but Unwilling to Charge*. Washington DC, USA

WSP (2002), *Small town water supply system tariff designs for Ghana, Field Report*, Washington, DC, USA.

WSP (2002) *Summary Statement of the 'Small towns water supply and sanitation conference* held in Addis Ababa on 11 –15 June 2002

Yepes, G. (1998) *Do Cross Subsidies Help the Poor Benefit from Waste and Wastewater Services?* World Bank TWU Infrastructure. Washington, DC, USA.

Annexes

Annex A
Option descriptions used in Bushenyi, Uganda

Enumerators, please show the picture of each option and describe it in full before going to the bidding, explain that the respondent will be able to discuss their preferred options in more detail, and that they can choose more than one option or just one option.

Option 1 – Protected spring
Description and attributes

- A spring will be protected with pipes that go underground and a concrete surround.
- The water will be fresh rainwater that has filtered underground. It will be clean because of the pipes and the protection.
- You may have to walk to the spring because the location will depend on where the fresh water is.
- Drainage will be built around the spring.
- There may be some queues at the spring.
- The water should be available throughout the year, although during a very dry season there is a risk that it will run dry.

Payment method
To use the spring you will be expected to pay a contribution to the cost of installing the improved protection around the spring. Only people who contribute to the scheme will be allowed to use it.

Options 2 – Handpump
Description and attributes

SHOW PICTURE

- Under this option there will be a handpump which is supplied from a borehole sunk deep into the ground.
- The water will therefore be reliable and very clean.
- Water will be available at all times during the day.

- There will be less queuing at peak times. However, there may be small queues with this service because it takes longer to pump the water out.
- You are likely to have less distance to walk to the handpump than your current source.

Payment method

You will be expected to a pay a lump some contribution. There will not be an operator but there will be a monthly fee which will cover repairs and maintenance.

Option 3 – New improved water kiosks

Description and attributes

- In this option a number of new kiosks will be built in your community.
- The water will come from a new rehabilitated piped network.
- The kiosk will be open from 7am to 7pm with an hour off at lunch time.
- You will have a RELIABLE AND CLEAN source of water at all times.
- There will be less queuing at peak times.
- You are likely to have less distance to walk to a tap than your current source.

Payment method

You will have to contribute to the capital cost of providing new community kiosks. And we would like to know how much you are willing to pay per jerry can for this service.

Option 4 – Shared yard tap

Description and attributes

SHOW PICTURE

- Option 3 is a shared tap connection in your own yard or in your neighbour's yard. This will involve connection to a new improved piped water system.
- There will a number of benefits for your family.
- There will be no queuing.

- You – or others in your family – will not have to spend time each day collecting water and so will have time for other activities.
- The water will be available between 7am and 10am in the morning and between 4pm and 6pm in the evenings – that is five hours per day.
- You can share the cost of providing and running the tap with other families – we can imagine about three to five families will share each tap.

Payment method

- There will be a contribution towards building the system, that will include improving the piped system in the town and the cost of additional pipes to your house. Your contribution will also cover the meter and tap.
- Remember that if there is more than one family wishing to share this tap you might be able to split the cost between all the families. Also you will have to negotiate with the families sharing the tap to work out how much each household should pay.
- There will also be operating and maintenance costs. The price of water will be about the same as the price of water sold at community kiosks. However, it is possible that you will use more water with a shared yard tap and so will also have higher operating costs.
- You will be issued with a monthly metered bill but remember you must be able to work out how much each household should pay towards this bill per month.

Option 5 - Private house connection

Description and attributes

- Option 5 is a private tap connection in your own home or yard. This will be a connection to a new improved piped water system.
- You – or others in your family – will not have to spend time each day collecting water and so will have time for other activities.
- The water will be reliable all day so long as you pay for it.
- You will not have to share the water with your neighbours or negotiate how to pay the bill because it will be your sole responsibility.

Payment method

- There will be a contribution towards building the system, that will include improving the piped system in the town and the cost of additional pipes to your house. Your contribution will also cover the meter and tap.
- Remember your family will be the only ones paying for the private connection so you will not be able to share the costs.
- There will also be operating and maintenance costs. The price of water will be about the same as the price of water sold at community kiosks. However, it is possible that you will use more water with a private connection and so will also have higher operating costs.
- You will be issued with a monthly metered bill.

Now we have seen all five options I would like to ask you some questions about whether you would be interested in them, and whether you can afford to contribute some money to make sure they are built and maintained properly.

Note for enumerators:
Go to the WTP questionnaire, remember which bidding model you have been assigned for the day.

Annex B
Example annuity factor table

This table can be used to calculate replacement costs and the amount that should be saved each year to ensure that major repairs are met. It is referred to in the main text on page 86.

Estimating the cost of a handpump can be relatively simple. The following example is based on the Finnish Nira handpump, used in many countries including Tanzania, from where the following data originates.[26] In 2000, the local cost of a Nira handpump in Tanzania was about US$625 (for a shallow well about 8 metres deep). If the pump is well maintained, after 10 years its life can be extended by a further 10 years by replacing a number of critical components. These have a 2002 price of US$314. The amount that needs to be set aside each year to raise the equivalent amount that will be required to purchase the same component in 10 years time, can be calculated using an annuity factor. Once again, an appropriate annuity factor can be looked up and used to calculate the annual amount which must be 'saved' or 'paid' by users, referring to the annuity factor table below.

In this case, assuming an interest rate of 5% over a 10-year period, the annuity which should be set aside each year is US$40.6.

$AF_{(5,10)}$ = 7.72 (read off the annuity table)

$$\text{Annuity} = \frac{314}{7.72} = \text{US\$40.60 per year}$$

In addition, replacement costs for the handpump valued at US$625 can calculated, based on a 20-year life span. Again, applying an annuity factor to the present value of the handpump (US$ 625) results in an annual cost of US$50.20.

$AF_{(5,20)}$ = 12.46 (read off the annuity table)

$$\text{Annuity} = \frac{625}{12.46} = \text{US\$50.20 per year}$$

[26] For further details see Quest Consult (2000).

Table 4 shows that in order to enjoy the benefits of the handpump in the future, its users should set aside almost US$150 a year for the first ten years. Assuming the pump is used by 30 families and there is a flat-rate payment system, this is equivalent to an annual O&M tariff of US$5 per household per year. This figure does not include the costs of tool replacement, everyday caretaking, and the administration of the cost recovery system itself.

Annuity Factor Table

No of years (n)	Interest Rate (r)							
	3%	5%	6%	8%	10%	12%	15%	20%
1	0.9709	0.9524	0.9434	0.9259	0.9091	0.8929	0.8696	0.8111
2	1.9135	1.8594	1.8334	1.7833	1.7355	1.6901	1.6257	1.4726
3	2.8286	2.7232	2.6730	2.5771	2.4869	2.4018	2.2832	2.0146
4	3.7171	3.5460	3.4651	3.3121	3.1699	3.0373	2.8550	2.4611
5	4.5797	4.3295	4.2124	3.9927	3.7908	3.6048	3.3522	2.8306
6	5.4172	5.0757	4.9173	4.6229	4.3553	4.1114	3.7845	3.1378
7	6.2303	5.7864	5.5824	5.2064	4.8684	4.5638	4.1604	3.3944
8	7.0197	6.4632	6.2098	5.7466	5.3349	4.9676	4.4873	3.6096
9	7.7861	7.1078	6.8017	6.2469	5.7590	5.3282	4.7716	3.7909
10	8.5302	7.7217	7.3601	6.7101	6.1446	5.6502	5.0188	3.9443
11	9.2526	8.3064	7.8869	7.1390	6.4951	5.9377	5.2337	4.0746
12	9.9540	8.8633	8.3838	7.5361	6.8137	6.1944	5.4206	4.1857
13	10.6350	9.3936	8.8527	7.9038	7.1034	6.4235	5.5831	4.2807
14	11.2961	9.8986	9.2950	8.2442	7.3667	6.6282	5.7245	4.3624
15	11.9379	10.3797	9.7122	8.5595	7.6061	6.8109	5.8474	4.4328
20	14.8775	12.4622	11.4699	9.8181	8.5136	7.4694	6.2593	4.6681
22	15.9369	13.1630	12.0416	10.2007	8.7715	7.6446	6.3587	4.7264
25	17.4131	14.0939	12.7834	10.6748	9.0770	7.8431	6.4641	4.7910
30	19.6004	15.3725	13.7648	11.2578	9.4269	8.0552	6.5660	4.8597

Annex C
Example socio-economic and water supply questions for the household survey component of a CVM Questionnaire

These questions particularly focus on attempts by the team to ascertain the income and expenditure levels for the complete household. They are only for basic guidance, and many more detailed questions might be needed depending on the particular circumstances of the project. One copy of the data code sheet was given to each enumerator – this had the introductory speech and the various intervals required to fill out the household information table. The data code sheet reduced the length of the questionnaire, and so the need for photocopying.

DATA code sheet and introductory statement

My name is............................and I am working for a research team from a university in the UK who are looking at how to improve water supply systems in towns such as this one. We have been granted permission to talk with people in this local council area about their current water practices as well as ask them what kind of water supply services they would like in this town, and whether people are prepared, able, and willing to pay for them. We particularly would like to discuss this with the head of the household and/or spouse. Your answers will be used for the purpose of this study only and will be kept very confidential. During the interview if there are any questions that you would like to ask please feel free to do so, we hope that this is a consultative process and are very interested in your views.

Household Data Code sheet: Use to fill in codes on household data table
Position in HH
1 – Male – who is head of household
2 – Female – who is head of household because there is no husband, he is away or deceased
3 – Female of household who is not the head
4 – Brother or sister of head of household
5 – Other relative
6 – Servant or paid employee
7 – Other

Sex 1 = Female 0 = Male

Age – years (ageinyrs)
0 – less than one year old
1 – 1 to 5 years old
2 – 5 to 10 years old
3 – 11 to 20 years old
4 – 21 to 35 years old
5 – 36 to 50 years old
6 – 51 to 65 years old
7 – over 66 years old

Employment (employme)
1 – Unemployed – no work
2 – Street vendor/small informal business
3 – Shop attendant/employee of a small business
4 – Sells food in market
5 – Government employee
6 – Works for a large private company
7 – Business man/women, owns a small business
8 – Business man/women, owns a large business
9 – Casual labourers
10 – Occasional skilled freelance work
11 – Retired and not earning any more money apart from pension
12 – Subsistence farmer
13 – Commercial farmer
14 – Other_____________

Income per person per year (Sh) INSERT ACTUAL AMOUNT IN TABLE AS WELL. If they give you a monthly amount, calculate per year.
0 – No money earned
1 – 100,000 per year
2 – 100,001 to 200,000 per year
3 – 200,001 to 300,00 per year
4 – 300,001 to 400,000 per year
5 – 400,001 to 600,000 per year
6 – 600,001 to 800,000
7 – 800,001 to 1 million per year.
8 – 1.1 to 2 million per year
9 – 2.1 to 4 million per year
10 – 4.1 to 8 million per year

Note: For new surveys it will be necessary to develop appropriate figures for each area.

Household details

1. Insert the name and details of the person answering the questionnaire in the first box and ANY OTHER PEOPLE WHO EARN MONEY FOR THE HOUSEHOLD. DO NOT INCLUDE CHILDREN OR NON-WAGE EARNERS.

Use the codes sheet to insert the right code for each answer (except for income).

Household details							
Name	Position in house-hold	Sex	Age	Education level	Work type Is it seasonal? check	Work (Sh) per month per person PUT IN REAL AMOUNT AND CODES – convert all prices into an annual amount (i.e. multiply by 12 or whatever is needed)	
						Actual Sh per year	Code
TOTAL household income per year							

2. What is the total number of people in your household unit? ____________

2a. How many children are there under 14 years old? ____________

3. How many other people who live away from Bushenyi send money to your household?____________________

4. How much do they send in total per year? (use approximate amounts, remember to include all transfers)______________________Sh per year

4b. How much do you spend on the following items per year? (HELP THEM WORK IT OUT, this may take some time)

Food purchases (per week, day or year)________Sh (include units at all times)
School fees and uniforms __________________Sh
Household bills __________________________Sh
Medical expenses ________________________Sh
Transport _____________________________Sh
Clothes ______________________________Sh
Agricultural inputs________________________Sh
Livestock inputs, vets _____________________Sh
Hired labour, (restaurant staff, agric.)__________Sh
Others please list _________________________Sh

TOTAL Expenditure per year________________________

5. Considering the employment of key wage earners and transfers, work out *approximate* (Sh) TOTAL income per household per year. To do this add up the totals of Question 1 and Question 4a.

0 – No money earned
1 – 100,000 per year
2 – 100,001 to 200,000 per year
3 – 200,001 to 300,00 per year
4 – 300,001 to 500,000 per year
5 – 500,001 to 700,000 per year
6 – 700,001 to 1 million per year
7 – 1.1 to 2 million per year.
8 – 2.1 to 4 million per year
9 – 4.1 to 8 million per year
10 – more than 8 million per year – how much ________?

6. How long have you been living in this town?_____________years **(timeinhh)**

1 = Less than 1 year
2 = 1 to 5 years
3 = 6 to 10 years
4 = 11 to 15 years
5 = more than 15 years

House observation:

6b. Do you rent or own this house **(housetyp)**

1. Privately rented – landlord lives away
2. Privately owned
3. Rented but landlord lives within our compound or house
4. Owned by the parastatal/company
5. Other (describe)________

7. Number of rooms for use by household unit **(roomshh)** (include bathroom but not pit latrine)

Number____________

8. Enumerator please make an assessment of income based on the criteria we discussed and the observation of this house and discussion on their jobs. **(hhpov)**

1 – Very poor
2 – Poor
3 – Middle Incomes
4 – Wealthy family
9 – Too difficult to assess

9. How much money do you pay per month(Sh)? **(rent)**

1 – 0 to 5000
2 – 5001 to 10,000
3 – 10,001 to 15,000
4 – 15,001 to 20,001
5 – 20,001 to 30,000
6 – 30,0001 to 50,000
7 – 50,001 to 100,000
8 – more than 100,000
9 – Not applicable owns house

10. Do you have electricity? **(electric)**

0 – No
1 – Yes

11a. Do you own a TV? **(TV)**

0 – No
1 – Yes

11b. How do you run your TV? **(TV power)**

1 – Mains power
2 – Generator
3 – Solar Power
4 – Battery
5 – other

Existing water supply questions

12. What is your household's main source of water for bathing and washing clothes? **(wshwat)**

If more than one source put in ranking for main and secondary sources.

Code: ....
Protected spring or well 1______
River or stream 2______
Public handpump 3______
Rainwater or local swamp 4______
Water vendor 5______
Own private well 6______
Own private connection from a government piped scheme 7______
Kiosk/ standpost 8______
Water bought from a neighbour 9______
Shared yard tap 10______
Other (specify) 11________________

13. What is your household's main source of drinking water during the wet season? **(watersup)**

If more than one source put in ranking, number 1 for main source, number 2 for secondary source.

Code: ....
Protected spring or well 1______
River or stream 2______
Public handpump 3______
Rainwater or local swamp 4______
Water vendor 5______
Own private well 6______
Own private connection from a government piped scheme 7______
Kiosk/ standpost 8______
Water bought from a neighbour 9______
Shared yard tap 10______
Other (specify) 11________________

14. What is your household's main source(s) of drinking water during the dry season? **(watersup)** (remember ranking)

Code: ....
Protected spring or well 1______
River or stream 2______
Public handpump 3______
Rainwater or local swamp 4______
Water vendor 5______
Own private well 6______
Own private connection from a government piped scheme 7______
Kiosk/ standpost 8______
Water bought from a neighbour 9______
Shared yard tap 10______
Other (specify) 11________________

If respondent answers code 6, 7, or 10 **for primary use go to** Question 15.

If respondent answers code 1, 2, 3, or 4 **for primary use go to** Question 20

If respondent answers code 5, 8, or 9 **go to** Question 24.

If respondent answers 11 (other) **decide which section is most suited (does the water supply involve buying water, or free supplies?)**

15. Is the connection shared with other households? **(privconn)**

No........0 If no go to Question 17
Yes.......1

16. How many households share the connection? **(numshare)**

______number

17. How much did it cost to install the connection/well (Sh)? This includes the connection fee and any additional costs you had to pay for pipes, etc. **(costpc)**

0 – no charge
1 – up to 10,000
2 – 10,000 to 50,000
3 – 50,001 to 75,000
4 – 75,001 to 100,000
5 – 100,001 to 150,000
6 – 150,001 to 200,000
7 – more than 200,000_______how much?
8 – Don't know

18. Do you sells water to neighbours, or other organisations or groups? **(sellwat)**

1 – Yes
2 – No If no go to 19b

19a. How much do you sell water for (Sh) per jerry can? **(pricewat)**

1 - up to 10
2 - 10-25
3 - 26-50 Sh
4 - 51-75 Sh
5 - 76 - 100Sh
6 - >100, How much? _________

19b. How many hours a day does the tap/well supply water (on average)?

1 – up to 2 hours
2 – 2-4 hours
3 – 4-6 hours
4 – 6-8 hours
5 – more than 8 hours
6 – other______________

Now go to straight to Health questions.

20. How far is the water source from your home? **(distwat)**

Water is < 20m.......0
Water is 20-99m.....1
Water is 100-499m...2
Water is 500 to 999m......3
Water is 1-2km away.......4
Water is >2km away.........5

21. How long does it take to walk to the water point and back again?**(timewat)**

0 – Up to 14 mins
1 – 15-29 mins
2 – 30-44 mins
3 – 45-59 mins
4 – 1 hour to 1 hr 29 mins
5 – 1 hour to 1 hour 59 mins
6 – more than 2 hours

22. How long on average at peak time do you have to queue at the water point? **(queuetim)**

0 – No queuing at all
1 – I queue for 10 minutes
2 – I queue for 20 minutes
3 – I always have to queue for 30 minutes
4 – I sometimes have to queue for _____ mins (insert amount) but other times I don't have to queue at all.

Now go straight to Health questions.

23. How much do you pay during the rainy season? **(priceven)**

________Sh/jerry can

24. How much do you pay in the dry season? **(dryvendp)**

________Sh/jerry can

25. What do you think of the quality of the water that this supply delivers? **(qualvend)**

1 – Very clean, I know he/they get it from a good source.
2 – Quite clean, we don't need to boil it.
3 – Not very clean, we boil it for drinking.
4 – It varies, sometimes it is very dirty and we boil it, sometimes we think it is clean and do not boil it.
5 – Very dirty.

26. What do you use this water for? **(venwtusse)**

1 – We use it for ALL water uses.
2 – We only use it for drinking.
3 – We use it for drinking and washing ourselves, but not for washing clothes.
4 – Other_______

Disease episodes

27. What type of diseases have effected any members of your family over 12 years old, in the last two months?

Insert number of people that were affected by each disease (diseases) (numdise)

	Yes	**Number?**
Diarrhoea	1	_______
Blood or mucus in faeces	1	_______
Vomiting	1	_______
Malaria	1	_______
Cholera	1	_______
Typhoid	1	_______
Other_________________________		

28. Have any of the children in the household who are under 12 had any of these conditions during the last two months?

Insert number of people affected by each disease. (diseasch) (childise)

	Yes	Number?
Diarrhoea	1	_______
Blood or mucus in faeces	1	_______
Vomiting	1	_______
Malaria	1	_______
Cholera	1	_______
Typhoid	1	_______
Other_______________________		

Remarks about the house – any useful comments or observations.

Annex D
Example willingness-to-pay questions for a CVM Survey

The following questions are based on a split sample bidding game. Enumerators were asked to start at one of three prices, either the highest, middle or lowest price. The respondent was then given the opportunity to raise or lower their bid in the increments offered.

Option 1 – Protected spring

Do not show ANY prices, select a different starting point each time, and raise or lower the bid according to the answer. RECORD THE STARTING POINT WITH AN S AND THE FINAL BID WITH AN F.

QUESTION 1 – Would you use this option and are you willing to contribute a certain amount towards its construction or running costs?

Yes I would like to use this option, and would be willing to contribute something towards its construction.

No I would not use this option and would not like to pay anything for it.

Enumerator: If answer is No please go to next option.

QUESTION 2 – As you know the local council does not have enough money to improve the springs in your area, therefore households will need to make a contribution. Everyone who contributes will be allowed to use the spring. How much are you prepared to contribute, in a one off lump sum, to help with the construction of the spring? This price is per family.

1 – Sh1000 lump if NO how much Sh________________
2 – Sh5,000 lump sum
3 – Sh10,000 lump sum
4 – Sh15,000
5 – Sh20,000 If YES what is the maximum amount Sh____________

QUESTION 2b What monthly fee, per family, are you prepared to pay towards general maintenance of the spring and pipes?

1 – Sh100
2 – Sh250
3 – Sh500
4 – Sh1,000
5 – Sh5,000 If yes what is the maximum amount? Sh _____________

Option 2 – Handpump over borehole

QUESTION 3 – Would you use this option and are you willing to contribute a certain amount towards its construction or running costs?

Yes I would like to use this option, and would be willing to contribute something towards its construction and/or running costs.
No I would not use this option and would not like to pay anything for it.

Enumerator: If answer is No please go to next option.

QUESTION 4 – As you know, the local council does not have enough money to build new boreholes, therefore households will need to make a contribution. Everyone who contributes will be allowed to use the handpump. There are two options you can choose:

Payment choice 1: You can pay a lump sum contribution and then a small monthly fee.
Payment choice 2: You do not make a lump sum contribution but pay a higher monthly fee.

Which payment method would you prefer?

A – I would prefer payment choice 1: to pay an upfront contribution and then pay a smaller monthly fee.

B – I would prefer payment choice 2: to pay a higher monthly fee and not pay an upfront contribution.

If respondent answers A, then go to question 5a. If respondent answers B then go to question 6.

QUESTION 5a – How much are you prepared to contribute, in a one-off lump sum, for the installation of handpumps connected to a borehole? This price is per family.

1 – Sh5000 lump If NO how much? Sh_________________
2 – Sh10,000 lump sum
3 – Sh25,000 lump sum
4 – Sh50,000
5 – Sh100,000 If YES what is the maximum amount? Sh____________
Now complete question 5b

QUESTION 5b – What monthly fee are you prepared to pay? Remember how much people normally pay per jerry can in Bushenyi.

1 – Sh500 If not how much? Sh_______
2 – Sh1000
3 – Sh2000
4 – Sh5000
5 – Sh10,000 If yes how much is the maximum amount? Sh_____________

OR

QUESTION 6 – What monthly fee are you prepared to pay, (if you do not contribute a lump sum)?

1 – Sh1000 If not how much? Sh_______
2 – Sh5000
3 – Sh7,500
4 – Sh10,000
5 – Sh15,000 If yes how much is the maximum amount? Sh_____________

Option 3 – Kiosk selling water from a standpost connected to the piped system

QUESTION 7 – Would you use this option and are you willing to contribute to it?

Yes I would like to use this option, and would be willing to contribute something towards its construction.
No I would not use this option and would not like to pay anything for it.

Enumerator: If answer is No please go to next option.

QUESTION 8 – How much are you prepared to contribute (Sh), in a one-off lump sum, for the installation of new community kiosks in your community. If people do not pay at least some of the costs of installation the kiosks cannot be built, therefore people who do not make contributions will not be able to use the kiosk. This price is per family.

1 – Sh10,000 If not how much? Sh_________________
2 – Sh25,000
3 – Sh50,000
4 – Sh75,000
5 – Sh100,000 If yes what is the maximum amount? Sh_________

QUESTION 9 – What are you prepared to pay per jerry can (Sh)?

1 – Sh25
2 – Sh33
3 – Sh50
4 – Sh75
5 – 100, if yes what is the maximum amount?__________

Option 4 – Shared yard tap option

QUESTION 10 – Would you use this option and are you willing to contribute to it?

Yes I would like to use this option, and would be willing to contribute something towards its construction.
No I would not use this option and would not like to pay anything for it.

Enumerator: If answer is No please go to next option.

QUESTION 11 – For the capital cost to install the yard tap how much are you prepared to pay in a lump sum per family? Remember there will be a few families who will also use this tap and will also have to contribute?

1 – Sh25,000 If no how much? Sh____________
2 – Sh50,000
3 – Sh100,000
4 – Sh150,000
5 – Sh200,000 If yes how much? Sh__________________

QUESTION 12 – You will be charged for the amount of water you consume. You will need to work out how much each household that shares the tap consumes, in order to work out how much each household pays each month. You will probably consume more water because the tap will be located close to home. How much would you be able and want to pay per month for this service per household?

1 – Sh2,500
2 – Sh5,000
3 – Sh10,000
4 – Sh25,000
5 – Sh50,000 If yes what is the maximum amount? Sh______________

Option 5 – Individual house connection

QUESTION 13 – Would you use this option and are you willing to contribute to it?

Yes I would like to use this option, and would be willing to contribute something towards its construction.
No I would not use this option and would not like to pay anything for it.

If answer is no finish questionnaire.

QUESTION 14 – For the capital cost to install the private connection how much are you prepared to pay in a lump sum per household (Sh)?

1 – Sh50,000 If no how much? Sh____________
2 – Sh100,000
3 – Sh200,000
4 – Sh300,000
5 – Sh400,000 If yes what is the maximum amount? Sh_________________

QUESTION 15 – How much would you be willing to pay per month for the amount of water you consume? The water will be metered and you will be billed monthly. You will probably use more water than you use at the moment.

1 – Sh5,000
2 – Sh10,000
3 – Sh25,000
4 – Sh50,000
5 – Sh75,000

Annex E
Data entry table

This table was set up for the enumerators to use. The table is in Excel and each column represents a question from the questionnaire. Each horizontal line represents one completed questionnaire. By this stage, all of the answers should be in some form of numerical code, although some words can be used for so-called 'string' variables, such as the names of diseases. Care must be taken to ensure that the numbers are entered in the same way and that spaces are not used for zeroes. If the answer is missing nothing should be entered into that particular box.

Annex E. Extract from Data Entry Table

Interview number	Code For Interviewer (see advice)	Date of interview use format 26 May 27 May	Number of minutes interview lasted, only write the number, no words	Location (see advice)	Q1Position of respondent	Q1 Sex of respondent	Q1 Age code of respondent	Q1 Education of respondent	Q1 Employment of respondent	Total Income per family (real amount)	Total income per family (code)	Q2 Total number in household
1	7	27-May	30	4	1	0	7	0	9	90000	1	6
2	3	26-May	42	2	1	0	4	3	12	1,416,000	8	8
3	6	25-May	0	2	1	0	7	0	12	72000	1	4
4	2	28-May	24	4	1	0	6	2	12	300000	3	8
5	1	26-May	65	2	1	0	4	0	14	480000	5	2
6	6	27-May	30	4	1	0	5	2	9	360000	4	3
7	5	26-May	0	2	1	0	5	7	6	7200000	10	1
8	4	27-May	20	4	1	0	5	4	5	2196000	9	4
9	3	26-May	33	2	1	0	4	3	2	5040000	10	7
10	3	27-May	39	4	1	0	4	3	9	690000	6	5
11	4	27-May	0	4	1	0	4	5	5	2560000	9	2
12	6	28-May	30	4	1	0	5	4	10	360000	4	6
13	5	27-May	0	4	1	0	4	2	2	720000	6	4
14	7	24-May	0	3	2	1	4	3	7	1200000	8	1
15	6	27-May	25	4	1	0	5	5	5	2160000	9	4
16	6	27-May	30	4	1	0	7	2	12	384000	4	8
17	7	25-May	19	2	1	0	4	3	9	1440000	8	4
18	4	25-May	30	2	1	0	5	3	13	3480000	9	6
19	6	25-May	0	2	2	1	4	2	12	126000	2	6
20	6	25-May	0	2	1	0	5	2	7	450000	5	9
21	4	25-May	20	2	1	0	5	3	12	150000	2	7
22	2	25-May	0	2	1	0	7	2	1	557000	5	3
23	2	25-May	0	2	1	0	6	0	12	260000	3	4
24	2	24-May	20	3	1	0	6	2	7	14400000	11	4
25	1	26-May	36	2	1	0	4	0	9	480000	5	1
26	7	26-May	0	2	3	1	5	2	3	144000	2	9
27	6	26-May	0	2	2	1	4	0	12	240000	3	1
28	6	26-May	0	2	1	0	5	2	9	720000	6	1

Annex F
Financial sustainability analysis

The attached spreadsheets represent the financial sustainability analysis completed for Bushenyi, Uganda, following the analysis of the willingness-to-pay survey results. A high-cost investment scenario is presented (four pages), as well as a low-cost investment scenario (four pages). Such investment models could be used and adapted for other town water supply investment analyses.

The model includes existing and projected use of service options and projected costs and revenues, leading to the projected deficit/surplus each year over a ten-year period.

The model user can change all of the numbers shaded on the table in Annex F. For example the data for 'existing water use in the core area' was taken from the results of the CVM Survey in Bushenyi. The 'target water use patterns from WTP survey' were also taken from the CVM Survey and are based on respondents' willingness to pay and choice of their preferred option. This model separates out core and fringe areas; more sophisticated models could disaggregate the data into varying income groups. This might prove useful if there is a willingness by the authority to charge higher rates to higher income households, with the aim of cross-subsidisation within the community.

Estimates are made of average consumption per person according to the water supply option used. The most interesting aspect of this model is the 'percentage change in use' columns. The values can be varied by the model user to show the growth or decline in the number of households using each option. The model aims to represent the difficult transition period between the existing water supply system and the changes in water supply use once the system has been rehabilitated. In many small towns the main pipes and water tanks/reservoirs are built in the first stages of a rehabilitation programme and then smaller pipes and house connections are built when funds/labour/user contributions are available. This on-going process can take a number of years. Individual sections of the model show:

- the percentage of the population in the fringe and core areas using each option. The percentages in Year 1 represent existing water use patterns;
- the actual number of people using each option. These change each year according to the growth/decline rates applied at the beginning of the model;

- the physical number of options within the fringe and core areas. The number of people using each option are used to calculate the actual number of protected springs, public kiosks, and house connections that exist in year one and will exist in the future;
- the costs of providing and maintaining the new and existing options, based on the Government of Uganda/World Bank investment analysis;
- tariffs for each option with the amount of revenue that will be raised each year. Tariffs for yard taps and house connections increase in small increments over the first eight years; and
- the total costs and revenues can be compared to show how changes in the tariff rates or the number of households connecting to the piped scheme affects cost recovery.

The final shaded boxes can also be changed to examine cost recovery according to:

- the amount of grant aid provided; and/or
- the interest rate for a commercial loan, which can be changed to show the levels of debt servicing and cost recovery if no grant aid is available.

The model is very useful because it enables sensitivity analyses, varying subsidy and tariff levels and other factors in order to inform key policy decisions on matters such as which are the preferred service options and what should be the subsidy and tariff levels over time.

High-cost scenario

In the high-cost scenario the pipe connections are extended to the core area. The proportion of households using each option are set out in Table 17 and in the first section of the spreadsheet. Capital costs are US$3.9 million. Tariffs vary according to the water supply option and increase at rates of 2 per cent per annum for protected springs up to 4 per cent per annum for piped connections. Tariffs are set out in the first part of the model. The interesting cash flow is the line **surplus/ deficit with grant aid and loan repayments.** This shows a realistic scenario with a percentage of grant aid used to pay capital costs and repayments on a loan for the remaining percentage. In addition the model includes all operating and maintenance costs and generates revenues from the tariffs. Under this scenario it would take eight years to re-pay the loan of 10 per cent of capital costs.

Low-cost scenario

The low-cost scenario ignores the high demand for private connections in the fringe areas and instead provides more protected springs and kiosks to the fringe areas; the piped system only covers the core areas, this reduces the capital costs significantly. Under this scenario it would take six years to repay the loan of 10 per cent of capital costs.

The tariffs remain the same as in the high-cost investment scenario but capital costs are significantly reduced to US$1.5 million. Under this scenario, it would take only eight years to repay the loan of 10 per cent of capital costs.

ANNEX F: HIGH COST INVESTMENT SCENARIO FOR BUSHENYI TOWN WATER SUPPLY SYSTEM

(numbers in shade can be changed to test the sensitivity of % of capital cost contributions, loan interest rates, existing and target number of users for each option, implemenation rates and tariffs)

High Cost Investment Scenario

Option	Existing Water Use Core Area	Existing Water Use Fringe Area	Target Water Use Patterns From WTP Survey - CORE	Target Water Use Patterns From WTP Survey - FRINGE	Vol of water consumed (pcpd) litres	% change in use CORE	% change in use FRINGE	tariffs in yr 1	Tariffs % annual increase
Protected springs	49	72	30	41	20	-10	-10	750	1
Public kiosks	4	1	15	9	20	20	25	50	2
Shared yard taps	12	2	30	40	50	20	50	1,250	3
Private connections	14	2	25	10	80	20	25	1,750	3
Other (vending, unprotected springs)	21	23	0	0	20				
Total	100	100	100	100					

High Cost Investment Scenario - Costs	
Piped Scheme Capital Costs US $	3,909,880
Protected Springs Capital Costs US $	147,618
% Grant Aid	90
O&M Cost of water production / m3 ($)	0.5
Loan (interest at %)	5

Year	1	2	3	4	5	6	7	8	9
TOTAL REVENUE FROM TARIFFS ($)	71,101	91,523	118,267	153,443	185,850	225,333	268,429	327,653	379,489
Surplus/Deficit with zero interest rates and % grant aid	-394,029	-374,733	-343,173	-293,130	-225,544	-134,631	-14,288	148,102	347,886
Outstanding Loan (with grant aid)	405,750	394,029	394,435	382,596	351,683	301,681	225,852	116,802	0
Debt Servicing		19,701	19,722	19,130	17,584	15,084	11,293	5,840	0
O&M Expenditure	59,380	72,228	86,706	103,401	118,264	134,420	148,086	165,263	179,705
Revenue	**71,101**	**91,523**	**118,267**	**153,443**	**185,850**	**225,333**	**268,429**	**327,653**	**379,489**
Surplus/Deficit with loan repayments and grant aid	**-394,029**	**-394,435**	**-382,596**	**-351,683**	**-301,681**	**-225,852**	**-116,802**	**39,748**	**199,783**

Tariff Model Calculations

Population Split (Existing)	
% of people living in fringe area	58
% of people living in core area	42

Year	**1**	**2**	**3**	**4**	**5**	**6**	**7**	**8**	**9**
Population	23,180	23,875	24,592	25,329	26,089	26,872	27,678	28,508	29,364
Core Area Population	9,736	10,028	10,328	10,638	10,958	11,286	11,625	11,974	12,333
Fringe Area Population	13,444	13,848	14,263	14,691	15,132	15,586	16,053	16,535	17,031
CORE AREA WATER CONSUMED									
Core Area Water Consumption %	**% existing**	**% future**							
Protected springs	**49**	44	40	36	32	30	30	30	30
Public kiosks	**4**	5	6	7	8	10	12	14	15
Shared yard taps	**12**	14	17	21	25	30	30	30	30
Private connections	**14**	17	20	24	25	25	25	25	25
Other (vending, unprotected springs)	**21**	20	17	12	10	5	3	1	**0**
Total	**100**	**100**	**100**	**100**	**100**	**100**	**100**	**100**	**100**
Core Area Population Using									
Protected springs	4770	4422	4099	3800	3523	3352	3453	3556	3663
Public kiosks	389	481	595	735	909	1123	1388	1716	1850
Shared yard taps	1168	1444	1785	2206	2727	3370	3487	3592	3700
Private connections	1363	1685	2082	2574	2739	2822	2906	2993	3083
Other (vending, unprotected springs)	2044	1996	1767	1323	1060	619	390	116	37
Total	**9736**	**10028**	**10328**	**10638**	**10958**	**11286**	**11625**	**11974**	**12333**
Core Area Number of Options									
Number of protected springs	32	29	27	25	23	22	23	24	24
Number of public kiosks	10	12	15	18	23	28	35	43	46
Number of yard taps	115	142	175	216	267	330	342	352	363
Number of house connections	267	330	408	505	537	553	570	587	605
Other (vending, unprotected springs)	409	399	353	265	212	124	78	23	7
Core Area Consumption (m3) per Annum									
Protected springs	34824	32282	29925	27741	25716	24470	25204	25960	26739
Public kiosks	2843	3514	4343	5368	6635	8200	10136	12528	13504
Shared yard taps	21321	26353	32572	40259	49760	61503	63646	65555	67522

Private connections	39799	49192	60801	75150	79990	82389	84861	87407	90029
Other (vending, unprotected springs)	14925	14567	12901	9660	7738	4521	2848	845	270
Total Exluding Springs	78888	93625	110616	130437	144122	156614	161491	166335	171326
FRINGE AREA WATER CONSUMED	**1**	**2**	**3**	**4**	**5**	**6**	**7**	**8**	**9**
Fringe Area Water Consumption %	**% existing**								
Protected springs	**72**	65	58	52	47	43	41	41	41
Public kiosks	**1**	2	2	3	3	4	5	6	8
Shared yard taps	**2**	3	4	6	9	14	21	31	40
Private connections	**2**	3	3	4	5	6	8	10	10
Other (vending, unprotected springs)	**23**	28	32	35	36	34	26	13	1
Total	**100**	**100**	**100**	**100**	**100**	**100**	**100**	**100**	**100**
Fringe Area Population Using									
Protected springs	9680	8973	8318	7711	7148	6626	6582	6779	6983
Public kiosks	175	225	290	373	480	618	796	1025	1320
Shared yard taps	242	374	578	892	1379	2130	3291	5085	6812
Private connections	269	346	446	574	739	951	1225	1577	1703
Other (vending, unprotected springs)	3079	3929	4632	5141	5386	5259	4159	2068	213
Total	**13444**	**13848**	**14263**	**14691**	**15132**	**15586**	**16053**	**16535**	**17031**
Fringe Area Number of Options									
Number of protected springs	65	60	55	51	48	44	44	45	47
Number of public kiosks	1	1	1	2	2	3	4	5	7
Number of yard taps	24	37	57	87	135	209	323	499	668
Number of house connections	53	68	87	113	145	187	240	309	334
Other (vending, unprotected springs)	616	786	926	1028	1077	1052	832	414	43
Fringe Area Consumption (m3) per Annum									
Protected springs	70664	65505	60723	56291	52181	48372	48048	49489	50974
Public kiosks	1276	1643	2115	2723	3506	4514	5812	7482	9634
Shared yard taps	4416	6823	10542	16288	25165	38879	60069	92806	124326
Private connections	7852	10109	13015	16757	21575	27777	35763	46045	49730
Other (vending, unprotected springs)	22475	28684	33812	37527	39315	38394	30362	15100	1556
Total Exluding Springs	36019	47259	59484	73295	89560	109564	132005	161433	185246
TOTALpiped WATER CONSUMPTION (ex.sp)	**114906**	**140884**	**170101**	**203731**	**233683**	**266178**	**293496**	**327769**	**356571**

CASH FLOW ANALYSIS									
Expenditures ($)									
Capital costs paid by scheme	390,988								
Capital Costs Springs	14,762								
O&M Piped Scheme	57,453	70,442	85,050	101,866	116,841	133,089	146,748	163,884	178,286
O&M Springs	1,927	1,786	1,656	1,535	1,423	1,330	1,338	1,378	1,419
TOTAL EXPENDITURE	465,130	72,228	86,706	103,401	118,264	134,420	148,086	165,263	179,705
REVENUES AND TARIFFS									
O&M Contribution For Springs per month Ug sh	750	758	765	773	780	788	796	804	812
O&M Contribution For Springs per month $	0.42	0.42	0.43	0.43	0.43	0.44	0.44	0.45	0.45
Total Revenue ($)	1,181	1,105	1,035	969	907	857	870	905	942
Price Per Jerry Can - Kiosks Ug shillings	50	51	52	53	54	55	56	57	59
Price Per Jerry Can - Kiosks $	0.03	0.03	0.03	0.03	0.03	0.03	0.03	0.03	0.03
Total Revenue ($)	5,720	7,305	9,332	11,925	15,245	19,497	24,943	31,924	37,652
Tariff For Yard Taps per m3 Ugandan Sh	1,250	1,288	1,326	1,366	1,407	1,449	1,493	1,537	1,583
Tariff For Yard Taps per m3 $	0.69	0.72	0.74	0.76	0.78	0.81	0.83	0.85	0.88
Total Revenue ($)	17,873	23,730	31,764	42,910	58,561	80,813	102,584	135,253	168,769
Tariff For House Connections Per m3 Ugandan S	1,750	1,803	1,857	1,912	1,970	2,029	2,090	2,152	2,217
Tariff For House Connections Per m3 $	0.97	1.00	1.03	1.06	1.09	1.13	1.16	1.20	1.23
Total Revenue ($)	46,327	59,383	76,136	97,640	111,136	124,166	140,031	159,570	172,125

ANNEX F: LOW COST INVESTMENT SCENARIO FOR BUSHENYI TOWN WATER SUPPLY SYSTEM

(numbers in shade can be changed to test the sensitivity of % of capital cost contributions, loan interest rates, existing and target number of users for each option, implemenation rates and tariffs)

Low Cost Investment Scenario

Option	Existing Water Use Core Area	Existing Water Use Fringe Area	Low Cost Investment Target Use Patterns CORE	Low Cost Investment Target Use Patterns FRINGE	Vol of water consumed (pcpd) litres	% change in use, per year CORE	% change in use, per year FRINGE	tariffs in yr 1	Tariffs % annual increase
Protected springs	49	72	35	60	20	-10	-10	750	1
Public kiosks	4	1	30	30	20	20	25	50	2
Shared yard taps	12	2	15	5	50	20	50	1,250	3
Private connections	14	2	20	5	80	20	25	1,750	3
Other (vending, unprotected springs)	21	23	0	0	20				
Total	100	100	100	100					

Low Cost Scenario - Costs	
Piped Scheme Capital Costs US $	1,500,000
Protected Springs Capital Costs US $	201,553
% Grant Aid	90
O&M Cost of water production / m3 ($)	0.5
Loan (interest at %)	5

Year	1	2	3	4	5	6	7	8	9
TOTAL REVENUE FROM TARIFFS ($)	71,101	91,523	114,623	129,064	144,211	156,895	170,686	186,518	204,857
Surplus/Deficit with zero interest rates and % grant aid	-158,434	19,295	30,229	38,633	49,171	58,804	69,652	82,453	97,671
Financial Summary									
Outstanding Loan (with grant aid)	170,155	158,434	147,061	124,184	91,760	47,177	0	0	0
Debt Servicing		7,922	7,353	6,209	4,588	2,359	0	0	0
O&M Expenditure	59,380	72,228	84,393	90,431	95,040	98,091	101,033	104,064	107,186
Revenue	71,101	91,523	114,623	129,064	144,211	156,895	170,686	186,518	204,857
Low Cost, Surplus/Deficit with loan and grant aid	-158,434	-147,061	-124,184	-91,760	-47,177	9,269	69,652	82,453	97,671

Tariff Model Calculations

Population Split (Existing)	
% of people living in fringe area	58
% of people living in core area	42

Year	**1**	**2**	**3**	**4**	**5**	**6**	**7**	**8**	**9**
Population	23,180	23,875	24,592	25,329	26,089	26,872	27,678	28,508	29,364
Core Area Population	9,736	10,028	10,328	10,638	10,958	11,286	11,625	11,974	12,333
Fringe Area Population	13,444	13,848	14,263	14,691	15,132	15,586	16,053	16,535	17,031
CORE AREA WATER CONSUMED									
Core Area Water Consumption %	**% existing**	% future							
Protected springs	**49**	44	40	36	35	35	35	35	35
Public kiosks	**4**	5	6	7	8	10	12	14	17
Shared yard taps	**12**	14	15	15	15	15	15	15	15
Private connections	**14**	17	20	20	20	20	20	20	20
Other (vending, unprotected springs)	**21**	20	20	22	22	20	18	16	13
Total	**100**	**100**	**100**	**100**	**100**	**100**	**100**	**100**	**100**
Core Area Population Using									
Protected springs	4770	4422	4099	3800	3835	3950	4069	4191	4316
Public kiosks	389	481	595	735	909	1123	1388	1716	2121
Shared yard taps	1168	1444	1549	1596	1644	1693	1744	1796	1850
Private connections	1363	1685	2066	2128	2192	2257	2325	2395	2467
Other (vending, unprotected springs)	2044	1996	2019	2379	2378	2263	2099	1876	1579
Total	**9736**	**10028**	**10328**	**10638**	**10958**	**11286**	**11625**	**11974**	**12333**
Core Area Number of Options									
Number of protected springs	32	29	27	25	26	26	27	28	29
Number of public kiosks	10	12	15	18	23	28	35	43	53
Number of yard taps	115	142	152	156	161	166	171	176	181
Number of house connections	267	330	405	417	430	443	456	470	484
Other (vending, unprotected springs)	409	399	404	476	476	453	420	375	316
Core Area Consumption (m3) per Annum									
Protected springs	34824	32282	29925	27741	27996	28836	29701	30592	31510
Public kiosks	2843	3514	4343	5368	6635	8200	10136	12528	15484
Shared yard taps	21321	26353	28274	29122	29996	30896	31823	32778	33761

Private connections	39799	49192	60318	62128	63992	65912	67889	69926	72023
Other (vending, unprotected springs)	14925	14567	14740	17370	17362	16516	15323	13694	11524
Total Exluding Springs	78888	93625	107676	113989	117985	121524	125170	128925	132793
FRINGE AREA WATER CONSUMED	**1**	**2**	**3**	**4**	**5**	**6**	**7**	**8**	**9**
Fringe Area Water Consumption %	**% existing**								
Protected springs	**72**	65	60	60	60	60	60	60	60
Public kiosks	**1**	2	2	3	3	4	5	6	8
Shared yard taps	**2**	3	4	5	5	5	5	5	5
Private connections	**2**	3	3	4	5	5	5	5	5
Other (vending, unprotected springs)	**23**	28	31	29	27	26	25	24	22
Total	**100**	**100**	**100**	**100**	**100**	**100**	**100**	**100**	**100**
Fringe Area Population Using									
Protected springs	9680	8973	8558	8815	9079	9351	9632	9921	10219
Public kiosks	175	225	290	373	480	618	796	1025	1320
Shared yard taps	242	374	578	735	757	779	803	827	852
Private connections	269	346	446	574	739	779	803	827	852
Other (vending, unprotected springs)	3079	3929	4392	4195	4077	4057	4020	3935	3790
Total	**13444**	**13848**	**14263**	**14691**	**15132**	**15586**	**16053**	**16535**	**17031**
Fringe Area Number of Options									
Number of protected springs	65	60	57	59	61	62	64	66	68
Number of public kiosks	1	1	1	2	2	3	4	5	7
Number of yard taps	24	37	57	72	74	76	79	81	83
Number of house connections	53	68	87	113	145	153	157	162	167
Other (vending, unprotected springs)	616	786	878	839	815	811	804	787	758
Fringe Area Consumption (m3) per Annum									
Protected springs	70664	65505	62473	64347	66277	68266	70314	72423	74596
Public kiosks	1276	1643	2115	2723	3506	4514	5812	7482	9634
Shared yard taps	4416	6823	10542	13406	13808	14222	14649	15088	15541
Private connections	7852	10109	13015	16757	21575	22755	23438	24141	24865
Other (vending, unprotected springs)	22475	28684	32063	30623	29762	29619	29345	28729	27664
Total Exluding Springs	36019	47259	57735	63509	68650	71110	73243	75441	77704
TOTALpiped WATER CONSUMPTION (ex.s	**114906**	**140884**	**165411**	**177498**	**186635**	**192634**	**198413**	**204366**	**210497**

CASH FLOW ANALYSIS									
Expenditures ($)									
Capital costs paid by scheme	150,000								
Capital Costs Springs	20,155								
O&M Piped Scheme	57,453	70,442	82,706	88,749	93,318	96,317	99,207	102,183	105,248
O&M Springs	1,927	1,786	1,688	1,682	1,722	1,774	1,827	1,882	1,938
TOTAL EXPENDITURE	229,535	72,228	84,393	90,431	95,040	98,091	101,033	104,064	107,186
REVENUES AND TARIFFS									
O&M Contribution For Springs per month Ug sl	750	758	765	773	780	788	796	804	812
O&M Contribution For Springs per month $	0.42	0.42	0.43	0.43	0.43	0.44	0.44	0.45	0.45
Total Revenue ($)	1,181	1,105	1,055	1,062	1,098	1,142	1,188	1,236	1,286
Price Per Jerry Can - Kiosks Ug shillings	50	51	52	53	54	55	56	57	59
Price Per Jerry Can - Kiosks $	0.03	0.03	0.03	0.03	0.03	0.03	0.03	0.03	0.03
Total Revenue ($)	5,720	7,305	9,332	11,925	15,245	19,497	24,943	31,924	40,874

www.ingramcontent.com/pod-product-compliance
Lightning Source LLC
Chambersburg PA
CBHW080926050426
42334CB00055B/2729

* 9 7 8 1 8 4 3 8 0 0 1 4 9 *